Anonymous

The Hawkeye ornithologist and oologist

Anonymous

The Hawkeye ornithologist and oologist

ISBN/EAN: 9783337808648

Printed in Europe, USA, Canada, Australia, Japan

Cover: Foto ©ninafisch / pixelio.de

More available books at **www.hansebooks.com**

VOL. I.   JANUARY, 1888.   NO. 1.

THE HAWKEYE ORNITHOLOGIST AND OOLOGIST.

+EDITED AND PUBLISHED BY+
WEBSTER & MEAD,
CRESCO, - - IOWA.

CONTENTS FOR JANUARY.

The Seagull, — Julia Goddard.
The Audubon Society.
Disappearance of the Bobolink, — — E. H. Lathrop.
The Tree Swallow, — — — Oliver Davie.
Canadian Flycatchers, — — Wm. L. Kells.
The Owl.
The Night-hawk.
Notes on Some of the Passeres of Fulton Co., Ky., L. O. Pindar.
What Shall the Harvest Be.
A Few Words From an Old Collector, — E. G. Ward
The Red-tailed Hawk, — — — H. W. Davis.
Suggestions for Forming Collections of Bird's Eggs, Smithsonian Bulletin.
Editorial and Notes.
Bird Dissection.
Leaf Photographs.
The Bowlder, — — Selected by M. R. Steele.
Home Science, — — — H. F. Hegner.
The Bad Lands of Dakota, — — — L. W. Stilwell.

Advertisements.—Read them carefully and state where you saw ad. when writing to advertisers.

The Hawkeye Ornithologist & Oologist.

"Better search the fields for health unbought,
Than fee the doctor for nauseus draught.
The wise for health on exercise depend,
God never made his work for man to mend."

THE SEAGULL.
BY JULIA GODDARD.

The sky was blue on a summer day,
    And the sea was blue below;
And the seagulls—whose wings flashed gleaming white—
    Were swooping to and fro.

The boatmen rested on their oars,
    And the marksman took his gun,
And he said, "My love wants a seagull's plume,
    And I will get her one.

He lifted his gun, he shot—and lo!
    With a thud upon the deck,
Fell the white-winged bird, whilst a scarlet stream
    Dripped from its wounded neck.

"A fine young bird! I've had good luck,"
    Quoth the marksman, in great glee;
Whilst round the boat hovered the parent bird,
    And ever nearer came she.

She uttered many a plaintiff cry;
    She would not her young forsake.
"O, marksman! marksman! your heart must be hard
    If pity you do not take."

The marksman he raised his gun again,
    But the brave bird did not care:
She was robbed of her nestling; she followed on—
    Ah! say if its fate she will share?

"Oh, marksman! marksman! a love so great
    Should with tenderest pity meet."
But the marksman aimed, and the marksman fired,
    And the bird fell at his feet.

Two happy creatures that God had made
    To play o're the restless sea!
Thank God, O reader, that he who fired
    Was neither you nor me!

Oh, fair ones who wear the seagull's plumes,
    And think that in feathers you're fine,
Close your ears when barbarous Fashion speaks,
    And think of this tale of mine.

                  —*Animal World.*

THE AUDUBON SOCIETY.

While the A. O. U. has been directing a fair share of its efforts to inquiries regarding the causes of the rapid destruction of birds and to the framing of laws of such character as to secure their complete protection, the Audubon Society, which was founded by Forest and Stream in February, 1886, has been rendering efficient service by creating and sustaining a strong public sentiment in support of such legislative enactments as already exist.

With its stated purpose, the protection of birds not used for food, from destruction for mercantile purposes, it has rapidly gained in membership, until now, scarcely two years old, it has a membership of about 40,000, distributed over a great portion of North America.

The Society is attempting to "arouse the people to the consideration of the consequences of the wholesale destruction of birds for millinery purposes, to instruct them in the importance of the functions performed by birds, to familiarize them with the investigations of specialists into the subject, and to popularize the somewhat dry reports of the more rigidly scientific societies; beyond this it aims at a national agitation which shall force the subject upon the most indifferent, and shall organize all friends of the movement in one compact phalanx for effective work, and provide for the general presentation of the subject in its ethical as well as its economical aspect."

Whenever the subject of bird protection is presented to the public through the agency of the newspapers, intelligence and right feeling are to be found arrayed in its favor, but the prevailing indifference and thoughtlessness must be overcome before the nation at large shall consider as a crime the wanton slaughter of entirely harmless creatures which are of such inestimable importance to mankind. The people must be brought to a fair understanding of man's dependence on his feathered friends, and the moral faculties quickend to a just recognition of their ethical relation with everything that has life.

THE DISAPPEARANCE OF THE BOBOLINK.

The bobolink, sweetest and best of our New England meadow singers, is gone. The pied dandy of tussock and springing golden rod no more in this vicinity tinkles his tangled bell music in our fields. Around our city and especially in the West Springfield meadows, as all up and down the valley of the Connecticut, used to be the resort and home of this characteristic and blithe bird. This is the first season that I have failed absolutely to see or hear a single one.

Of late years they have been fewer, each season being made melancholy in a measure by the steadily depleted numbers of the birds, and now I believe there are none. Others may have seen or heard them, but after diligent seeking, foreseeing as I have the inevitable, I fail to find a single songster.

One great cause of this is the shooting of this song bird by our friends further south for food. Garbed in russet, in the fall he becomes in Maryland the rice bird or the ortolan and is shot and strung up in Baltimore and Philadelphia markets by the hundreds to be eaten.

I should feel as if I were eating dead music if I attempted to eat one of these. There are bigger and better things to eat than they. Why not leave in life this epitome of tremulous melody, instead of reducing him to the level of an oyster or a clam? Our southern friends have dainties enough for the table without him, in their terrapin and canvasbacks.

Will our southern Audubon societies think of this and let us see if the bobolink cannot be saved from extinction.—*E. H. Lathrop, in Forest and Stream.*

For the Hawkeye O. and O.

THE TREE SWALLOW.
(*Tachycineta bicolor* (VIEILL.))
BY OLIVER DAVIE.

This plain and delicate looking little Swallow is a common bird throughout North America, breeding from latitude 38 degrees to high Arctic regions, many residing the entire year in Mexico, Central America, and in the West Indies. As its specific name, *bicolor*, implies it is a bird of two colors—greenish-black above and pure white beneath. The bird's favorite resorts are in the vicinity of ponds, marshes and rivers. It seems to love the picturesque and beautiful in nature, lingering throughout the long summer months by the margin of rivers, where the music of running waters mingle with the zephyrs that blow and seem to whisper to its young and tell them of a world in whose elements they will soon take wing and soar into boundless space. From morning's dawn until nightfall it may be seen soaring high in air, wheeling and playing in graceful evolutions or skimming along the surface of the stream, now and then dipping into the rippling waters, then flitting merrily away into the azure sky.

It dwells along those streams upon whose banks the lofty trunks of trees, with leafless tops, that stand like sentinels watching over the lovely scenes which nature's magic hand changes from winter's russet-brown to summer's lively green. Even in its migrations this bird is seldom seen far away from running water.

In the old excavations made by woodpeckers or in the natural cavities of those weather-beaten trunks it constructs its nest of straws and a thick lining of feathers. These are usually chicken or tame geese feathers, carefully gathered from a neighboring barn-yard. They are laid in the nest so that the tips curl upwards and nearly conceal the eggs. In this warm bed the bird deposits from four to seven pure white eggs, and occasionally a nest is found containing nine These measure from 70 to 80 hundredths of an inch long by 50 to 55 hundredths in diameter.

Mr. Edson A. McMillan informs me that he took from a single nest in regular succession no less than five sets each containing five eggs. This was in the Adirondack Mountain region, beginning with set No. 1 the first part of June. Mr. C. S. Shick of Sea Isle City, N. J., writes that a pair of these birds had taken possession of a box which he had put up in his yard. This seems to be a common occurrence in the Eastern States; the birds forsake their primitive breeding places and resort to bird-boxes for that purpose.

The song of the White-breasted Swallow, as it is often called, seems to be nothing more than a mere chatter, and again when heard under favorable circumstances one might imagine that it somewhat resembles the low warble of the Song Sparrow, as on several occasions I have heard it while at rest on a fence or on telegraph wires; my presence at the time being unknown to the bird. On account of its musical notes it is called by some the Singing Swallow.

During the nesting season this Swallow is less gregarious than the Barn Swallow and others, but often associate in large communities in their autumnal gatherings. In many of the islands of the sea its nest is elegantly lined with feathers of the Eider Duck and Herring Gull.

The flight of the Swallow is one of its most wonderful powers. An experiment to test the speed of the swallow's flight was recently (1887) made at Pavia. Two sitting birds were taken from their newly hatched young, carried to Milan and there released at a given hour. Both made their way back to their nests in thirteen minutes, which gave the rate of speed at 87½ miles an hour. Wilson estimates the flight of the Barn Swallow at the rate of a mile in a minute, the time spent on wing each day to be ten hours, and its length of life at ten years. This shows that it would thus pass around the globe eighty-seven times.

For the Hawkeye O. and O.

CANADIAN FLYCATCHERS.
BY WM. L. KELLS, LISTOWEL, ONTARIO.

THE FLYCATCHER FAMILY.

This is a numerous and widely diffused family of birds, of which there are some nine representatives, to be found as summer residents of the Province of Ontario. Some of these are common in all parts of the country, others only rarely met with anywhere. And while some of them have their summer homes and nesting places near by human dwellings, others are seldom seen or heard except in the deep wilds of the forest. Of these the kingbird and the phœbe flycatcher are the most familiar, while the scissor-tailed species is so rare as scarcely to be regarded as a Canadian bird. The olive-sided and the yellow-bellied flycatchers are also rarely met with, and the former more as a spring migrant than a summer resident. The wood pewee and the least flycatcher are commonly met with, generally in the woods, sometimes in orchards. The crested species is more rare and generally confined to the tops of the trees in deep woods, while Traill's flycatcher is sometimes common in certain low, second-growth woods, where there is deep concealment. They are all insect feeders and expert in capturing their winged victims. In the form and position of their nests, as well as the marking of their eggs, there is a good deal of variation. Most of them have songs, but their notes possess little melody.

THE KINGBIRD.
(*Tyrannus tyrannus.*)

This famous little warrior is well known through all the temperate regions of eastern North America. It frequents all parts of Ontario, and most of the other Canadian Provinces. Its favorite habitats are orchards, plantations and patches of woods bordering on water courses. It is also often observed along the public roads, as well as in meadows, and pasture fields. It returns to this country from its winter sojourn in the south in the early part of May, and till the female begins to construct her nest is comparatively peaceful and silent, but after that period the male bird is the terror of all the small birds in the vicinity, as he will attack them without the slightest provocation if they have the misfortune to approach the place which the female has chosen for her nesting site; no matter how innocent or non-combative may be their character. His whole life during the breeding season is one continual scene of attacks and battles, in which he is always victorious. He is strangely attached to his mate, and while she attends to her nestling duties, he is stationed near by and will attack with daring and gallant courage any feathered intruder; not excepting the white-headed-eagle. His mode of attacking the larger species is to mount in the air above his enemy, and then by a rapid movement dart upon its back, and sometimes fix himself there and ride off a considerable distance, picking out feathers and uttering notes of triumph, to the great annoyance of his adversary.

who by various turnings endeavors to rid itself of its troublesome little opponent. But the kingbird, from his natural abilities and constant practice, is not easily dismounted; nor does he give up the contest until the object of his dislike has left the neighborhood, and his passion has exhausted its fury.

The female is also courageous, and often joins her mate in the attack, but she seldom pursues the fugitive more than a few rods from her nesting place.

The nest of the kingbird is placed in various situations and at various elevations from the ground. Generally it is placed on the horizontal branch of an apple or shade tree near human dwellings, again you may see its nest on the limb of a high tree on the margin of the woods, or bordering a water course. Sometimes it will nest on the top rail of a fence, or inside the old nest of a robin, between the rails; a thornbush is also with it a favorite nesting site. This structure is commonly formed with wool, strips of bark, horse hair and fine rootlets. The eggs are usually four to the set, though sometimes three and even two are found undergoing the process of incubation. These are of a clear white color, marked towards the large end with a few brownish or black spots.

Although the kingbird is usually successful in his attempts to drive off the larger species of birds, yet he sometimes meets with trouble from the male baltimore oriole and purple martin, while the red-headed woodpecker at times highly irritates him by clinging to the side of a tree and playing bo-peep around it, though he makes many vain efforts to dislodge it. But the kingbird waits his opportunity; he retires a short distance and when the poor woodpecker imagines that the way is clear, leaves his perch and starts for some other retreat; then the tyrant with notes of exultation, darts off in pursuit, overtakes the fugitive in mid air, and either hurls it to the ground or causes it, with cries of distress, to take refuge on the nearest tree or fence. Sometimes when the kingbird becomes enraged he will even attack his female and cause her to take refuge among the thick branches of some tree until his passion has subsided. This species feeds much on insects, chiefly those of a medium size, which are generally captured on the wing or picked up off the grass. Sometimes he will take his stand on a mullen stalk or tall weed in the pasture field near where cattle or horses are feeding, and then make a series of sweeps around them in pursuit of insects, particularly the large black gad-fly which are so annoying to these animals, in which case he must be looked upon as a beneficial servant, but his partiality to the honey bee is not relished by the apiculturist. Some persons contend that it is only the drones that the kingbird makes use of for a morning or a noon-day meal, and that the working bees are not molested, but the probability is that the bird exercises no discretion in the matter, but snaps up whatever kinds of insects that are most easily procured, whenever it feels disposed to dine on these humming creatures. Notwithstanding this, however, the agriculturist may be assured that this bird renders him more service than injury by destroying great numbers of other insects which prey upon the fruits of his industry.

The length of this bird is about eight inches. The crown of the head has a flame-colored patch, the rest of the plumage on the upper parts is dusty black, the head and neck being darker than on the other parts. The lower parts are white, the tail also being fringed with the same color.

(TO BE CONTINUED.)

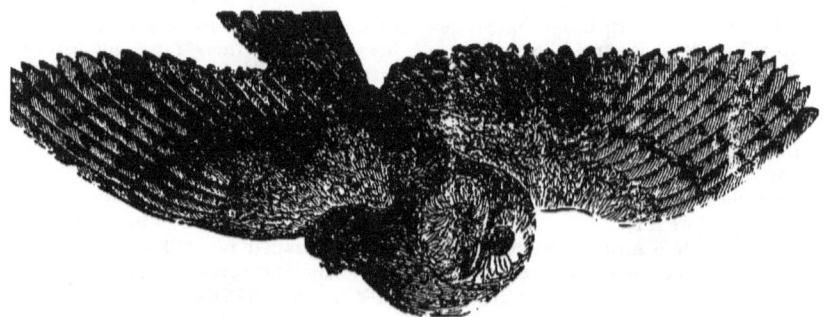

THE OWL.

"When cats run home and night is come,
And dew is cold upon the ground,
And the far off stream is dumb,
And the whirring sail goes round,
And the whirring sail goes round,
   Alone, and warming his five wits,
   The white owl in the belfry sits."
          —*Tennyson: The Owl.*

Owls are found in all parts of the world and in all climates, there being about thirty species in North America. The owl has from early times been deemed a bird of evil omen, and has been an object of dread to the superstitious. It is, perhaps, to be accounted for, partly by the sudden and unexpected manner with which it flys by in the shades of twilight, partly by the fact that most species haunt the deep woods or ruined buildings, and partly by the startling cry of some of the species, heard so often by the lonely wanderer. From this cry it is evident that the name owl is derived.

They are an extremely well defined group of birds; their large heads, wierd, cat-like faces, great eyes directed forwards, which are surrounded with discs of radiating feathers, the small, half concealed hooked bill; and the downy character of the plumage distinguishing them at once from all other birds. The bill is curved almost to the base, being hooked at the tip. The claws are sharp and curved, but less powerful than in the diurnal birds of prey. The toes are generally opposed two and two, the outer one being reversible at pleasure. The downy plumage and the recurved outer web of the primaries makes the flight almost noiseless, thus enabling them to capture their prey by surprise, their weak wings rendering them almost incapable of pursuit. The peculiar plumage adds a great deal to the apparent size of the body, but the head owes its really large size to the large cavities in the skull, between the outer and inner layers, which cavities communicate with the ear, and are supposed to add to the acuteness of the sense of hearing. The ear in many species is very large and is furnished with an external arch, which is found in no other birds. The feathers which radiate from the eye completely conceal the ear; but the feathers surrounding the ear are arranged in the shape of an ear trumpet, thus rendering the sense still more acute. The feathers surrounding the eye serve to collect the rays of light and throw them on the pupil so that owls can see as well in twilight and moonlight as other birds can in the day.

They feed on all small animals, such as rabbits, mice, birds, lizards, fishes and insects. Their voracity is wonderful, killing even more than they eat.

Their prey is usually swallowed entire, the indigestible parts being thrown up in the form of pellets.

THE NIGHT-HAWK.
(*Choridiles popetu.*)

This bird is very generally distributed over the temperate regions of the United States; generally eastern, found in no small numbers in the Mississippi Valley, and is abundant from northern Maine to southern South Carolina.

The name of this bird is in striking contrast with its habits. From its name one would suppose it to possess nocturnal habits; but such is not the case, being seen almost entirely in broad daylight, although it seems to be most frequent at early twilight. This supposition is due to the utterance of those peculiar cries which at once catch the ear; for who has not cast his eyes Heavenward on hearing those strident notes to discover their origin. These notes are made in the greatest abundance in the early evening, soon after his arrival from the south, and incubation in progress. He may be seen rising in wide circles, propelled by quick and slow movements, in alternation, of the wings, until he is almost invisible to the eye, and his whereabouts are known only by his harsh squeaks. Then with a headlong rush he suddenly falls from fifty to ninety feet, and then as quickly wheeling up, when a hollow whirr is heard which has been compared to the blowing of the wind in the bunghole of a barrel. This noise by some writers on ornithology, is attributed to the action of the air on the wings; by others to the action of the air on the wide-open mouth. Our opinion is that it is produced by the first-named cause, a good deal after the manner of that produced by the ruffed grouse, on which there is some considerable discussion, but that the action of the wings of the partridge on the air causes the noise is sustained by several writers, notably one calling himself "Hermit," in *Our Dumb Animals*, who claims personal observation of said cause. This certainly seems more feasable than the second theory.

His food consists of insects, chiefly of the larger kind, such as beetles, wasps, moths, etc., in the pursuit of of which its motions are most graceful, engaging the admiring eye of every beholder.

Toward the close of April the night-hawk arrives in the Middle States, and in early May it makes its appearance in Iowa; according to my migration reports of 1887 it was first seen the fifth of May.

Soon after their arrival from the South they may be seen in pairs, circling the heavens in pursuit of food. Less than a month later the female selects some suitable spot on the ground, on which to deposit her eggs. The nest is always placed on the ground and frequently on the bare rocks of some field with scarcely any show of a nest whatever.

The eggs, according to Davie's Egg Check List, are "greyish, thickly mottled with tints of darker grey, slate and yellowish brown; the pattern and tints are very variable; elliptical; size, 1.25 by .85." The number of eggs in a set is always two.

About the middle of August the fall migration begins, moving southward in large scattering flocks, and we bid them good-bye till another year.

An eagle died in Vienna, Austria, last November, that had been kept in confinement 114 years. It probably was a young bird when caught, so that its age must have been not far from 120 years. A record of the eagle's condition was made from year to year.

For the Hawkeye O. and O.

NOTES ON SOME OF THE PASSERES OF FULTON CO., KY.

FIRST PAPER, BY L. O. PINDAR, PRES. Y. O. A., HICKMAN, KY.

This article must not be taken for a *list* of Fulton county passeres, as I only write of those that I have most observed. I follow the A. O. U. code and wish all writers on ornithology and oology would do the same, as it prevents the confusion which necessarily arises from a multiplicity of names. Almost all these notes were made at Hickman, Ky., a small town on the bank of the Mississippi river.

And now to the birds: I will devote this paper to the family *Tyrannidae*.

KINGBIRD.

(*Tyrannus tyrannus*.)

A summer resident, but not so common as the next species. Its colors are simple but pleasing and may be thus described: above, black; below, white; a few red feathers on crown. These red feathers can be displayed or concealed at will. Some writers think they are displayed with a view of attracting insects which take them for a flower but others do not think so. I agree with the former class.

Four eggs in my collection, collected in Jefferson Co., Texas, by Jas. H. Rachford May 22, 1886, have a ground color of white, with bold markings of dark and reddish brown and faint lavender.

The nest was "of grass lined with a downy substance."

TRAILL'S FLYCATCHER.

(*Empidonax pusillus Trailli*)

A common summer resident. Coloration as follows: above, olive brown, darker on head; below, grayish white, wingbars same color.

I have only one set of eggs, which is a set of three, collected in Wayne Co. Mich., by James Purdy, May 9,

1886. The eggs are very pretty, cream colored with reddish spots.

I found an empty nest which I take to be of this species at this place last year.

In the next paper we will tell of the *Corvidae*, with notes on the Crow and Blue Jay.

There are swans on the river Thames, in England, that are known to be 150 years old. For five centuries, the Vintner's Company there has kept a record of certain swans, and the ages of the specimens of this long-lived species of water-fowl are known to a day.

The above lifelike cut shows us, better than words can describe, the but too uselessness of the crow.

'Tis thou, oh sable bird of prey
   In deepest mourning, darkly dressed,
That eateth of the farmer's corn,
   And leaveth him so sore distressed.

'Tis thou that knows when death is near
   And from afar off scents the stear,
That died of direst, dread disease—
   'Tis thou that picks those fleshless knees.

With dismal croak you rob the nest
   Of happy, warbling birds,
And then, with devilish intent,
   You next uproot the early dent.

N. B.—The above was written by our junior editor during a sudden attack of insanity. He is now slowly recovering and will soon be able to attend to his regular duties. We will see that he is caged should he have another like attack.

OOLOGY.

For the Hawkeye O. and O.

A FEW WORDS FROM AN OLD COLLECTOR.

BY E. G. WARD, THREE RIVERS, MASS.

It is surprising to note what changes have taken place in the methods of collecting eggs among amateurs since we first commenced our little collection more than twenty years ago. We commenced by getting two eggs of a kind, and, with a few exceptions, have always followed that rule. We think that is a sufficient number for the average collector. The new craze is to collect in sets, which is all right where they are collected in the interests of science, but young collectors who wish a set for themselves and have a dozen or more sets of the same kind for their exchanges, make it look too much like wholesale robbery of the birds. No wonder some states have made laws forbidding collecting eggs and shooting certain kinds of birds. Massachusetts has such a law, but she has kindly made provision for those collecting in the interest of science. The teachers in our public schools are calling the attention of their pupils to that law, and encouraging them to protect the birds and their nests. This is a necessity, for birds are not as plenty as they were a few years ago, and many kinds which were quite common then, are either very rarely seen, or have entirely disappeared from certain localities: for instance, in Franklin county, Mass., our old home, the meadow larks were quite plenty a few years since, and it was an easy matter to find several nests during the nesting season; now we haven't seen or heard of one being seen for several years. The bobolinks also are few in numbers compared with those early days, and it is quite difficult to find a nest. The same is true of the yellow-birds, partridge woodpeckers, least flycatchers, etc. We use the common local names because they recall old times and bring more vividly to our minds certain very interesting excursions after eggs in which we had the satisfaction of adding certain desirable specimens to our collection.

Now, what causes the scarcity of birds or the disappearance of certain species from certain localities? Do they move from place to place on account of the scarcity of food like the squirrels? Is it owing to climatic changes? These are questions that naturally arise in the mind of the keen observer. We think all of these have a bearing, and to these we can add the mowing machine and horserake, which have something to do with thinning out, if not in driving back, into wilder portions of our towns and counties, those birds that nest on the ground. These causes taken in connection with the depredations made by their natural enemies, the foxes, cats, snakes, hawks, etc., have caused the scarcity of ground nesting birds. The English sparrow, an *imported nuisance*, is driving away from our cities and villages some of our most desirable feathered songsters. New England is subject to so many extremes in temperature, especially in spring, that some seasons the birds commence to nest so early that their eggs or young broods are destroyed.

The hunter is almost wholly responsible for the scarcity of our game birds. To these causes we may add the collector of "sets" who sees nothing but the *Almighty dollar*. This class who collect simply to make money out of the birds, bring reproach upon that class who love the study of Ornithology and Oology. We will find them in every branch of science that has any money in it, so we must make the best of the matter and give them a wide berth.

Most of the common varieties of eggs in our collection were collected when it was rulable to "*blow*" them by making small holes in the ends. We haven't replaced them by eggs *blown* on the side because of the associations connected with them, still some of our eggs collected in the past few years have been prepared for the cabinet in the manner now in use.

For the Hawkeye O. and O.

THE RED-TAILED HAWK. 436.
(Buteo borealis.)

BY H. W. DAVIS, NORTH GRANVILLE, WASHINGTON CO., NEW YORK.

The above bird is quite abundant around this locality in the breeding season, but their eggs are quite difficult to obtain, owing to the great heighth and large trees they select for their nests.

To do any collecting one must be accompanied by climbers and a good determination. On April 25th in company with a friend of mine who most always accompanied me on my collecting trips, because he was a fine climber, we took a fine set of three of this species. We entered a thick, heavy timber in which no sign of opening buds were to be seen, but plenty of hard wood trees with the dead leaves clinging to them. It was in one of these the nest was placed, being only about thirty feet from the ground.

The nest was in about the center of the woods. We crept up as slowly and still towards it as we could and were soon informed that it was inhabited by the fact that the tail of the female was sticking out over the edge of the nest. Arriving at the foot of the tree and hammering on the same with a stick, thought of course I could make the female fly off, but could not stir the bird from its comfortable position until my partner had got about half way up, then the startled bird left the nest and was soon joined by her mate. They would start and fly straight for your face as if they were going to swoop down and get their eggs, but just before they would get to you they would take a quick sharp turn and alight on some tree near by, so that I could have shot both birds very easily.

On reaching the nest he reported "three eggs." They were all placed in a handkerchief with the four corners in his mouth, and all three were safely brought to the ground.

The nest was a large bulky affair composed of sticks and twigs, mixed together with dead grass, moss, etc., and lined with a few feathers.

The eggs were a bluish white, spotted with brown and umber of varying shades.

The color of the bird is a rich dark brown; the wings are spotted with dusky and white; the tail is a bright chestnut red. The under parts are generally white with a streak of brown across the breast. The legs and feet are a bright yellow.

SUGGESTIONS FOR PROPERLY FORMING COLLECTIONS OF BIRDS' EGGS.

The following article, which was published in the late *Hoosier Naturalist*, and credited to the *Smithsonian Bulletin, No. 139*, contains such valuable suggestions that we republish it for the benefit of those of our readers who may not have read it before.

The collection of birds' eggs for scientific purposes requires far more discrimination than the collecting of specimens in almost any other branch of natural history. While the botanist, and generally speaking, the zoologist, at home is satisfied as long as he receives the specimens in good condition, with labels attached giving a few concise particulars of when and where they were obtained, it should be always borne in mind that to the oologist, such facts, and even the specimens themselves, are of very slight value unless accompanied by a statement of other circumstances which will carry conviction that the species to which the eggs belong has been accurately identified, and the specimens subsequently carefully authenticated. Consequently precision in the identification of his specimens should be the principal object of an egg-collector, to attain which all others must give way. There are perhaps few districts in the world, and certainly no regions of any extent, whose faunas are so well known that the most rigid identification may be dispensed with. Next to identifying his specimens, the most important duty of an egg-collector is to authenticate them by marking them in some manner and on some regular system as will leave no doubt, as long as they exist, of their having been obtained by him, and of the degree of identification to which they were subjected. Neatness in the mode of emptying the shells of their contents, and other similar matters, are much to be commended; they render the specimens more fitted for the cabinet. But the main points to be attended to, as being those by which science can alone be benefited, are identification and authentication.

IDENTIFICATION.

Of course the most satisfactory, and often the simplest, way of identifying the species to which a nest of eggs, when found, belong, is to obtain one of the parents, by shooting, snaring or trapping. But it sometimes, in practice, happens that this is found to be difficult, from one cause or another—such as the wary instincts of the birds, or the necessities of his position compelling the traveller to lose no time, or the scarcity of the species making him unwilling to destroy the individuals. In any of these cases there is nothing to be done but to make as careful an examination as circumstances will admit, of the precise situation of the nest, the materials of which it is composed (supposing the collector cannot bring it away with him), and accurately to survey the surrounding locality, to observe by what species it is frequented; all the particulars which examination should be fully noted down at the earliest opportunity possible. Should, however, either or both birds be killed, they should be skinned, or at least some characteristic part of the bird preserved, and duly labelled to correspond with the inscriptions subsequently put upon the eggs, and *always* with a reference to the collector's journal or note-book, wherein fuller details may be found.'

The oologist is especially warned not to be misled by the mere fact of seeing birds around or near nests. Many of the crow family (*Corvidæ*) are great eaters of eggs, and mistakes are known to have originated from birds of that kind being seen near nests of which they were certainly not the owners. Others, such as the titmice (*Paridæ*), though not plunderers, obtain their food by incessantly seeking it even in the very localities where many species build. It often happens, also, that two different birds have their nests situated very close to one another, and if they be allied species, the collector may be easily deceived. Thus, it has come to the writer's knowledge that the dunlin (*Tringa alpina*) and the purple sandpiper (*Tringa maritima*) have had their nests only a few feet apart. At first a pair of the latter only were seen, which by their actions betrayed their uneasiness. A short search discovered a nest with four eggs. The observer was one of the best practical oologists then living, and his eye at once saw that it was not the nest which he wanted; but a less experienced man would doubtless have immediately concluded that he had found the eggs of the rarer species.

[TO BE CONTINUED.]

THE HAWKEYE
ORNITHOLOGIST & OOLOGIST

A MONTHLY MAGAZINE
DEVOTED TO ORNITHOLOGY AND KINDRED SUBJECTS, AND GEOLOGY.

EDITED AND PUBLISHED BY

E. B. WEBSTER.   F. D. MEAD.

TERMS OF SUBSCRIPTION.

Per year, - - - - - 50 cents.
Per year to foreign countries, - 65 cents.
Single copies, - - - - 5 cents.
Remittances for subscriptions must be made by postal note—stamps will be returned.

TERMS OF ADVERTISING.

1 line, 1 insertion, - - -	$	.10
1 Inch, " - -		1.00
2 inches, " - -		1.75
½ column, " - -		2.50
1 column, " - -		5.00
1 page, " - -		9.00

A large discount on standing ads. Special rates can sometimes be given.

GENERAL AGENT.— Ph. Heinsberger, 183 Ludlow St., and 89 Delancy St., New York.

All books, periodicals, specimens, etc., sent us will be reviewed.

Correspondence and items of interest relating to the several departments solicited from all. All matter for publication must be in by the last of each month in order to insure insertion in the next number.

WE'VE COMMENCED.

Magazines have been published for the suppression of evil, for the diffusion of general knowledge, for the interests of fashion, for the benefit of the needy, for the good of various causes, for the advancement of business interests, for the advocacy of certain principles, for the defense of the innocent, for the justification of wrongs, for the comfort of the afflicted—this magazine is published for 50 cents per annum.

NOTES.

For a limited time we will give to raisers of clubs a free copy with every five cash subscriptions.

Next month we shall commence a series of articles on the new preservative method of taxidermy, as our teacher learned it of F. Kaempfer, Chicago's leading taxidermist, many years ago.

Harry G. Parker of Chester, Pa., who is connected with the scientific department of the government informs us that he intends to start in a short time for Arizona on a six month's collecting trip.

Just before going to press we received a sample copy of the ressurected *Hoosier Naturalist*, Vol. III, No. 1. It appears as a four page monthly magazine; subscription price 50 cents a year, advertising space $40 per page. Send six cents for sample copy.

We are indebted to Prof. Oliver Davie for a complimentary copy of his "Nests and Eggs," of which we have bought his remaining stock. This is a valuable work, which is in the hands of a majority of collectors, and those not having bought a copy should procure one at once for use during the coming spring.

Our thanks are due Prof. H. W. Davis for fine sets of scientifically prepared eggs of the California Quail and Chaparral Cock or Road-runner. We can recommend Mr. Davis as being a thorough gentleman in every respect, and as he deals only in strictly first-class specimens, he should receive the liberal patronage of all northern oologists.

During the coming spring migration, we will publish an extended report on bird migration in the Mississippi valley. The list of observers we have secured in our county numbers fourteen; the territory consisting of 430 square miles of greatly diversified surface, attracting wood-land, swamp and prairie birds. During the year 1887 our list numbered 183 birds (a good many of the smaller varieties, such as warblers and sparrows, were unknown to our observers). This list embraces about one-half the number of Iowa birds, but with our own observations and those of others on the start, we hope to greatly enlarge this list. All persons are requested to send to us for blanks on which to record their observations, as each addition, however small, will help us in giving a complete record.

Upon reading Mr. Kell's article in which he describes the pugnacious habits of that rightly named little warrior, the kingbird, we were reminded of the actions of a pair of these birds that nested in our city. Their nest was in the top of a tall black-oak tree, which grew very near the sidewalk, over which there was considerable travel. From the time their nest was completed till the young had flown, their time was almost continually spent in warfare upon other birds and all pedestrians. Without the slightest warning whatever, you were suddenly made aware of their whereabouts by a rush of wings and their war-whoop is sounded in your ears; and woe to the passer-by who tarried, a peck on the head was liable to be his reward. In fact, they became so troublesome that the more timid ladies and children, who ordinarily passed under the tree, were compelled to walk on the opposite side of the street, and even then they were not entirely free from attack. We might also add that for three successive years this has been the nesting site of a pair of these birds, no doubt the same ones each year.

TAXIDERMY.

BIRD DISSECTION.

Taking the pigeon as an example we will give, for the benefit of those not possessing either of the works, a series of articles on the structure of birds, using Coues' Key as authority and following the general plan of the work of Prof. Martin. It will be the intention to present the matter in a condensed form convenient for actual work.

1 GENERAL EXTERNAL APPEARANCE.

Supposing the bird to lie before us we will first notice
 a. The tapering of the body toward either end, thus enabling the bird to pass through the atmosphere with as little resistance as possible.
 b. The main divisions of the body and the modification of the fore limbs to form wings.
 c. The *feathers* covering all of the body but the eyelids, bill and lower portions of the legs.

2. OBSERVE ON THE HEAD.
 a. The conical *bill* and the upper and lower *mandibles* with the mouth opening between.
 b. The mandibles are generally of a hard or horny nature near the head.
 c. The opening of the *nostrils*, under the soft swellings of the posterior portion of the upper mandible.
 d. The tip of the upper mandible overlaps the lower, and is in a slight degree flexible.
 e. The circular *eye* with its orange or red *iris*; the opaque *eyelids*, and the *nictitating membrane*, capable of being drawn over the entire eye.
 f. The external portion of the *ear*, found behind the eye by lifting the loose vaned feathers which cover it.

3. SPREAD THE WINGS AND NOTE
 a. Their comparatively large size, due to the stiff feathers.
 b. The concavity of the wings above, and the convexity below.

c. The division of the wings proper into *arm, forearm* and *manus*.
4. ON THE LEGS, STUDY
 a. The *thigh, crus,* or leg proper, and *foot*. The foot consisting of the unfeathered tarso-metatarsus and the four digits, one of the toes being turned backward.
 b. The *claws*.
 c. The peculiar scales (scutellæ) on the upper portions of the legs and toes.
 [TO BE CONTINUED.]

LEAF PHOTOGRAPHS.

A pretty amusement, especially for those contemplating the study of botany, is the taking of leaf photographs. One very simple process is:
At any druggist's get five cents' worth of bichromate of potash. Put this into a two-ounce bottle of sodawater. When the solution has become saturated—that is, the water has dissolved as much as it will—pour off some of the clear liquid into a shallow dish. On this float a piece of ordinary writing paper till it is thoroughly moistened.
Let it become nearly dry in the dark. It should be a bright yellow. On this put the leaf, under it a piece of soft black cloth and several pieces of newspaper. Put this between two pieces of glass—all the pieces should be the same size—and fasten them all together with spring clothes-pins. Expose to a bright sun, placing the leaf so that the rays will fall upon it as nearly perpendicular as possible.
In a few minutes it will begin to turn brown, but it requires from half an hour to several hours to produce a good picture. When it has become dark enough, take it from the frame, and put it in clear water, which must be changed every few minutes, until the yellow part becomes white.
Sometimes the venation of the leaves will be quite distinct. By following these directions it is scarcely possible to fail, and a little practice will make perfect. The photographs, if well taken, are very pretty, as well as interesting.

GEOLOGY.

THE BOWLDER.
SELECTED BY M. R. STEELE.

Though I'm but a granite bowlder,
 Little children, I am older
Than the limestone rocks, that moulder
 On the Upper Iowa's shore.
Torn by glaciers from the mountains,
 From the rivers' snowy fountains,
I, and many thousand more,
 Strew the prairies far and wide,
 Ocean-shore and bleak hillside.
High on Greenland's mountain crest
 See the glacier's silvery breast
Granite rocks upon it crashing;
 Rushing, crushing, dashing, splashing,
To the sea a pathway tearing,
 To the South a burden bearing.
Hark! the crashing iceberg's thunder!
 Man is mute with fear and wonder—
Silent now, o'er ocean's breast
 Towers aloft its gleaming crest.
Far it floats upon the tide,
 Tow'rd a rocky island shore,
Now it strikes! it rolls and tumbles,
 Like a wounded beast it grumbles,
Roars and rages, topples o'er,
 Drops its bowlders on the shore,
On the wild Newfoundland shore.
Thus, in ages past, the bowlders,
 Torn by ice from mountain shoulders,
Scatter'd on the frozen tide,
 Strewed the prairies far and wide,
Ocean shore and bleak hill-side.
 Now the children go a-Maying,
Through the woods and meadows straying,
 See the pebble and the bowlder,
Ask of those who're wiser, older,
 "Pa, do rocks from pebbles grow?
"Surely, papa, you must know!"

For the Hawkeye O. and O.

HOME SCIENCE.
BY H. F. HEGNER, DECORAH, IA.

In this material universe of ours, the laws of nature are repeated from age to age and cycle follows cycle as sure as night follows day. If we were to sum up the flights of time, adding epoch to epoch and age to age, the sum total would be: Time is long! Quickly it passes away. Year follows year in a uniform repetition of the laws of nature. That all benignant sun that shone so brightly during the past summer is but repeating the lesson which he learned in his youth: for the sun is old. Yes, the sun is old and weary, rapidly passing away into feeble age. Those waves of light and heat, without which no life could exist, are gradually losing their strength.

The vital power of the sun is ebbing into eternity, and even this land on which we live is covered with the foam of age. I would that some power could take us back to the time when the earth was young. Would not those mysterious hills come to us in another form, and teach us of marvelous things?

The history of Egyptian wonders (Rameses and all of his idolatrous successors) cannot compare with the history of the section of country that we plow from year to year, and call our own. Those elements around us that give life to all vegetation now, formed the very ground on which our dwellings now stand. I have often heard men complain of the weather—how this is wrong, and that is wrong—how the whole world is wrong, if things do not shape themselves to their minds, but don't you know that the elements around you are your friends?

Without the rain, your crops would'nt grow, and the springs would run dry, the poor, weary cattle would suffer unto death, and all vegetation would die.

No life could exist if deprived of this precious boon. Aye, even the wind would droop and die away; but without the sun we could have no rain.

The elements around us, the sun above us, 92,000,000 miles away,—yes, 'twill bear repeating; these are the agents which have formed the soil that you plant with corn and take such pride in. In what way has the sun done this work? The heat of this fiery sphere evaporates the oceanic waters, and thus forms clouds. The rain comes down and forms rills, creeks and rivers; and these agents spread rich alluvial soil over the land and have finished this expanse of country that we might profit by it—all for us! God in His wise and all powerful plan has done part of His work in this way, and as we enjoy the light and heat of this brilliant orb we are but enjoying the power that formed the solid hills and fertile soil of our mountainous regions and and prairie lands.

[TO BE CONTINUED.]

For the Hawkeye O. and O.

THE BAD LANDS OF DAKOTA.

BY L. W. STILWELL.

A region lying between the White and Cheyenne rivers, where those streams flow near together, in Ziebach, Washington and Jackson counties, and touching the "Bad River," is a barren tract constituting what is known as the heart of the "Bad Lands," (*Mauvaises Terres*). Once covered with an ocean whose waters in the late ages laved the shores of the uplifted island which is now known as the Black Hills, subsequently covered with brackish or fresh water lakes following the subsidence of Old Ocean, this "Bad Lands" region is now left a dry, sterile, desolate waste. The appearance of the soil and rock is that of a marine deposit of clay, sand and calcareous compact. A wierd feeling creeps over the visitor as he stands amidst the towers, pyramids and serrated ridges carved here and there by water erosion; a loneliness steals over him as he perceptibly *feels* the solemn stillness of nature's gray city of pinnacled forms; and he finds himself looking around him, almost expecting to see arise ghosts of the huge mammals that perished with the Tertiary age, whose remains lie buried in the detritus at his feet.

The *Brontotherium* and *Titaotherium* of Marsh, Hayden and Weeks are exhumed in this locality. These animals were of elephantine proportions, and are said to reach the dimensions of twenty-eight feet in length and nine feet in height. I have teeth of the *Brontotherium* three and one-half inches square at the crown. The enamel of the teeth remains in a state of preservation for untold centuries. The bones and teeth of the *Oreoden*, *Anbhitherium* (three-toed horse) *Hyrtcodon*, etc., are found here. The Tertiary turtle is also found fossilized; I have one weighing sixty pounds.

Following up the Cheyenne river and its tributaries, many cretaceous shells are found over quite an extent of margin bordering their banks. The *Scaphties Nodussus*, here illustrated.

are from one inch to three and even four inches across. Most of those discovered have four rows of nodes, two upon each side, as seen in the cut. They are well preserved, mostly imbedded in concrete boulders of a blueish gray, fine-grained calcareous compact that may be called limestone. The specimens come out clear and distinct. Also associated with the *Scaphites* in the same mass are *Baculites*

of all lengths and sizes from one-fourth to two inches in diameter, and from two to ten inches in length. Many are irridescent, and many display very beautifully the sutures as shown in the cut. Figure 2 is only a short portion of a *Baculite*, however it is extremely rare to find the tail termination of these shell-fish. The head portion of this cephalopod was an open shell.

Figure 3 represents an *Ammonite Placenta*, a flat shell-fish with sharp edges, found also in concrete boulders, from the size of an old penny to eighteen inches to two feet across. I sent one to a college in Massachusetts weighing forty-nine pounds, but they are procured from five to seven inches across.

Associated with these three species in the same locality are the *Nautilus DeKayii*, *Inoceramus* in variety, gasteropods, etc.

The Jurassic fossil, *Belemnite Densus* in very fine condition is found at the "foot-hills" of the Black Hills, especially near the volcanic column of *Sanadin Trachyte*. One of the greatest of nature's wonders is this column called the "Devil's Tower" of which we will write at another time.

EXCHANGE NOTICES.

Notices under this heading inserted for one-half cent per word but no notice will be inserted for less than 25 cents.

TO EXCHANGE—First class eggs in sets with full data for V nickels without the word cents on; also for 10, 25 and 50 cent shin plasters, HENRY W. DAVIS,
North Granville, N. Y.

TO EXCHANGE—Bird's eggs in sets with full data for such sets as I may want; also one new Ballard rifle, 22 cal., for sale or to exchange for eggs in sets. Wanted the following single eggs, Red-shouldered Hawk, Sharp-shinned Hawk, Broad-winged Hawk, Marsh Hawk and Osprey.   HENRY W. DAVIS,
North Granville N. Y.

ADVERTISEMENTS.

"He who by his biz would rise must either burst or advertise."

BIRD'S EGGS.

Any of the following first-class sets with full data will be sent by return mail at prices named. Safe delivery guaranteed.

No.	Set of	Name	Per set
20	4	Blue-throated Warbler	$2.00
21	2	B'ack-crested Flycatcher	1.00
52	4	Red-bellied Nuthatch	1.80
394	5	Am. Barn Owl	1.80
42	3	Little Screech Owl	1.25
407a	4	European Hawk Owl	3.00
422	5	European Kestrel	1.30
447	4	Am. Rough-legge'l Hawk	3.00
501	4	Glossy Ibis	1.60
514	4	Golden Plover	1.25
518	4	Ringed Plover	.80
564	4	Northern Phalarope	1.80
558		Long-billed Curlew	1.60
705	1	Fulman Petrel	.80
714	2	Black-throated Diver	2.50
710	2	Red-throated Diver	1.00

Two fine mounted Great-horned Owls and one mounted Bald Eagle for sale cheap. Send for price. Have more than 200 different sets besides the above. Send stamp for full list.

HENRY W DAVIS,
NORTH GRANVILLE, N. Y.

1885.   3 PAGE   1888.

LARGE, ILL'S'T'D CATALOGUE

ELEGANT POLISHED AGATE GOODS, BLACK HILLS MINERALS, BAD LANDS, D. T., CRETACEOUS AND TERTIARY FOSSILS, SIOUX, APACHE AND PUEBLO BUCKSKIN RELICS; 3000 OREGON BIRD ARROW POINTS. WHOLESALE AND RETAIL.

SEND FOR CATALOGUE.

L. W. STILWELL,
DEADWOOD,   -   -   -   D. T.

TO CLOSE OUT

My entire stock of New Mexico and Southern California

BIRD SKINS

I now offer them at greatly reduced rates. Price List sent for stamp. All skins first-class.

CHARLES H. MARSH,
San Diego Co.   DULZURA, CALIFORNIA.

Europe.   Established 1850.   America.

Ph. HEINSBERGER,
108 Ludlow St. and 89 Delancey St.,
NEW YORK, U. S. A.

International Gen. Agency.

Advertising, collecting, patents, addresses furnished in all parts of the world. Stamp Directories $1. U. S. and Foreign stamp papers, 10 papers $1. Postage and Revenue of all countries for sale. 1000 assorted European postage stamps $1. 100 postage stamps of South and Central America, West India Islands $1. 100 different postage stamps of Asia and Australia $5. 10 asst. Confederate notes $1. 4000 gummed hinges? $1. Mercantile agency, news depot, printer. Circulars sent on application with enclosed postage. Correspondence in English, German, French, Dutch and Spanish.
Agent for the Hawkeye Ornithologist and Oölogist.

BARGAINS!

Every intelligent collector will find the collections that I am now offering under the name of

"PECULIAR OCCURRENCES"
— OF —

MINERAL BODIES.

The best thing in the world.
PRICE,   -   -   -   - $2.00.
With a Cabinet, $2.50.

W. S. BEEKMAN,
BOX 108.   -   WEST MEDFORD, MASS.

JOB PRINTING.

We can do any variety of Job Printing, in the finest style and at your prices. Neatness and dispatch guaranteed.

WEBSTER & MEAD,   -   -   CRESCO, IOWA

DAVIE'S EGG CHECK LIST
AND
KEY TO THE NESTS AND EGGS OF
NORTH AMERICAN BIRDS.
SECOND EDITION, REVISED AND ENLARGED.
FINE ILLUSTRATIONS BY THEODORE JASPER, A. M., M. D.

This work has taken a permanent place in the literature relating to the Nesting Habits of our North American Birds. It contains accurate descriptions of the Color and Size of the Eggs of all the Land and Water Birds known to breed in North America. No Oologist can afford to be without this work and it takes the place of expensive works which are usually beyond the reach of many collectors.

WHAT OTHERS SAY OF IT.

"The illustrations are new and far ahead of the old cross-eyed owls and the like which are found in so many ancient and modern works on the subject."—*Thomas McIlwraith, Author of the "Birds of Ontario."*

"I consider it a valuable contribution to ornithological literature. It should be in the hands of every collector."—*Thomas G. Gentry; Author of "Nests and Eggs of Birds of the United States," "Life Histories of the Birds of Eastern Penn,"* etc.

"I must say the illustrations are beautiful, and true to life. You deserve great credit for getting out such a book. It is the only work of the kind I have ever seen that exactly filled the wants of the egg collector."
E. C. Davis, Greenville, Texas.

"Your last work I am more than pleased with; it ought to be in the possession of every collector." — *Edwin A. Chapen, Author of "Cology of New England."*

"It will be of great value to me and I shall prize it highly."—*N. S. Goss, Topeka, Kansas.*

"I am sure you have made a most useful little book, one that every young collector (and many who are not young) ought to have."—*B. W. Everman.*

"I take pleasure in acknowledging the receipt of your "Key to the Eggs of North American Birds." It is very handsomely gotten up and unique. It will certainly take a permanent place in the ornithological literature of the U. S. Fifteen years ago what would I not have given for such a volume? and to-day I welcome it heartily. I wish it great success, which it will surely have, unless I misjudge the sense of all working oologists."—*Dr. Howard Jones, Author of the "Illustrations of the Nests and Eggs of the Birds of Ohio."*

"I cannot refrain from telling you direct how much I welcome this helpmeet in my studies and researches, in short, in a concise and thorough manner it fills a long felt want. Add my name to the long list of admirers, which this charming little book must have made for you."—*Harry G. Parker, Chester, Pa.*

"Have looked it over, and find it invaluable to the egg collector. The work meets a long felt want. The topography of the work is perfect, and the price is within the reach of all."—*A. K. Fuller, Lawrence, Kan.*

Price by mail, - - - $1.00.

Having purchased all the remaining copies of Davie's "Eggs and Nests" we will offer them, until all are sold, at the above price. Those ordering before March 1st, will receive the Hawkeye O. and O. free. Postal note or money order preferred.

WEBSTER & MEAD, Cresco, Iowa.

VOL. I. FEBRUARY, 1888. NO. 2.

THE HAWKEYE
ORNITHOLOGIST
AND OOLOGIST

❧EDITED AND PUBLISHED BY❧
WEBSTER & MEAD,
CRESCO, - - IOWA.

CONTENTS FOR JANUARY.

The Wild Swan's Dying Strain, - - - - Coues' Key.
A Merciless War Upon Birds, - - - - Hon. C. Aldrich.
Canadian Flycatchers, - - - - - Wm. L. Kells.
The Wood Ibis.
Suggestions for Forming Collections of Bird's Eggs, Smithsonian Bulletin.
Animals as Teachers.
Notes.
Bird Dissection.
To Mount Crawfish, - - - - - John O. Snyder.
Home Science, - - - - - - H. F. Hegner.
The Devil's Tower, - - - - - L. W. Stilwell.
    Advertisements.—Read them carefully and state where you saw ad. when writing to advertisers.

R. E. RACHFORD & SON,
COLLECTING NATURALISTS
——AND WHOLESALE DEALERS IN——
BIRD SKINS & EGGS,
BEAUMONT, TEXAS.

COLLECTORS & DEALERS
OF OOLOGICAL AND ORNITHOLOGICAL SPECIMENS.

"The Collector's Hand-book" will be a paper bound book of 50 or more pages devoted to Birds, their Eggs and Nests, Curios., etc. I have engaged some most eminent writers to contribute to it. It will also contain a few advts. from reliable dealers only. The pages are 5x7 inches, and the book has a *guaranteed* circulation of 2500 copies. The following are the

ADVERTISING RATES:

½ inch .25.   1 inch .40,   2 inches .70,   ½ column 1.20,
1 column 2.00,   1 page 3.50.

Terms for ads.:—Cash *after* book is delivered. The price of book alone is a silver dime, in advance. ☞ As to my honesty I can refer to Two Bank Corporations, the Sheriff of Fillmore Co., Nebraska, and others. Address everything to

ANTON DWORAK,
LINCOLN, NEBRASKA.

The Hawkeye Ornithologist & Oologist.

"Better to search the fields for health unbought,
Than fee the doctor for a nauseus draught,
The wise for health on exercise depend,
God never made his work for man to mend."

VOL. I. CRESCO, IOWA, FEBRUARY, 1888. NO. 1.

THE WILD SWAN'S DYING STRAIN.

FROM COUES' KEY.

How sadly sweet, how soft and low
   Is the music born of pain—
How mournful sounds the ebb and flow,
What measured beats, what throb and throe,
   In the wild swan's dying strain.

The archer, Death, and the twanging bow,
   And the fateful shaft on-sped,
All state and grace and pride laid low,
Disordered plumes and crimson flow—
   For the wild swan's heart has bled.

But hear the mournful cry that rings
   On the startled air of night!
As a spirit form in the darkness wings
Its way unseen, the wild swan sings
   His psalm of life and light.

How sadly sweet the solemn strain—
   The dirge of the dying swan!
That wondrous music, child of pain,
That requiem, sounding once again—
   And a bird's soul passes on.

A MERCILESS WAR UPON BIRDS.

Condensed from an Address by Hon. CHARLES ALDRICH, before the Iowa State Horticultural Society.

There can be no doubt that the birds of Iowa, as of the country at large, are yearly diminishing at a rate which should excite our most serious apprehensions, though we would seem to be less merciless in some respects, in the treatment we give them, than the people of certain other regions. Though we are, just now, enjoying beautiful winter weather, there is a wonderful dearth of birds. The noisy jays, troops of charming little chickadees, the busy horned larks, creepers, nut-hatches, winter sparrows, robins and blackbirds, that once enlivened our woods in winter, are gone with few exceptions.

Many species that breed in the wild regions of the far north, come here to winter. These, and still more, our own summer birds, are rapidly disappearing from the land. As to the cause of this alarming change, the rapid settlement of the land may be the first mentioned. The breaking-plow and the tile-drain are constantly transforming the prairie sloughs into dry land, and thus destroying the haunts of red-wings, yellow-headed blackbirds and marsh wrens, that build their nests in the tops of reeds and coarse grasses, above the water, to protect their young from foxes and other vermin. We have in Iowa one hundred or more tile factories. They rapidly aid the removal of these beautiful birds to other regions, never to return. The consequent loss to the farmer, gardener, and orchardist, may be faintly imagined from an estimate made by Wilson, the father of American ornithology. He stated that these three species above—red-wings, yellow-headed blackbirds and marsh wrens—annually destroyed in the then limited area of the United States, 16,-000,000,000 insects. They are among the earliest birds to return from the Sunny South; for many of them are singing in the tree-tops in February, while the ground is still covered with snow. They are the last to leave us in autumn or winter. They do little damage, so little indeed, in comparison with their useful work, that a decent Christian should be ashamed to mention it; though it was once attempted with marvellous stupidity and monumental wickedness to pass a law in Iowa offering rewards for their destruction. The bill made good progress, but was ridiculed to death by Hon. Thomas W. Clagett, then a Representative from Lee County. Without his timely interposition this most disgraceful proposition might possibly have become a law of the state. That the beautiful red-wings do a world of good, that they are most emphatically "feathered friends," the observations of Alexander Wilson fully proved almost a century ago.

Mr. Aldrich then speaks of the rapid destruction of forests, and the fact that we are not planting enough of the right kinds of timber to hold our own with the birds.

But there are, he continues, two modes of bird destruction in active, increasing operation, which occasion more wholesale losses than all others. They ought to be easily preventable, and would be, if we had an enlightened public sentiment on the side of the birds and humanity. The first mode referred to is the universal slaughter of birds for millinery purposes, which has at last aroused a general protest, and a determination to change the fashion. "Live skins" are considered the best! Who would encourage so inhuman a practice?

Lastly, the mania for stealing eggs is referred to. Sharp eyed small boys are allowed to range the fields and woods for the purpose of making "collections" of birds' eggs. Every accessible nest is harried; the eggs are "blown," and then arranged in "strings" or boxes. People who are very strict in sending their boys to Sunday School, and requiring perfect lessons, still encourage this wicked and unlawful business of robbing nests! Yes, we have laws, but they are not enforced.

America's ornithologists should see that public sentiment is aroused to a just sense of the magnitude of the fashion evil, and that the laws forbidding "collecting" for unscientifical purposes be enforced.

ORNITHOLOGY.

For the Hawkeye O. and O.

CANADIAN FLYCATCHERS.
BY WM. L. KELLS, LISTOWEL, ONTARIO.

THE CRESTED FLYCATCHER.
(*Myiarchus Crinitus.*)

This species receives its name from the remarkable crest that adorns the back part of the head. It is between seven and eight inches in length. The plumage on the upper parts is a greyish-olive hue; the throat and fore breast, dark ash, the lower parts yellow. It arrives in central Ontario in the early days of May, and makes its advent known by loud warning notes, as if announcing to the woods and fields, and all animated existences therein, that it was time to "wake up, for the coming of summer is nigh." It does not appear to be abundant in any part of this province, though sometimes the rural ornithologist notes its call on the margin of high, hardwood lands, and again in the depths of the swampy woods its notes direct him to its perch on the top of some monarch of the forest; and again he may observe a pair sportively chasing each other among the trees of an orchard.

It appears also to have a partiality for the vicinity of small lakes, and the rolling margins of rivers, and near such places its loud call suddenly uttered, often startles the wanderer in the woods, who would not otherwise be aware of its existence. It feeds largely on the various species of insects that make the woods their home; many of these being captured on the wing with the grace and dispatch peculiar to its family. In disposition it sometimes manifests some of those irritable propensities which are characteristic of its relative, the kingbird; and when the female is nesting she is occasionally subjected to treatment, like the female bobolink for which there appears no reason, except the bad temper of her partner. This species makes its nest in the hollows of trees, or in woodpecker's holes and in the older settled parts of the country, the boxes put up for martins and blue-birds are sometimes occupied. The nest is composed of wood, strips of bark, fine dry grass and hair, and sometimes in it are found the cast off skins of snakes. The set of eggs numbers from four to six; they are of a buffy white color, marked all over the surface with purplish brown lines.

THE PHŒBE FLYCATCHER.
(*Sayornis Phœbe.*)

This is the commonest and best known of the flycatcher family found in Canada, and is among the earliest of our returning spring birds. In the early morning, while the air is still cold and patches of snow still lingering in the woods, and around the fences, and while but few others of our feathered visitants have returned from their tropical exile, perched on the top of some building, on a fence post, or on the leafless branch of some tree; the pleasant and familiar "phœbe" of this little wanderer may be heard greeting the new born day and returning spring, to the delight of the rural Canadian and the observant student of nature. Its simple notes seem always pleasing, not for their variety or melody, but rather for their pleasing ideas of renewed life and animation with which they are associated; and the confiding nature which the performer itself evinces.

This species remains in Ontario for about five months in each year, and during that period it may be found ranging the outskirts of the woods, the vicinity of farm buildings, and the streets of towns and villages; and especially is it to be found frequenting the margins of watercourses in the vicinity of bridges, where it is always sure to find a suitable nesting place, and under some of these structures, which span the streams on every road, a nest is found. It is an expert insect catcher, and generally captures its victims on the wing, by a series of darting evolutions, though it will also alight upon the grass or drop down among the grain in order to secure a prized morsel, and at times it may be observed skimming over the plowed fields in quest of its favorite food. Those who choose the woods as their summer habitat, make their nests in the roots of fallen trees, while those who prefer to abide near the habitations of man, find nesting places in the barn, the wood shed, or porch, or on some projection beneath the eaves of the dwelling house. Its nest has also been found in chimneys, old wells, caves, sawmills, and on pieces of bark hanging from logs crossing streams. The nest is composed externally of a species of moss gathered from stones in damp places, wool and fibers of bark; with a little mud, and neatly lined with fine dry grass and hair. The set of eggs, of a white color, sometimes with a few small reddish dots towards the large end, is from four to six in number. If the first effort at brood raising is successful, it does not appear to nest more than once in the season, otherwise it will nest a second time. When perching, either repeating its ditty or watching for a passing insect, the tail is constantly jerked up and down with a wagging motion. In length, this species is between six and seven inches The plumage on the upper parts is a dusty olive-black; darkest on the head, the lower parts has a lighter hue, the feathers on the head are loose and crested, and there are short bristles at the base of the bill. Though it is an early spring visitant; yet it generally leaves this country early in September, or as soon as the first severe frost indicates the approach of autumn.

THE OLIVE-SIDED FLYCATCHER.
(*Contopus Borealis.*)

This bird is but rarely met with in this section of country, and it seems to be rather uncommon in any part of Ontario as well as the other provinces of Canada, though solitary individuals are generally met with in various places every year. It has always been in the early springtime that I have observed it in the neighborhood of Listowel. The first time that I noticed a specimen of this species, was seven or eight years ago. It was among some fruit and ornamental trees in front of a private residence on Main street near the center of the town; it was quietly seeking its food, flying down to the ground after some food-stuff, and as soon as it had picked it up, returning to a branch overhead, in a quiet, leisurely manner. Some days after I saw it again in a piece of low woods, a mile east of the town. Two or three seasons afterwards I saw another in a piece of dry hard-wood, undergrowth, southwards of this place. This was also in the early springtime, before the leaves had begun to make their appearance on the trees. It may yet become a summer resident in this vicinity as several other species have done in recent years. In the early days of the past October, when at Niagara Falls, soon after crossing the bridges, from the mainland, on the eastern side to Goat Island, and taking the road to the right towards the cataracts I heard a rustling in the leaves overhead, and looking upwards, saw at an elevation of about twenty feet, a fine plumage individual of the olive-sided flycatcher. It was then actively gleaning among the leaves, and seemed not in the least alarmed by the many tourists who were passing below. A little farther on, the notes of a kinglet caught the ear; and then several robins were noticed; and the "cawing" of a number of crows sounded overhead. These were the only evidences of bird-life then observable in that celebrated place. But when my companion and I reached the turning point towards the Horse-shoe Falls, between the island and the Canadian shore, as we gazed down the mighty chasm where the waters of the Niagara tossed and foamed after their tremendous plunge, we saw, unalarmed by the sound of many waters, or the actions of the "Maid of the Mist" three beautiful ospreys busily pursuing their winged evolutions over the still raging torrent.

The olive-sided flycatcher is between seven and eight inches in length; and, as its name implies, the plumage on the sides of the body is of a bright olive-yellow hue, while that on the upper part of the body and wings is more of a dusky color. I have never yet seen its nest or eggs, but am informed that its nest is much like that of the kingbird, and that the eggs, three or four in number, are of a creamy-white color, speckled with reddish brown.

[TO BE CONTINUED.]

THE WOOD IBIS.

(Tantalus loculator.)

The wood ibis, a southern bird, is at once remarkable and interesting to the observer. In its size and shape, it much resembles the crane, being about four feet in height and even more when standing erect. It is white in color with wings and tail tipped with black. This bird's head is very peculiar, being entirely bald, and is furnished with an enormously thick and heavy bill.

This bird is in some sections of its habitat called the "gannet;" in others it is known as the 'water turkey.'

The wood ibis is distributed over nearly all the Southern States from the Carolinas to Colorado, although assembling in the greatest numbers along the Colorado and Gila rivers. This habitat is extended eastward to the Ohio river; but the swamps and lagoons of Louisana, Mississippi and Florida, are their favorite resort.

They are gregarious in habits. Audubon speaks of their being seen in flocks "composed of several thousand;" but large flocks are not always the rule, as very often single individuals may be seen flying or wading.

Their carriage is very firm; walking about very sedately, lifting each leg with the greatest deliberation and precision. They never run rapidly; when alarmed they always take flight.

They feed entirely upon fish and other aquatic animals, of which they destroy an enormous quantity; fishes, frogs, young alligators and snakes being their prey. Its method of obtaining food is very singular; as soon as its prey is discovered, it begins a dance, roiling the water so that the fishes, etc., rise to the surface, when it strikes them with its bill.

The eggs are elliptical in form; a dull white color, without markings, and rather rough to the touch, with a coating of flaky calcareous substance. Two or three constitute a set.

The young are entirely dusky-gray, with brownish-black wings and bill. The heads is at first covered with a downy plumage, but gradually becomes bald. About four years are required for the bird to attain the adult plumage.

OOLOGY.

SUGGESTIONS FOR PROPERLY FORMING COLLECTIONS OF BIRDS' EGGS.

Indeed it may, generally speaking, be said of most birds, that whenever they have nests of their own they are acquainted with those of their neighbors, which by their actions they will often betray to the collector who may be patiently watching them. Birds, again, will occasionally lay their eggs—accidentally, as it were—in the nests of other species, even when they were not of a parasitic nature, as the Old World cuckoos (*Cuculus, Eudyamis* and *Oxylophus,*) or the cow blackbird (*Molothrus ater;*) thus eggs of the eider duck (*Somateria mollissima*) have been found in the nest of a gull (*Larus*) and other similar cases are on record in some of which from the species being nearly allied, confusion might easily have arisen, though at the time, no doubt may have occurred in the collector's mind.

It would be impossible in this paper to treat of the various methods which may be successfully employed to obtain the birds, to whom a nest belongs, and, in fact, these methods can generally be learned only by experience. It is sufficient to indicate here the use of traps, snares, hingles or bird-lime, in cases where the individuals are too shy to admit of being shot by the gun or rifle. Much may often be gathered by the collector from the practice of the natives, especially if they be savages, or half civilized. In like manner it would too much extend these suggestions to give a detailed account of the different ways in which the nests of birds are to be found. The experience of a single season is to most men worth a whole volume that might be written on the subject. Nevertheless, a few hints are given further on, which might not occur to the beginner.

AUTHENTICATION.

The most complete method of authenticating eggs is that of writing in ink on their shells, not only the name of the species to which each belongs, but also, as far as the space will admit, as many particulars relating to the amount of identification to which the specimen was subjected, the locality where, date when, and the name of the person by whom they were taken, *adding always* a reference to the Journal or note-book of the collector, wherein *fuller details* may be given. It is advisable to do this on some regular system, and the following method is suggested as one that has already been found to work well in practice. The *scientific* names *only* to be used, except with a mark of doubt or within brackets, when the specimens have *really been satisfactorily identified*; and if the identification has been made by obtaining one or both of the parent birds, a memorandum of the fact to be added, thus: "Both birds snared;" "Bird-shot;" or in smaller space, "Bd. st."

[TO BE CONTINUED.]

ANIMALS AS TEACHERS.
SELECTED.

How much we are indebted to the lower animals! Some of them labor for us. Some furnish us food, clothing and shoes. Bees make honey for us, and silk-worms give us the most beautiful garments. Various insects carry pollen from plant to plant, which, without this cross fertilization, would not produce seed and fruit. Even earthworms, as Darwin has informed us, are very useful as drainers and plowers of the soil.

But animals also teach us mechanic arms, showing their own bodies as models. Builders of boats and ships have only imitated the forms, and studied the motions, of fish and waterfowl. These are so made as to unite buoyancy with speed. The nose of a fish and the stiff fins on his back act as cutwaters, and his flexible side fins as oars. His tail, combining the rudder and oar, makes a sculling motion familiar to all boys who use boats. John Ericsson, the inventor of the Monitor and the caloric engine, after studying the motion of a fish's tail, invented the screw propeller, which is now generally used on large steamers instead of side wheels.

The octopus or devil fish, and the beautiful nautilus, of the same family, swim by sucking water into a tube, and ejecting it behind them, the reaction producing a forward motion. A steamer has been propelled in the same manner, but not fast enough to suit American travelers.

The sails of a ship imitate the wings of a bird. The long bones and plumes of a bird's wing resemble the spars of a ship and the sails attached to them. The bird in flying and the dog in swimming use their tails as rudders.

The slime, that covers the bodies of fish, is supplied by glands in the head, and, like paint on a boat, makes the scales waterproof, and helps the fish to glide easily through the water. The scale armor of the ancients was suggested by the scales of a fish. The Roman soldiers employed in mining hostile walls worked with one hand, while they covered themselves with a continuous roof, made of their overlapping shields and named *testudo*, or tortoise.

The *teredo navalis*, or ship-worm, bores with an auger attached to his head. Another borer preys on bivalves. He makes a round hole, reamed out like a screw-hole, and sucks the shell-fish dry. Hard rocks are honey-combed by shell-fish armed with files; and crabs and lobsters have terrible forceps for holding and crushing their prey. The large eyes of the octopus suggested one of the most powerful lenses used by microscopists. This animal's long arms are furnished with many cups and lancets, similar to those used by physicians in drawing blood. The "fishing frog" or angler is a fish with a huge mouth, in front of which a bait hangs on a slender spine or rod, to allure the small fry to their doom.

If man is ever able to traverse the air at will, as he sails the ocean, his vessel must imitate the form and propellers of a fish.

Of all insects the most interesting for study is the honey-bee, the subject of many learned works, and hardly yet understood. Who can solve the mystery of the bee-hive? By sprinkling bees with flour they have been tracked from a clover field forty miles to their hive. How do they know their way home?

It has lately been discovered that the sting of the bee is not merely a defensive weapon, but is also a tube used to puncture each filled honey cell, when filled and capped with wax. The bee then injects a drop of formic acid, which prevents the honey from spoiling. The *tremex*, or saw-borer fly carries her tools within a sheath, and deposits her eggs in the hole she has made.

Disturb an ants' nest, or throw crumbs or seeds where ants will find them, and you will soon see ants, even far from the nest, conversing in pairs, by rubbing their feelers together, and afterward hurrying to gather the harvest or to repair the ant-hills. Solomon says: "Go to the "ant, thou sluggard; consider her "ways, and be wise, which, having no "guide, overseer or ruler, provideth "her meat in the summer, and gathereth her food in the harvest." Animals are endowed with a subtile instinct unknown to man, and mistaken by some, for reason. Cats and dogs, birds and fish return from distant places by land, air or water, to their early homes.

We have so much in common with the lower animals, and they are so serviceable to us, that we owe great kindness to these "poor relations." They teach us lessons of family affection, and of trust in the providential care of Him who feeds and guards us all. Birds delight us with their curious nests, their airy flights, their wide diversity of character.

Their beauty and song please our senses, and cheer us in the dull round of daily toil. Kindness to inferior creatures ennobles us. "The merciful man regardeth the life of his "beast."

THE
ORNITHOLOGIST & OOLOGIST

A MONTHLY MAGAZINE DEVOTED TO ORNITHOLOGY AND KINDRED SUBJECTS, AND GEOLOGY.

EDITED AND PUBLISHED BY

E. B. WEBSTER. F. D. MEAD.

TERMS OF SUBSCRIPTION.

Per year, - - - 50 cents.
Per year to foreign countries, 65 cents.
Single copies, - - - 5 cents.
Remittances for subscriptions must be made postal note—stamps will be returned.

TERMS OF ADVERTISING.

1 line, 1 insertion,	- -	$ .10
1 inch,	" - -	1.00
2 inches,	" - -	1.75
½ column,	" - -	2.50
1 column,	" - -	5.00
1 page,	" - -	10.00

A large discount on standing ads. Special rates can sometimes be given.

GENERAL AGENT.—Ph. Heinsberger, 138 Ludlow St., and 80 Delancy St., New York.

All books, periodicals, specimens, etc., sent us will be reviewed.

Correspondence and items of interest relating to the several departments solicited from all. All matter for publication must be in by the last of each month in order to insure insertion in the next number.

NOTES.

Our article on the "new preservative method" has been indefinitely postponed owing to the ad. of Mr. Gibbs in this issue.

Orders have already been received from several for those migration blanks. Send ahead for them—we want everyone to help us out in our report.

The present month's magazine is somewhat smaller than the last, owing to the fact that we expect to be crowded for time on the March issue, of which we intend to print several thousand copies.

For several nights large flocks of screech owls have been hovering around the cornices of big buildings in Columbus, Ind. A dispatch says an investigation was instituted, and the discovery made that, "the owls are catching and devouring hundreds of English sparrows. They drag them from their nests or roosting places beneath the cornices, carry them away and devour them."

A four-footed bird has been discovered in South America. The "cigana" (*Opisthecmu cristata,*) or "gipsy," as it is called by the natives, lives on the Anabiju River, in the island of Marajo, at the mouth of the Amazon, and builds its nest in the reeds of the "aninga," a large-leaved semi-aquatic plant, which grows in dense masses in the island swamps. The bird resembles a pheasant, and is only fourfooted in early life, as, after a few days' existence, one pair of legs develops into wings.

There is at Leeds, England, an ornithological association. Among other things, they study the songs of wild birds. Not long ago they pitted a full-song, acclimated nightingale against an American mocking-bird. They sang together, and then they sang apart. First the nightingale led off, until everything he sang was duplicated and improved upon by our national songster. Then the mocking-bird struck off into a new field of song. The nightingale listened, but did not repeat. He pined away and died within a week.

Mr. Hegner, of Decorah, writes us that he has been studying the "ice cave" of that place and intends to issue a pamphlet next summer giving measurements, currents of air, etc.,— also a theory more accurate than the one he has already published. He says: "To tell you the truth, this theory will unfold a marvelous cause for the formation of this ice. I never dreamed of the real cause until I carried my investigations to actual experiment. Before the appearance of this theory I would be glad to give you an article bringing forth the salient points in it."

At a public school-house near Topeka, Kansas, there is a drinking cup that attracts the attention of all who catch a glimpse of it. The cup was brought from Melbourne, Australia, by an uncle of the young man who teaches at the school. There are many such cups in Melbourne, where they are made of emu eggs. The eggs of the emu are like pebbled leather and they are very strong. Being of a myrtle-green color, they are handsome objects. The ostrich eggs are sometimes used for similar purposes. They are like ivory, both in hardness and in color, and weigh as much as three pounds when full.

The native clergyman in some of the Pacific islands correspond with each other by means of the frigate bird. For instance, two islands in the Ellice group are about sixty miles apart, and the carrier birds are very useful in bearing messages from island to island. The note is usually concealed in a bit of reed and tied to one of the wings. In the olden times pearl fish-hooks were in this way sent from one island to another. During a cyclone the frigate bird flies so low that it is easily knocked down by a long stick. When sitting on her solitary white egg the mother bird will allow herself to be seized by the hand.

TAXIDERMY.

BIRD DISSECTION.

5. FEATHERS.
Note on one of the larger feathers of the wing.
a. The main stem, called *scapus*.
b. The quill, or *calamus*, cylindrical, translucent and hollow. That portion which was imbedded in the skin, the end of which is perforated as if by a needle, contains a reddish pulp; the opposite end being filled with scales.
c. The remainder of the scapus is called the *rachis*. Rectangular in shape, it tapers to a point. The color is whitish; it is opaque, and contains a dry pith.
d. The slender filaments, fringing a depression in the under side of the scapus, where the rachis and calamus meet. There is in this depression another opening leading into the calamus.
e. The large, flat portions of the feather, called *vanes*, or *vexillæ*. These are situated on the opposite sides of the rachis. In most feathers they are of the same size. The vanes will be found to be composed of a considerable number of
f. *Barbs*. These are fastened together firmly enough to make the whole vane a continuous membrane. Each separate barb is triangular in shape and is set obliquely on the rachis with the base sloping towards the calamus.
g. By examining the vane with a microscope the *barbules*, a number of thin plates on each side of the barb may be seen. The barbules of each barb cross ob-

liquely the barbules of the next barbs.

h. The barbules on the side of the of the barb towards the calamus end in closely packed slender filaments, *barbicels*. The barbules on the opposite side are looser, and consist of larger filaments, bearing fine processes and knobs, these knobbed threads are hooked on the slender filaments of the neighboring barbules, so that the whole forms a membrane which gives a firm resistance to the air.

6. FEATHERS—VARIETIES.

a. A feather of the kind described is known as a *penna* or a *contour feather*.
b. Under these feathers are the *plumulæ*, or down feathers. There are but few of these on the pigeon. They resemble the contour feathers, with the exception that the barbules do not interlock.
c. The hair feathers (*filo plumæ*) may be found among the others upon plucking the belly of the bird. But few barbs and no clear distinctions between calamus and rachis.
d. The *semi-plumæ*, differing from the penna by the vanes being loose and downy, are found on the under surface of the body.

TO MOUNT CRAW FISH.

Taking a specimen (just killed) by the back, between the thumb and finger, press or pull the tail downward with the other hand in such a manner as to separate the shell of the back from the tail and breast. Now with a small knife, scrape out all soft matter from the body and also the flesh from inside the tail. Replace the shell of the back and arrange the legs and claws in their natural shape. Drying it in a slow oven or under the stove will color it a bright red. Drying it in the sun will give it a purple and red color.

But to preserve its natural color, it should be dried in a dark box.—[*John O. Snyder in Hoosier Naturalist.*

GEOLOGY.

HOME SCIENCE.
BY H. F. WEGNER, DECORAH, IA.

[CONCLUDED FROM LAST NUMBER.]

I remember a time when I classed the rough, unsightly stones and bowlders, found in our river beds or on our fields, as a nuisance. They were in the way and interfered with the cultivation of the land, and in this sense might have been called a nuisance; but now these stones and bowlders have a language for me, and I love to read it. They tell me that these fields were not always here, and that the dry land was not always where it is at present.

Far to the west, where the continental backbone stretches from the peninsula of Alaska to the isthmus of Panama, the ocean extended. The Rocky Mountains were not yet formed, and the sea shells, which are found to-day embedded in the solid rock, lived in this ocean. But here comes this all important question. If these shells lived in an ocean and died there, how is it that we find them turned to solid stone hundreds of miles from an ocean?

'Tis by years of study that the geologist has acquired the power to answer this question. If you desire to learn the geologist's method of study, my friends, come with me to the Iowa river, and let us dig into one of these sandy banks.

What is this we have come to? 'Tis a clam shell filled with hardened sand. As we dig deeper we find more similar specimens.

Where did they come from? They came from the Iowa river to be sure. You will notice that the current has eaten its way into the bank opposite us. While the current was doing this work, the sediment on which we are now standing was deposited, and these shells as they died, were buried in this sediment, being first filled with sand.

The shells which lived in that aged ocean, of which we have been speaking, died and were buried in the sediment brought down by the Silurian rivers, which drained the continent, the same as our river systems drain our continental bodies now. This continent, though, extended far to the north. The pressure of the ocean, about 9,000 pounds per cubic foot, together with internal heat, hardened this sediment, making rock of it. Since then it has been raised from the ocean's bed, and beautified for the advent of man.

Fossils is the name given to all such petrified remains of vegetable and animal life, and 'twas by studying the fossils of our country that the geologist has been able to trace the history of animal life, even from that remote sea where all was so dark and gloomy, the Azoic sea. From the first appearance of life in the Eozoic seas, he has been able to trace the different forms of animal life, which increased in species and order, but decreased in number, until the order next lower to man was reached. Then man was created, not by evolution, but as a separate, holy creation; and the last touch was thus added to this beautiful earth.

This is what the geologist has accomplished by his persistent study; and his work has been practical as well. Our coal mines are valuable, and it is beautiful to think of these grand treasures stored away for centuries by a kind and benevolent God, that we might use them for our own benefit and comfort. But God has done more than this: He not only stored away the coal for us, but also sent us the geologist, that is, gave us minds that can be developed by studying the works of God through nature.

If we were to dig for coal and other valuable minerals where they do not exist, much labor would be wasted. The science of geology, though still in its youth, enables us to locate the presence of valuable minerals, if they are to be found; and, if geology tells us that no coal exists in a certain region, 'twould be foolish for us to search for it.

"The geologist may be mistaken," you say. You would hardly wish to invest your money in such vague speculations as this. The geologist has studied this subject well; he ought to know, and the outcome will be a loss of the money that you invest in digging for coal in such regions.

There is no coal in the north eastern part of Iowa. The coal regions are to the south west of us, along the Des Moines river; therefore it would be useless to dig for coal here. My space is too limited to give the reasons in full why coal is not found in strata below the carboniferous; but in the near future I intend to write an article giving these reasons in detail. In closing, let us bear this in mind, there is nothing that improves the intellect like a study of the Natural Sciences. Observe and investigate, no matter where you are. Even the roughest stones can teach you a valuable lesson. There is history in Nature. You can read it if you try. Go, then, and do your best. Use all your spare moments in studying these wonderful works of God.

Lieutenant Greely believes that there is an ocean 1500 miles in diameter round about the pole, that never freezes, and conjectures that the pole itself is the center of an ice-capped land, covered with ice from 1000 to 4000 feet thick.

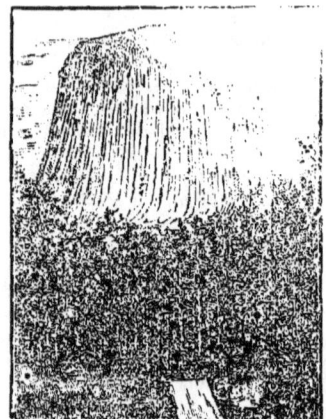

For the Hawkeye O. and O.

THE DEVIL'S TOWER.
BY L. W. STILWELL.

There are a number of peaks and buttes in the Black Hills of volcanic origin. Crow Peak, Terry's Peak. Bear Butte, Inyan Kara, etc., are wonderful, but none stand out to the wondering gaze of the over-awed admirer as does the Devil's Tower.

The indications of these peaks, generally in the northern part of the hills, is not that of overflowing erruption, but rather of the pushing through the crust of the earth of a plastic material by volcanic force from beneath. The bases of the peaks show strata turned up edgewise and *porphyritic trachyte* and *rhyolite* abound at the places of intrusion. The Devil's Tower *seems* to be the core of a volcano, the walls having eroded and crumbled away.

This great rectangular obelisk consists of an aggregation of crystal like columns; nearly every individual column extending unbroken from base to summit, giving the entire structure the appearance of a fascicle of gigantic fibres.

The rock is a greenish-gray *Sanijin Trachyte.* The great crystals having generally a rectangular or rhombic section, with sometimes a triangular or hexagonal form, have sides measuring two to four feet. One crystal 30 feet long has cleaved from the mass and fallen flat to the ground with a sharp edge upward, broken out of place like one-eighth of an orange.

The height from the Belle Fourche river is 1126 feet and it rises 625 feet from the mound on which it stands. Its width at the base is 796 feet, and at the summit 376 feet.

The Indians named it "Mato Tipi" or Bear Lodge and called it "The bad god's tower," hence the name Devil's Tower.

Eminent geologists who have examined it say "it is a remarkable structure and appears not to have been repeated elsewhere in nature but stands alone, unique and mysterious."

EXCHANGE NOTICES.

Notices under this heading inserted for one-half cent per word but no notice will be inserted for less than 25 cents.

WANTED—First-class eggs of Swallow-tailed Kite, Prairie Falcon, Pigeon Hawk, American Bittern, Wilson's Snipe, Solitary Sandpiper, Bartram's Sandpipe, Baldpate, Blue and Green-winged Teal, Hooded Shelldrake, Noddy and Sooty Terns. I can offer sets of Golden Eagle, Iceland Falcon, Iceland Gulls, Skua Gulls, and other eggs from the Arctic regions
W. RAINE. Walton St,
Toronto, Canada.

TO EXCHANGE—Bird's eggs in sets with full data for each set as I may want; also one n w Bizzard Rifle, 22 cal., for sale or to exchange for eggs in sets. Wanted the following single eggs; Red-shouldered Hawk, Marsh Sharp-shinned, and Broad-winged Hawks and Osprey.
HENRY W. DAVIS,
North Granville N. Y.

TO EXCHANGE—First class eggs in sets with full data for V nickles without the word cents on; also for 70, 25 and 50 cent skin plasters.
HENRY W. DAVIS,
North Granville. N. Y.

ADVERTISEMENTS.

"He who by his biz would rise must either burst or advertise."

EVERYONE
SHOULD HAVE IT!

Write and receive a large sheet of printed explanations regarding our new and easy process of preserving birds, etc.

EMBALMING:

Easy to learn; scarcely any expense; no time or money wasted; few tools required, and those made at home; simple and effective; no difficult complicance to dishearten the amateur or beginner; satisfaction guaranteed.

ALWAYS SEND 2c STAMP FOR REPLY!

Eggs. Skins. etc., to exchange.
Wanted—All kinds of Natural History Specimens, also Indian Relics.

R. M. GIBBS,
KALAMAZOO, MICH.

Gem arrow points from the Willamette river, Oregon, at wholesale and retail 3000 on hand.

SANIDIN TRACHYTE

From the "Devil's Tower, (described elsewhere in these columns,) for sale in cabinet specimens. Black Hills.
mineral,
bad I. nd's. D. T., fossils
Sioux and Apache buckskin beaded relics. For 8-page illustrated catalogue write to

L. W. STILWELL,
Deadwood, D. T.

BIRD'S EGGS.

Any of the following first-class sets with full data will be sent by return mail at prices named.
Safe delivery guaranteed.

No.	Set of	Name	Per set
20	4	Blue-throated Warbler	$2.00
26	2	Black-crested Flycatcher	1.00
52	4	Red-bellied Nuthatch	1.80
394	5	Am. Barn Owl	1.80
4 2	3	Little Screch Owl	1.25
407a	4	European Hawk Owl	3.00
422	5	European Kestrel	1.30
447	1	Am. Rough-legged Hawk	3.00
503	4	Glossy Ibis	1.60
514	4	Golden Plover	1.25
518	4	Ringed Plover	.80
564	4	Northern Phalarope	1.80
558	7	Long-billed Curlew	1.60
03	1	Fulman Petrel	.85
7.68	3	Black-throated Diver	2.50
740	2	Red-throated Diver	1.00
1-3	3	Roseate Spoonbill	3.00
264	4	Am Osprey	1.25
375	2	Great Horned Owl	3.00
108	2	Barred Owl	1.00
531	5	Lawrence Goldfinch	1.25

Two fine mounted Great-horned Owls and one mounted Ba ld Eagle for sale cheap. Send for price. Have more than 200 different sets besides the above. Send stamp for full list.

HENRY W. DAVIS,
NORTH GRANVILLE, N. Y.

BIRDS EGGS AND SKIRS

At reasonable prices. Send stamp for price list.

J. A. SINGLEY,
GIDDINGS, TEXAS.

Europe.   Established 1859.   America

Ph. HEINSBERGER,
138 Ludlow St. and 89 Delancey St.,
NEW YORK, U. S. A.
International Gen. Agency.

Advertising, collecting, patents, addresses furnished in all parts of the world. Stamp Directories $1. U. S. and Foreign stamp papers, 10 papers $1. Postage and Revenue of all countries for sale. 1000 assorted European postage stamps $1. 100 postage stamps of South and Central America, West India Islands $1, 100 different postage stamps of Asia and Australia $5, 10 asst. Confederate notes $1. 4000 gummed hinges $1. Mercantile agency, news depot, printer. Circulars sent on application with enclosed postage. Correspondence in English, German, French, Dutch and Spanish.
Agent for the Hawkeye Ornithologist and Oologist.

DAVIE'S EGG CHECK LIST
AND
KEY TO THE NESTS AND EGGS OF
NORTH AMERICAN BIRDS.
SECOND EDITION, REVISED AND ENLARGED.
FINE ILLUSTRATIONS BY THEODORE JASPER, A. M., M. D.

This work has taken a permanent place in the literature relating to the Nesting Habits of our North American Birds. It contains accurate descriptions of the Color and Size of the Eggs of all the Land and Water Birds known to breed in North America. No Oologist can afford to be without this work and it takes the place of expensive works which are usually beyond the reach of many collectors.

WHAT OTHERS SAY OF IT.

"The illustrations are new and far ahead of the old cross-eyed owls and the like which are found in so many ancient and modern works on the subject."—*Thomas McIlwraith, Author of the "Birds of Ontario."*

"I consider it a valuable contribution to ornithological literature. It should be in the hands of every collector."—*Thomas G. Gentry; Author of "Nests and Eggs of Birds of the United States," "Life Histories of the Birds of Eastern Penn," etc.*

"I must say the illustrations are beautiful, and true to life. You deserve great credit for getting out such a book. It is the only work of the kind I have ever seen that exactly filled the wants of the egg collector."—*E. C. Davis, Greenville, Texas.*

"Your last work I am more than pleased with; it ought to be in the possession of every collector."—*Edwin A. Chapen, Author of "Oology of New England."*

"It will be of great value to me and I shall prize it highly."—*N. S. Goss, Topeka, Kansas.*

"I am sure you have made a most useful little book, one that every young collector (and many who are not young) ought to have."—*B. W. Evermann.*

"I take pleasure in acknowledging the receipt of your "Key to the Eggs of North American Birds." It is very handsomely gotten up and unique. It will certainly take a permanent place in the ornithological literature of the U. S. Fifteen years ago what would I not have given for such a volume? and to-day I welcome it heartily. I wish it great success, which it will surely have, unless I misjudge the sense of all working oologists."—*Dr. Howard Jones, Author of the "Illustrations of the Nests and Eggs of the Birds of Ohio."*

"I cannot refrain from telling you direct how much I welcome this helpmeet in my studies and researches, in short, in a concise and thorough manner it fills a long felt want. Add my name to the long list of admirers, which this charming little book must have made for you."—*Harry G. Parker, Chester, Pa.*

"Have looked it over, and find it invaluable to the egg collector. The descriptions are accurate and the work meets a long felt want. The topography of the work is perfect, and the price is within the reach of all."—*A. K. Fuller, Lawrence, Kan.*

Price by mail, - - - $1.00.

Having purchased all the remaining copies of Davie's "Eggs and Nests" we will offer them, until all are sold, at the above price. Those ordering before March 1st, will receive the Hawkeye O. and O. free. Postal note or money order preferred.

WEBSTER & MEAD, Cresco, Iowa.

VOL. I.   MARCH, 1885.   NO. 3.

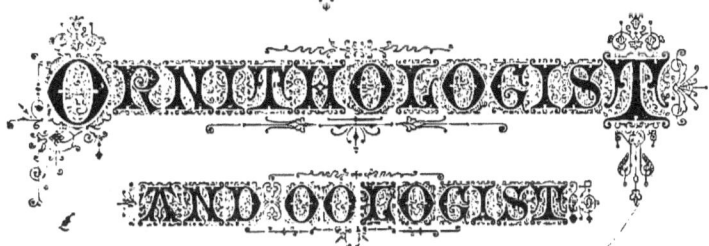

☙EDITED AND PUBLISHED BY☙
WEBSTER & MEAD,
CRESCO,   ·   ·   IOWA.

CONTENTS FOR MARCH.

Facts About the Birds. - - - - Dr. F. W. Langdon.
Bird Nesting in the North of England, - - Walter Raine.
Canadian Flycatchers, - - - - - - Wm. Kells.
Carolina Wren, - - - - - - J. W. Jacobs.
Habits of Some American Grebes, - - - - Oliver Davie.
Notes on Some of the Passeres of Fulton Co., Ky., - - - L. O. Pindar.
The Traill's Flycatcher, - - - - - - James Purdy.
The Bobolink, - - - - - - - Frank L. Burns.
Remarks on Bobolink and Kingbird, - - - - J. A. Singley.
Reminiscences of the Early Life of a Tame Crow.
Migration Report.
"Protect Our Birds." - - - - - - E. G. Ward.
Notes.
Kind Words.
Home Science, - - - - - - Herman F. Hegner.
Tertiary Fossils of the Bad Lands, Dak., - - - L. W. Stilwell.
Advertisements.—Read them carefully and oblige us by stating where you saw the ad. when writing to advertisers.

R. E. RACHFORD & SON,
COLLECTING NATURALISTS
AND WHOLESALE DEALERS IN

BIRD SKINS & EGGS,
BEAUMONT, TEXAS.

The Hawkeye Ornithologist & Oologist.

"Better to search the fields for health unbought,
Than fee the doctor for a nauseus draught,
The wise for health on exercise depend,
God never made his work for man to mend."

VOL. I.　　CRESCO, IOWA, MARCH, 1888.　　NO. 3.

FACTS ABOUT THE BIRDS.

MISLEADING STATISTICS RESPECTING FASHION'S DEMANDS.

Dr. F. W. Langdon, of Cincinnati, recently delivered an address before the Society of Natural History, of that city, in which he discussed the object of "The Destruction of our Native Birds" from what he admitted to be the unpopular side A portion of his address will be found of much interest to general readers, nevertheless, and it is here given:

"The main proposition," he said, "sought to be established by the report of your committee, the Committee of the American Ornithologists' Union, and papers of similar tenor by various individuals, is: That our song birds, insect-eating species, and smaller birds generally are in danger of suffering a notable decrease in numbers, or even extermination, by reason of the demands of fashion for millinery and dress ornaments; the bloodthirsty disposition of the 'bad small boy;' the market gunner or 'pot hunter' and the ornithological collector and student.

"In support of the claim that the demand for millinery purposes is the chief cause of an anticipated extermination of song birds, we find numerous high-sounding figures in the various papers referred to. Let us see what these figures are and to what birds they apply. Mr. William Dutcher states (quoted also by your committee) 'that 40,000 terns were killed on Cape Cod in one season; that at Cobb's Island, off the Virginia coast, 40,000 bird's, mainly gulls and terns, were contracted for by an enterprising woman from New York to ship to Paris; that 11,018 skins were taken on the South Carolina coast in a three months' trip of one dealer; that 70,000 were supplied to New York dealers from a village on Long Island. Note, if you please, that these large figures apply to 'coast' birds, mainly or entirely, therefore composed of gulls, terns, and the 'shore' birds. My friend Mr. George B. Sennett is also quoted as stating that he overheard the agent of a millinery firm endeavoring to make a contract in Texas for 10,000 plumes of egrets (a species of heron, or fish-eating wader). Then, in another place is an estimate that the number of grebes shipped, mainly from the Pacific slope of North America, must range far into the tens if not hundreds of thousands. And my friend Mr. Dury has drawn your attention to the fact that the herons and other water birds have been destroyed by thousands in the swamps of Florida.

"Now, the argument sought to be sustained by this startling array of figures is that we are in danger of allowing the extermination of species desirable to man on account of their song, or economically valuable to the agriculturist as insect destroyers; and the poetical quotations and crude generalizations which are invoked to excite our sympathies are such as relate to the latter species—*i. e.*, song birds. In other words, while in the statistics cited, mainly gulls, terns, herons, and 'shore birds' appear prominently in the foreground, the moral is pointed chiefly, if not entirely, at 'song birds'—so that the non-ornithological reader is extremely liable to the impression that the figures themselves apply to the 'song birds' as much as to any others, and to have his sympathies aroused accordingly. But when informed that these are almost wholly a marine species—gulls, terns, and 'shore birds' —the scavengers of the ocean and ornithological tramps, so to speak, most of them being migrants, whose home is far beyond the confines of civilization; whose only 'song' is a mere 'screech or squawk,' anything but musical to human ears, and which are not in any degree beneficial to man except for their feathers—these facts considered, does it really seem so bad to make merchandise of their plumage for ornamental purposes?

"As for the destruction of thousands of herons and other water birds in the swamps of Florida and Texas, this effects neither song birds nor civilization, since their notes are no more pleasing than those of the gulls and terns; and they are doomed to extirpation regardless of milliners and fashion whenever civilization drains and cultivates their nesting and feeding places. If we look at this part of the subject in an economic light, we shall see that these birds, chiefly herons, are the natural enemies of fish, so that their destruction, in the long run, directly favors the increase of food for man. Furthermore, their habitat is in districts entirely uninhabitable to the human species, and they would forever remain unknown to man but for the ornithologist, the sportsman, and the milliner.

Now, leaving the gulls, terns, shore birds, grebes, and herons for the present, let us examine some of the figures of our pessimistic friends which do apply to song birds, and their use for millinery purposes. Here we are struck at once with the absence of definite figures, and in their place find such generalization as 'many song birds, and 'war of extermination' on catbirds, robins and thrushes. One New York taxidermist is quoted as having 30,000 skins of 'crows, crow blackbirds, red-winged blackbirds, and snow buntings.' The first three species of disputed or doubtful benefit to man on account of their omnivorous diet, and with no song worth mentioning, excepting the clear whistle of the red-winged blackbird; while the fourth species is a far northern sparrow, a winter visitor only in the United States, irregularly distributed, subsisting chiefly on seeds, and with no more song while with us than the European sparrows in our streets.

"Again, the extent of territory from which this 30,000 skins were derived is not mentioned—a very important item, as I shall hope to show later.

"The most definite observations as to the use of song birds are those of Mr. F. W. Chapman as the result of two afternoon walks in the 'shopping' districts of New York. He gives a list of 40 species observed, of which 15 only can, by the most liberal classification, be denominated song birds, including two sparrows, which are only winter visitors in the United States. The aggregate number of individuals belonging to this lot is stated at 174, which may be classified as follows: Song birds and useful species 30; useful but not song birds, 38; birds of doubtful and negative value, 106. Among those classed as of negative value are some really objectionable as destroyers of useful species, namely, the shrikes and jays. The others in the negative list are chiefly terns, gulls, grebes, and shore birds.

"To this I may add my own observation, made yesterday, of a large wholesale milliner's stock in this city. Taking a dozen or two of boxes at random from the stock, here is the list: Twenty-four tropical blackbirds (South American;) 24 tropical orioles; 20 tropical kingfishers–habitat Mexican border to Brazil, 12 tropicals, (South American;) 6 large and very wicked-looking jays, (not recognized as North American;) 6 pigeons of a species whose habitat is West Indies, Central and South America; 12 white-shouldered blackbirds, not North American; 24 maroon tanagers, Brazilian; 6 heads of California quail; 1 red-shouldered blackbird; 137 skins, of which 7 only are undoubtedly North American, and none of these 7 song birds.

"I should not omit to mention the statement of my friend Mr. Dury as to seeing 'bluebirds by the bushel' in a taxidermist's stock in New Jersey. Now Mr. Dury does not say how many bushels, but we may suppose three bushels at one hundred skins to the bushel to be a pretty fair stock. Three hundred bluebirds killed in the State of New Jersey, with an area of 8,320 square miles, is equal to one to about every thirty square miles and we are not assured that they were taken all in one season either. Does any one suppose that this one bluebird to thirty square miles would create a noticeable gap in the fauna? but how small are these figures, and how scanty the facts as compared with those relating to the gull, terns, herons, &c. To be sure, we find mentioned by Mr. Allen, and quoted by your committee, 'the million of rail and bobolinks' killed in a single season near Philadelphia. These, however, have been destroyed annually for the benefit of Philadelphia and New York epicures for many years before bird wearing came into fashion, so it is out of the question to charge their destruction to 'bird wearing ladies.' And even with this formidable rate of destruction we do not see that either species has become extinct or even noticeably diminished in numbers. But suppose we consider, for the sake of argument, that birds are destroyed equally for millinery purposes— songsters and beneficial species along with those of negative value economically considered. To what extent are bird wearers responsible for their destruction?

"Prominent among the statements made in Mr. J. A. Allen's paper, and quoted by your committee in the use of birds for millinery purposes, is the assertion that 10,000,000 American women are of a 'bird-wearing age and proclivities.' Some might consider this an exaggeration, which it probably is, but for the sake of a basis we will admit it to be true. Mr. Allen further estimates, allowing for the making-over necessities of the economically disposed ladies, that 5,000,000 birds per year will be required to satisfy the demand.

"Now, what effect practically will this have on the bird fauna of America, for as two-thirds or more of the birds of any one North American locality are migrants, and many of them pass from South to North America, and *vice versa*, we must estimate the effect on the continent at large, as we do not limit the bird-wearing ladies to any one locality. Moreover, the ornithologist who attempts to identify the contents of boxes of bird skins in our millinery establishments will find the vast majority of exotic forms, as I have already noted. The ultimate influence of the destruction of birds, then, must be estimated by the number of birds in the whole country. Now, unfortunately for our purpose, we have no reliable census of American birds, as applied to individuals, but, following the example of Mr. Allen, we may estimate that the 15,000,000 square miles comprised in North and South America and the West India Islands will average at least 200 birds to the square mile, (and I think my ornithological friends that are present will agree with me that this is an exceedingly moderate estimate.)

"According to our estimate, then, we would have a bird population in the Americas of 3,000,000,000—that this is not an excessive estimate is evidenced by the fact that Alexander Wilson computed the number of pigeons alone in a single flight at over 2,000,000,000 or 1,500,000,000 pairs. Now, another very moderate estimate would allow at least two birds to each pair for natural increase, so that 3,000,000,000 birds must be destroyed annually, by all causes, in order that the bird fauna shall remain at its present proportions; in other words, until that number are destroyed there will be no decrease in numbers. Now, the proportion destroyed for millinery purposes taken at Mr. Allen's estimate of 5,000,000, and allowing another 5,000,000 for South America, Canada, Mexico, and the West Indies, would be as 10 to 3,000, or as 1 to 300; the other 299 meeting their death from other causes. In other words, a death mortality rate of $3\frac{1}{3}$ per 1,000, while a rate of 20 to 25 per 1,000 in the human species excites no comment whatever.

"The actual rate in the birds is manifestly much less than that above stated, since a section of the country with only 200 birds to the square mile would probably be the rare exception rather than a frequent occurrence. Be it noted, furthermore, that the constant demand for novelty to which fashions are due prohibits a continuance of even this low mortality rate for many years in succession.

"Figures aside, however, it is a self-evident fact that all species of animals and plants require checks to their maximum rate of increase. (The human population of the United States, at the ordinary rate of increase, would number four to every square yard of the earth's surface in less than 700 years.)

"Now, of the many natural checks upon the increase of birds, some are removed by civilization, others are increased. Then, again, there is even a higher factor that governs the increase or decrease of different species —which is unknown to us except by its effects, namely, the inherent capacity of the species itself to increase. As an instance of the disappearance of a species without known cause we have the case of our own paroquet, a bird abundant in large flocks throughout the Ohio Valley in the first quarter of the century, noted by Audubon in 1831, as rapidly diminishing in numbers; by Kirtland and others, in 1838, as only met with irregularly, and as straggling flocks. While we have no recorded date of their appearance in this State between 1840 and 1862, when a single flock of stragglers were noted in Columbus. Throughout their range we have the same accounts of constantly diminishing numbers, as we had before the days of bird wearers, taxidermists, or pot hunters, or ornithological collectors in the West. In accordance with this capacity some species are to-day increasing, while others are dying out, much as they did in for-l..er geologic times before the human biped made his appearance; and man to-day is only one check upon species in nature's vast game of chess, and not by any means so important a one as he is apt to imagine.

"To sum up, then, the practical influence of bird wearing upon our fauna, we may note:

"*First*—That the North American birds used in greatest numbers are gulls, terns, herons, and others, not song birds, nor species beneficial to the agriculturist.

"*Second*—That our most desirable and familiar song birds, such as thrushes, wrens, greenlets, and finches, are in limited demand, on account of their generally plain colors.

"*Third*—That of the brilliantly plumaged birds a vast majority come from South America and other foreign countries.

"*Fourth*—That probably enough of shrikes, jays, crows, and other predatory species are destroyed to more than compensate for the few song birds actually killed by man for all purposes.

"*Fifth*—If all were song birds and equally beneficial, the reduction in numbers from this cause would be inappreciable in its effects on the fauna of the country at large.

"Coming down to the consideration of the birds of our own locality and surrounding territory, Mr. Dury has given us a very interesting reference to the abundance of the wild pigeon in this region 25 years ago, and has noted their scarcity at the present day. The last great flight of these birds that I remember here was in the fall of 1865, when the air was darkened with them for the greater part of two days. Now, their disappearance is certainly not due to the demands of the milliners; and while the pot hunter and the 'bad small boy with a gun' have probably destroyed their share, much more influential factors in causing their disappearance in my opinion have been the demands of agriculture and commerce, causing the destruction of the mast-bearing forests where they fed and nested. The same factors account mainly for the disappearance of our larger game and water birds—*i. e.*, clearing forests, draining swamps, and so on. And we might as well attempt to stay the progress of Old Father Time himself as to check civilization in order to save these birds.

"'But,' it may be asked, 'must our civilization eventually cause a birdless country?' Not by any means; on the contrary, we shall find if we study the comparitive abundance of birds in general in most civilized sections of our country, that birds are probably more numerous, both in species and in individuals, than they were in the earlier days of its settlement.

"While I am in favor of increase of desirable birds, of the utmost dissemination of knowledge respecting all birds, of the formation of Audubon societies, if you please, and of the popularizing of ornithology in general, I do not think we gain anything in a scientific or practical sense by distorting, mistating, or suppressing facts, exaggerating figures, or by denouncing the well established right of man to use all natural objects for the furtherance of his necessities, his convenience, or his pleasures."

"The fishermen—this being a dull season—employ their seines in catching birds. They set their seines between tall poles on the beach, and *catch thousands of robins in a morning or afternoon*. At one flight a man caught over 2,000. He put away part for food for his family and shipped the others. On Bogal Banks, with a small net, last Monday, a Mr. Ross caught 500 robins."—*Our Dumb Animals.*

ORNITHOLOGY

For the Hawkeye O. and O.

BIRD NESTING IN THE NORTH OF ENGLAND.

BY WALTER RAINE, TORONTO, CANADA.

Yorkshire, being the largest county in England, has more species of birds nesting within its limits than any other English county. Bounded on the east by the North Sea, it has many species of sea birds resorting annually to nest amongst the cliffs of the sea coast. Those majestic chalk cliffs stretching from Flamborough Head to Speeton are the nesting places of thousands of guillemots, razorbills, puffins, cormorants, kittiwake and other gulls, as well as kestril hawks and jackdaws, whose eggs are collected in baskets by the hundreds, and still their numbers do not seem to diminish. At the report of a rifle the birds rise *en masse* in the air and darken the sun, whilst their cries are almost deafening to the ear. It is here that the peregrine falcon still finds a place to build a nest and lay its eggs, whilst the raven has forsaken the place some years ago. Along the sea beach from Flamborough Head to the mouth of the Humber may be found nesting oyster-catchers, ringed plovers and several species of terns.

Through the west of Yorkshire, runs the Pennine Chain from north to south and here are some of the highest hills in England, which are drained by the river Humbur and its tributaries. In this mountain limestone district of Ingleborough, Whernside and Pennyghent, may be found some of the grandest scenery in the British Islands, whilst the numerous and wonderful caverns in this locality, as well as the romantic limestone cliffs over 300 feet high, are of great interest to the geologist.

For many years I have made frequent journeys to this district during spring and summer, which I must say offers a charm to the ornithologist; and as many species of birds nest here that are included in the American fauna, I trust my readers will just accompany me on a visit to this place and let us spend a few hours amongst our feathered friends.

Leaving Leeds by an early train, in company with my brother, in two hour's time we arrive at Ingleton and at once make for the banks of the river Greta, intending to follow up this mountain stream to Thornton Force, the most lovely of Yorkshire waterfalls. This stream can only be followed by the sure footed; ladies need not attempt it, as much climbing over huge boulders must be done ere we reach Thornton Force. Two years ago a young lady was killed by falling over a cliff, up the face of which we shall have to scramble a mile further on.

We now enter Swilla Bottom, which is a romantic gorge with perpendicular cliffs on either side. Geologists say this once was a lake; it has but one entrance through which we have just passed. It is a paradise for birds; different species of warblers, finches and thrushes are singing away, each one trying to surpass the other, but the sweet song thrush may be heard above all the rest, perched upon a Yew tree growing out of the face of the cliff to our left. Vegetation here is very luxuriant, hartstongue ferns, spleenworts, parsly, oak, beech, and other ferns are peeping out of the crevices of the rocks, whilst the banks of the stream are covered with sweet scented violets, primroses, lilies of the valley, forget-me-nots and other flowers.

Proceeding along the banks of the stream, we startle a yellow wagtail, and on examining the mossy bank from whence it flew, we find its nest containing five eggs. The nest is composed of dried grass, lined with cows hair; the ground color of the eggs is buff, mottled all over with yellow-brown. The eggs are carefully packed and we prepare to scramble up the side of a cascade, when we notice a water ouzel fly from the rocks on the opposite side; with a slight wetting of the feet we reach the other side and are pleased to find a nest, which is a beautiful ball of moss, as large as a man's head, with a small hole at the side for the bird to enter. It contains five white eggs, average size 1.05 by .70. Further on we find two more nests in similar situations near the side of a cascade, one was ready to receive eggs and the other contained four eggs slightly incubated. The water ouzel or dipper is a common bird in this district; nearly every cascade has its pair of water crows as the bird is called here.

Two other species of wagtail occur in this gorge, the pied wagtail and the grey wagtail, but we do not find nests on this visit. Over our heads hangs a kestril hawk, and in front of us we disturb a heron, whose slow, lazy flight tells us he is gorged with trout. The Heronry is a few miles away at Gargrave, where about thirty nests are occupied every season. On striking an old tree stump all covered over with ivy, a winter wren flies out and exposes to us the nest and seven eggs. We do not touch the eggs. The nest is something like that of the water ouzel, only much smaller, with an entrance at the side; it is made of twigs and moss, lined with feathers. The eggs are crystal white, spotted with brown and purple. The nest of this bird is seldom disturbed, for in Yorkshire, they say:

"The robin and the wren
Are God's cock and hen."

The robin nests in this district. How beautiful are its eggs, something like those of the cactus wren, but more pinky and much smaller. The American robin was called after the English robin, having a red breast like that bird, and both frequent the habitation of man; one is a warbler, the other a thrush. Passing under a cedar tree, we notice a beautiful little nest resting on a branch about six feet above the ground. It contained five eggs of the common redpoll, of a pale bluish-green ground, with a zone of rich rusty brown round the large end; size .65 by .50. This bird is plentiful in Yorkshire, where I have found many nests, but it is never found breeding in the south of England. After examining a nest and eggs of the chaffinch, a beautiful specimen of bird architecture, we reach the end of the gorge. Here a waterfall prevents us following the stream further, so we begin to climb the cliff on our left and in ten minutes reach the top safely.

Turning back on the cliff top we enter a small fir wood and startle a magpie from its nest. My brother climbs the tree like a squirrel and finds it to contain seven well marked eggs, though five is the usual number of eggs laid by this bird. The kestril hawk breeds in this wood, and usually lays four or five eggs in a magpie's nest. The eggs are light red, blotched with deeper red. A series of forty eggs before me, show great varieties in color. A small bird is noticed climbing up a trunk of a tree, and approaching quietly, we find it is a creeper. Close by was its nest, a mass of twigs and rubbish crammed between the loose bark of a fir tree; it contained six white eggs, spotted with red-brown, chiefly at the larger end. In this wood the golden-crowned kinglet, called in this district gold-crested wren, breeds. Its nest, one of the most beautiful of all are English nests, is usually built below the branch of a fir tree, being suspended to two or three small twigs. It consists of a ball of moss with an opening at the top, lined with feathers and down, and contains from six to ten eggs not much larger than those of the humming-bird. They are creamy-white, sometimes pinky-white, covered with obscure speckles of purple-grey. Their nests are from six to twenty feet above the ground. This is the smallest of British birds.

[TO BE CONTINUED.]

For the Hawkeye O. and O.

CANADIAN FLYCATCHERS.

BY WM. L. KELLS, LISTOWEL, ONTARIO.

THE WOOD PEWEE.

(*Contopus virens.*)

In form and plumage this species strongly resembles the more common phœbe flycatcher, but it is smaller in size, and its song-notes and habitat are very different. Among our summer visitors it is late in its arrival, and as its sojourn here is passed chiefly in the wild woods, and it seldom comes out in the open fields, it is very fitly called the wood pewee, though there are other members of this family, much less known, whose homes are also in the wilderness.

The wood pewee does not frequent low swampy places, but takes up its abode in the high, hardwood timbered districts, where there is deep shade, and an abundance of dead twigs and branches shooting across the gloom, and where it finds its insect food abundant. Taking its stand on a naked limb, it for a few moments glances around; its tail meanwhile wagging with that 'peculiar motion common to the flycatchers, then darting off, and after a circling sweep of a few rods returns to its starting place, quivering its wings, and uttering its peculiar notes, "*wir-a-we we-too*," and which are often repeated by another of its species at a distance. These rather dismal notes, uttered in a sad tone, are but little noticed until most of our other summer songsters have become silent; then when the fallen leaves and chilly winds of autumn herald the approach of winter, this sad and doleful ditty becomes conspicuous, as it echoes in the silent woods in melancholy strains, as though the little performer was bewailing the departing glories of summer, the approaching desolation of nature, and the loss of all that is lovely and gay; which noticed in conjunction with the scenery of the surrounding landscape, may often fill the mind of the student of nature with sad reflections, and gloomy anticipations. As the fall advances and the leafless woods assume a barren and desolate aspect, no longer able to procure its insect food, the pewee ceases to battle with the elements of nature, leaves our woods and forests for a season to the sway of the icy monarch, and seeks a refuge from the winter's storms in the evergreen valleys of the South.

Though the summer habitat of this species is mostly in the high woods, yet some pairs of them will occasionally take up their homes in large orchards, and have their nesting places near human habitations.

This species is about six inches in length. The plumage on the upper parts of the wings, tail and head, is brownish-black; inclined to olive on the back; the throat and breast is white, and the lower parts yellowish. Its nest is usually placed on a horizontal branch, sometimes where it is forked, and sometimes where small twigs project on each side, and generally high from the ground. The nest, a shallow structure, is composed of moss, fibers of various barks; neatly lined with fine dry grass and hair, the outside being patched with lichen corresponding to the color of the branch on which it is placed. The set of eggs,—three or four in number, are of a creamy white color, blotched towards the large end with reddish-brown.

THE YELLOW-BELLIED FLYCATCHER.
(*Empidonex flaviventris.*)

This species—which at a short distance bears a close resemblance, both in size and coloration, to the wood pewee, or the female *Traillii*—is the rarest of all the smaller flycatchers which make their summer homes in the wild woods of Canada; though owing to its songless character, and the wild places that it frequents, as well as the very limited number of those who take any interest in our woodland birds, it is possible that it may be more common than is now supposed. Only one nest of this species has ever come under my observation, and but for that I would not have distinguished the species from the wood pewee. It was about the summer of 1872, and I think the early days of July, or latter part of June, I was then residing on Emerald farm, in North Wallace, when having occasion to penetrate a piece of low, tangled, cedar swamp, near the house, I flushed from a mossy bank, formed by a partially turned up cedar root, a bird which at first appeared to be the wood pewee, but a glance at its nest, which contained three beautiful eggs, convinced me that it was a different species, and I have since become certain that it was the yellow-bellied flycatcher. The nest was placed in a little hollow, evidently made by the bird, in the side of the mossy bank, and composed of dry moss, some rootlets, fine dry grass, and cattle hair. The eggs were of a creamy-white hue, marked with an irregular ring of reddish-brown spots toward the large end, much in every particular like those of the wood pewee. While I was looking at these, the bird returned and scolded in an angry manner, in a sharp "chip"-like tone of voice; nor am I aware that this species utters any other notes. A set of four eggs, which I saw in the collection of a person, some ten miles south of this town, and which he informed me he found in a turned up root, in a swamp at that place, I also believe, belonged to this species.

For the Hawkeye O. and O.

CAROLINA WREN.

BY J. W. JACOBS, WAYNESBURG, PA.

I found my first nest of this species *Thryothorus ludovicianus* on May 7th, 1887. It was placed on a shelf under a skating rink; was five feet from the ground, and was composed of grass, leaves, bark, rags, strings, etc., nicely lined with feathers, and was partially arched over on top. The eggs were five in number, fresh, of a reddish-white; thickly covered, but chiefly at the larger end, with spots and dots of red and different shades of brown; very much resembling the eggs of the white-bellied nuthatch *Sitta carolinensis*. They measure as follows: .76x.58; .75x.59; .76x.57; .75x.56; and .75x.58 inches.

Set II; taken July 21. This set was taken from a nest built in a rudely made cupboard in a corner of an old paintshop. It contained four eggs, slightly incubated, and measuring about the same as those of the first set. I could have easily caught the old bird as she emerged from the entrance, but I was afraid she would the eggs in her struggles to get loose. The nest was large and bulky, being composed of a great variety of rubbish, strings, twigs, bark, paper, leaves, rags and grass, lined with feathers, a few stems of grass and a small amount of hair, which it pickup in the shop.

The parent birds of the first set experienced considerable trouble in raising their brood. They had built a former nest; in this the mother deposited five eggs, which some children destroyed; then she built and deposited the second set which I collected; a few days afterward she built again. This time she was successful. All three nests were but a few feet apart.

HABITS OF SOME AMERICAN GREBES.

BY OLIVER DAVIE.

The grebes are strange birds closely resembling the loons in their general structure. They are expert divers and, like the anhinga or snakebird, when alarmed quietly sink back into the water and disappear. Like all true divers they are awkward on land and from the posterior position of the legs, they stand almost upright, so that they have more the air of a small kangaroo than of a bird.

The Pied-billed Grebe, *Podilymbus podiceps* which is a common species throughout the United States, breeds in the marshes, lakes and large bodies of water throughout its range. The nest is a little floating island of decaying rushes, reeds or grass, mixed with mud and *debris* brought up from the bottom of the slough or reedy pool in which it is built. The structure is fastened to the flags and aquatic plants; these are pulled down and piled upon each other till the nest rises two or three inches above the water, where it measures 12 or 15 inches in diameter, or it is just large enough to hold the eggs. Beneath, the nest is usually very large and may extend from one to three feet in depth or to the bottom. Thick-billed and Carolina grebe, pied-bill, dabchick, dipper, waterwitch, "devil-diver," and "hell-diver" are some of the names applied to this species. The American eared grebe, *Colymbus nigricollis californicus* which inhabits North America west of the Mississippi, builds a similar nest but generally in open situations in flags and rushes or upon a floating foundation in shallow water.

The Western Grebe, *Æchmophorus occidentalis*, the largest of the North American grebes, nests also similar to the common dabchick and is found breeding abundantly in Dakota, and northward into British America.

A remarkable fact concerning the nidification of the grebes is, that they cover their nests with weeds and grass before leaving them; but when suddenly alarmed will often hurriedly slip off the nest and leave the eggs exposed. The habit of covering the eggs is either for the purpose of concealing them from enemies, such as hawks, owls and gulls; or, that by means of the artificial heat produced by the decaying vegetation they are more or less dependent for the hatching of them. When thus covered the birds are known to remain away from their nests during the entire daytime.

Holbœll's grebe, *Colymbus holbœllii*, which breeds in high latitudes, has some peculiar habits which are also common to the horned grebe, *C. auritus* and the loon. As soon as the young are hatched the mother takes them upon her back, and swims with them in this position for hours at a time. When diving for food the young remain on her back, while she feeds them with small fishes and vegetable substances. These habits remind one of that strange and extraordinary compound of an animal, the opossum, which is often seen with a dozen sharp-nosed, sleek-headed young sitting on their mother's back, around whose prehensile appendage they entwine their tails to hold fast. Mr. W. W. Cooke in the Auk (vol. 1, p. 249) says that the Chippewa Indians call the grebes *Shin-gi-bis*, which means deformed. He says that the Indian stories by which they account for this name are as follows:

"Once upon a time the Great Spirit looked down on all the beasts and birds and saw that their lives were one dull round of monotonous toil.

So he told them to assemble at a certain place and he would teach them many beautiful games. He built an immense wigwam, and at the appointed time all were there except the grebes. He made fun of the whole matter, and said he knew tricks enough already. While the Great Spirit was instructing the assemblage, the grebe danced in derision before the door, and finally, emboldened by the forbearance of his master, ran into the room, and by dancing on the fire, put it out and filled the wigwam with smoke. The patience of the Great Spirit could stand it no longer, and giving the grebe a kick, he exclaimed. "Deformed shalt thou go through this world for the rest of thy days!" The imiuperial foot struck him just at the base of the tail. It knocked the body forward, but the legs remained behind, and the grebe has ever since had the legs set so far back on the body that it cannot walk."

The smallest of our North American grebes is *C. dominicus*, or the St. Domingo Grebe. It has a breeding range extending from the valley of the Rio Grande southward into the tropical regions—nesting in the wild herbage of the lakes and ponds of Mexico and Central America, in many of the islands of the West Indies. and the sloughs of the immense level, tropical plains and pampas of South America.

Its entire life is spent in the water, and it possesses the same aquatic habits peculiar to all the grebes. Dr. James C. Merrill first established the claim of this species to our North American fauna. He found it a rather common resident in southwestern Texas. On May 16, 1877, he found several nests undoubtedly belonging to this species in a salt marsh a few miles from Fort Brown. "They were made of water-plants and pieces of reeds slightly fastened to one or two tule-stalks, and forming a wet, floating mass."

The eggs of the grebes range from four to eight and nine in number; their general shape is elliptical oval; and they are whitish or greenish-white in color, unspotted. On most of the eggs there is a rough, chalky substance over the entire surface. The eggs usually becomes soiled or stained by contact with the wet, decaying vegetable matter of the nests —in fact many of them are so much soiled that the ground color is totally obscured.

My experience with the grebes in Ohio has developed the fact that they are most always sure to be found in company with the loon, *Urinator imber*, during the spring migration. In some quiet pool or marsh, or on the surface of a swollen river, they dwell harmoniously together; and it is often curious to hear the hoarse cry of the loon answered by the peculiar note of the dabchick.

Standing on the bank of a river in early spring, looking over a dreary landscape with perhaps a channel of floating ice in view, and lowering clouds overhead to add gloom to a scene yet wrapped in winter's garb, one is almost startled to hear the wierd, long-drawn notes of some restless loon as it utters its hoarse, reverberating cry to die away upon the ear in a strange, echoing undertone which is immediately followed by the feeble, whistling note of the pied-bill grebe.

For the Hawkeye O. and O.

NOTES ON SOME OF THE PASSERES OF FULTON CO., KY.

SECOND PAPER, BY L. O. PINDAR, PRES. Y. O. A., HICKMAN, KY.

The family we are to treat of in this paper is known as the *Corvidæ*, which name is derived from the Latin *corvus*, a raven. It includes the magpies, jays, and crows. The magpies are not represented in Kentucky, so we will begin with the bluejay, *Cyanocitta cristata*.

The "jaybird," as he is popularly called, is larger than either of the species treated of in the first paper, being about a foot long and having an extent of 16 or 17 inches. The colors are striking; blue above, of a purplish hue fading to a greyish purple, below; the throat, belly and crissum, nearly white. The wings and tail are of a deeper blue and crossed by numerous black bars. All the tail feathers except the two central ones and the wing coverts and secondaries are broadly tipped with pure white. The female may be distinguished by more subdued colors and smaller size.

The negroes in the south, that is most of them, believe that the bluejay is compelled to serve the devil one day in every week. However this may be, his satanic majesty could not have found a bird to suit him better, for the jay is a veritable rowdy; stealing corn and fruit, sucking eggs, killing nestlings, and even full grown birds of the smaller species. Fighting, quarrelling, screaming, he goes through life a veritable Ishmaelite.

The next bird on the list occuring in Ky. is the celebrated raven, but it is extremely rare. I saw one flying down the Mississippi river near Hickman, Oct. 8, 1887. I had no gun with me and wouldn't have used it if I had had one, for there was a sublime majesty about this sombre bird as he battled with wind, keeping steadily on, swerving neither to right or left, with outspread pinions and ruffled plumage which would have disarmed me.

His near relative the crow, *Corvus americanus*, is very common here, although we have no large "roosts" such as are found in the pine woods of New Jersey. The plumage of the crow is simple, being entirely dead black, except for a metallic burnishing on the back, wings and tail. It is from 18 to 19 inches in length as a rule, though I have seen crows which I think would measure over twenty inches.

Every now and then we see a newspaper paragraph about a "talking crow" and I would like to ask my readers if they have ever *seen* a "talking crow."

The eggs of the bluejay and crow taken around Hickman, much resemble each other—a green ground color with blotches of lilac and purplish-brown. Very few sets of jays, eggs show the "drab ground color with brown spots," described by Dr. Coues.

I close this paper with best wishes for its publishers' success and that of every ornithologist who collects for the interest of science and not for the purpose of having a "large collection."

N. B.—An error crept into my last paper unnoticed till this moment.

I have set down the kingbird as "not so common as the next species," viz., Traill's flycatcher. The kingbird is much more common. The Traill's was much rarer in 1887 than 1886, why, I know not. I hope for an increase of this species in 1888.

THE TRAILL'S FLYCATCHER.

(Empidonex pusillus Trailli.)

BY JAMES B. PURDY.

Read before the Ornithological Society of Wayne County, Michigan, Sept. 24, 1887.

Mr. President and Gentlemen:—

Having been assigned to me for my subject this evening, the "Traill's flycatcher," and having no works at hand; on which I can rely, I am compelled to rely almost entirely upon my own observation. Mr. Davie's Key to the Nests and Eggs of North American birds, although a very reliable work, seems to make two and perhaps three great mistakes in describing its nest and eggs. Mr. Davie says, "the locality usually selected as a nesting place by this species is in a thick growth of alders bordering a stream, or in the deep solitude of a lonely wood." The first place is correct, but I have never been able to find one of the birds or its nest in the woods. Again, he says, "that the nest is more slovenly built than that of the Acadian flycatcher." Now, of all that I have examined, and I have examined a considerable number, the Traill builds, by far, the neatest and most compact nest. And again, he says, "In nearly all cases, three eggs is the usual complement, rarely four." Now, of all the nests that I have examined, four has been the usual complement, and rarely any other number. And again, another mistake by Mr. Collins, the well known naturalist and taxidermist of Detroit. While talking with him one day last spring, the subject of the Traill's flycatcher was brought up, in which he declared that there never was a traill's flycatcher's nest found in Wayne county or in Michigan; that they were a bird of passage with us and went farther north to breed, in which he is certainly mistaken. Therefore I flatter myself that I know at least as much of the Traill's flycatcher as any authority that has thus far came under my observations. And yet, it is not strange that so many are mistaken, for it is so retired in its habits that none but the closest observer and student of birds are aware of its presence among us. In the month of June, as you are walking through a low, wet piece of land with a creek running through, dotted here and there along its margin with clumps of alder, you come upon a nest. It is situated in the upright fork of an alder, generally close to the stream. It is composed, mostly, of wild hemp, and resembles, nearer than any other, that of the summer yellow-bird. It contains four eggs of a cream or a light-buff color, and are marked with larger or smaller dots of reddish-brown, chiefly at the larger end, and measure about .70 by .53. But where is the bird? She saw you coming and slipped off her nest almost with the quietness of thought, and hid herself in the deep foliage. Listen! from a thicket three or four rods off, at intervals of about ten seconds, you hear a low "twit." It is the note of the Traill's flycatcher; and the only one I ever heard her utter. You go closer in hopes of seeing the bird, but it is with difficulty that you obtain a fair view of her, so close does she keep to the thicket. I do not believe that the male takes much, if any, part in incubation, for I have never seen him around the nest, nor have I ever seen one of the birds in any locality, except at their nesting place in the nesting season. Nor do they seem to express that anxiety for their eggs and young, that is so common with most other birds. It is one of our true flycatchers, having a musca capa bill with recumbent hairs at its base, and in color and appearance resembles very nearly that of the common pewee, but is smaller, and so exactly resembles the Acadian flycatcher that I do not believe any one can tell the two birds apart. Two years ago last June I procured a specimen of each for comparison and had it not been for the manner in which they were shot it would have been impossible for me to have told them, one from the other. Nor can their eggs be identified one from the other with any degree of certainty. But these birds build a different nest in different localities, and their notes are not alike. If it was not for this, they would seem to be identical. As to the time of the Traill's flycatcher's arrival and departure with us, I am unable to speak, so silently do they come and go. More might be said of this interesting bird, but feeling that the time allowed me for this reading has about expired and thanking you for your kind attention I will close.

For the Hawkeye O. and O.

THE BOBOLINK.

(*Dolichonyx oryzivorus.*)

BY FRANK L. BURNS, BERWYN, CHESTER COUNTY, PA.

This bird is a common migrant in this state, and is known as the reed-bird in the fall. At this time thousands are shot along the Deleware river, where they fatten on the seed of the wild oats or reed; numerous small flocks pass through here, feeding on wild cherries, sheep-berries, etc. They are eagerly sought for, and bring about seventy-five cents a dozen in the Philadelphia markets.

A writer in the January number of the H. O. AND O. deplores the apparent decrease of this species; but residents of the New England States hear and see only the beautiful songster. Pennsylvanians regard it as a game bird; and the Southerners, as a destructive nuisance.

One has only to read the report of the ornithologist, in the 1886 report of the department of agriculture, to know something of the sad havoc they play in the rice fields of the South.

"To prevent the total destruction of the crop during the periods of bird invasion, thousands of men and boys, called, bird-minders' are employed; hundreds of thousands of pounds of powder are burned, and millions of birds killed. Still the number of birds invading the rice fields each year seems in no way diminished, and the aggregate annual loss they occasion is about $2,000,000." The bobolink rarely breeds in this state. I know of but two instances of their nests being found in this county.

Giddings, Texas, Jan. 12, 1888.

EDITORS HAWKEYE O. AND O:

Please accept thanks for Vol. I, No. 1, of your magazine, which came a few days ago. It is much above the average in many respects.

I have a few remarks to make on some of the contents of No. 1. On page 2, there is an æsthetic wail, because the "bobolink" failed to put in an appearance. The United States Ornithologist has been making some investigations about this species and I copy from his report on its ravages. "One of the most important industries of the southern states, the cultivation of rice, is crippled and made precarious by the bi-annual attacks of birds.........the bird which does more injury than all the rest combined, is the bobolink of the north ......called 'rice-bird' in the south, To prevent total destruction of the crop......thousands of men and boys, called 'bird-minders' are employed, hundreds of thousands of pounds of of birds are killed, still the number of gunpowder are burned, and millions birds......seems in no way diminished and the aggregate annual loss they occasion is about $2,000,000:" I've only given extracts from the report (a voluminus document) but enough to show how destructive the bird is and from a practical point of view the bobolink—like the Chinese—must go; æsthetic people to the contrary notwithstanding.

The kingbird may be a warrior unconquered with you, but a near relative of his, the scissor-tailed flycatcher, common here during the summer, can make him "vamoose the ranch" every time. I had proof of this during '87 when a kingbird tried to build in the same tree in which a pair of scissor-tails had commenced building. The kingbird was whipped twice (not satisfied with the first bout probably) in less than an hour. It was a fair fight and no "shenanegan." J. A. SINGLEY.

REMINISCENCES OF THE EARLY LIFE OF A TAME CROW.

Some years ago I came in possession of a young half-feathered crow. I had often heard extravagant stories told of the ability to talk which was, or had been, possessed by certain tame crows, and so resolved to try the experiment. I had had my new pet some fifteen minutes when its bill flew open with a spasmodic gasp and an agonized caw informed me that food was required—and that immediately. Suffice it to say that after the first day's experience it would not have taken much to convince me that the government reports concerning the enormous number of insects destroyed every year by birds was fully correct in every particular.

While young he would watch every opportunity to enter the house, with which he made himself perfectly familiar. On one occasion he was found solemnly perched on the top of a high silver castor in the center of the table, probably "grace before meat." He seemed to take great delight in turning over ink bottles, emptying work baskets and hiding the contents under rugs, the edges of the carpet, etc. A sleigh bell afforded much amusement, and it was his especial delight to get on a shelf where a box of nails was setting and drop them, one by one, for the sake of hearing them jingle as they struck the floor. But as he grew older and able to fly he gradually acquired the sagacity common to all crows and could no more be induced to enter the house.

When fully able to care for himself he made frequent visits to various neighbors in the town, and afforded much amusement for the children, whom he always hated indiscriminately owing to their practice of plagueing him. Occasionally he would come over to the high school building and attract considerable attention by rapping on the windows. While making his tour one day, one of these kind old gentlemen employed in guarding a few raspberries from the robins and bluebirds, shot him, breaking his wing. Since then he remained at home and instinctively recognizes a gun at sight, making a great ado whenever one is shown him.

When a few weeks old a friend tried scratching his head one day and was much surprised at his apparent satisfaction. He would bend his head forward and close his eyes, apparently sinking into a doze. We soon learned to sidle up to one and holding his head down, would indicate by a low "aw" what he wished. Though still allowing old acquaintances to scratch his head, he never shuts his eyes during the operation.

Seemingly always busy, he would follow the gardener around hour after hour, catching and killing or hiding the various insects and worms, but was never noticed to eat any himself. From this peculiar characteristic of hiding food for another meal comes the crow's hobby of gathering miscellaneous articles and secreting them in out of the way places. He always remembered perfectly well where he hid anything, and, even after a heavy fall of snow, could go to the exact spot and find what he wished. By keeping a careful watch we saw him ressurrect one of the door keys of the house after he had had it safely laid away for several weeks. One often noticed trait was, that he would never attempt to steal anything when one was watching him, but as soon as one's back was turned would get what he wished and move off with the greatest haste. His customary gait was a cross between a fly and a hop, although when not disturbed nor in a hurry he would walk away very sedately.

He liked to ramble through the flower beds and bite off such buds and blossoms within his reach as seemed to please his fancy, never molesting any but the choicest roses or other flowers. He caught, carried off and killed several young chickens once, hence he is imprisoned at the very time birds most enjoy liberty—spring. One day a neigabor observed him steal quietly up to a cat and give her a powerful blow on the head; then, taking advantage of her surprise, he seized a kitten and made off with it.

He would set like patience on a monument waiting for a hen to leave the nest in order that he might steal the newly laid eggs, which he was never known to impale with his bill, but always carried them off holding his head nearly perpendicular. If suddenly alarmed the egg, of course, slipped and was usually broken in the fall. One thing that seemed peculiar was, that he would never touch the china nor composition nest eggs. He had a partiality for green corn, peas, etc., but mice and gophers were his favorites. He once caught a full grown cedar bird, which he was made to release. The bird, by the way, was only slightly wounded and soon became tame. We kept it for several weeks.

Like many of the human family, he has his moods, and he may exercise his vocal powers for hours one day and not make the attempt again for weeks. Hello, what, who, why, a cackle, various imitations of barking, a peculiar rattling sound like the irregular running of cog wheels, and a variety of "caws" comprise his vocabulary. Those well accustomed to his various caws can readily tell what he intends to convey, as for instance, he has peculiar caws for hunger, danger, etc. I have often heard of crows being able to repeat full sentences, and of others that could whistle, but I have considerable doubt in regard to the matter. I have often tried to teach him to whistle but, though he would set and attentively listen, he could never repeat. A relative, foreman of the Chicago *Times* composing room, while here on a visit at one time, spent a long while trying to learn him to say "dry up." Though the crow made numerous attempts, still he could not strike it, and finally it was given up in despair. On going out the next morning, however, and greeting the crow with "hello" he was quickly told to "dry up." The crow never repeated the words again.

MIGRATION REPORT.

The following observations on bird migration were made at Cresco, Iowa, during the month ending February 29, 1888.

NAME.	FIRST SEEN.	NO S'EN.	NEXT S'EN.
Cedar bird	1—27	2	
Marsh Hawk	1—29	1	
Black Snowbird	2—5	2	2—6
Am. Goldfinch	2—5	5	2—17
Wh te-b. Nuthatch	2—11	3	

OOLOGY.

"PROTECT OUR BIRDS."

BY E. G. WARD, THREE RIVERS, MASS.

This is a familiar saying to many of us, but do all who hear it realize the full meaning of these three words? I fear not. It is a warning that all should heed, and take active measures to help protect our feathered friends. Are we aware how many old as well as *young* persons are engaged, in *one* way, or *another*, in helping on this wholesale destruction of our birds? There are too many "so *called*" collectors, who are taking the eggs of our rarer species in great numbers, either for parlor ornaments or for speculation and our amatuer papers are recording from month to month the wonderful *luck* some of these parties are having in thus robbing these birds. We read, "I took four sets or five sets from this or that kind of birds," as the case may be, as though the party had accomplished something wonderful, something that will be of great importance to the scientific world. Almost every village and hamlet has one or more of *these collectors.* Still the people wonder why the birds aren't so plenty as they were when they were young. This "*set*" business is a *nuisance* and all intelligent and honest collectors should do all they can to stop this wholesale business of collecting in sets by every new tyro. Next come the taxidermists, who kill birds and mount them to sell as the grocer sells sugar and tea. You will meet them in the country searching for scarlet tanagers and other highly colored birds, because they bring higher prices in market, either as parlor ornaments or to deck the hat of some city belle, who *must* have everything that fashion dictates, even if it does take the life of an innocent and harmless bird. I am sorry to say that the demands of fashion are *so strong* that even our country cousins are willing to fall into line and thus assist indirectly in depopulating our fields and meadows of these beautiful birds. Then these very same people *will wonder* why there are so many worms and insects, and they will say that our insect pests are rapidly increasing and we shall soon be eaten up if something isn't done. *We say* something *must* be done. "In Massachusetts, we have laws that will cover the ground," some one says. Yes we have, but they are like a good many laws on our Statute Books, no one is willing to enforce them. Let us show our better nature and each one do all he or she can to bring into disfavor indiscriminate set collecting and the fashion of wearing birds on the hats and bonnets of our lady friends. Another source of trouble is our Game Laws which appear to protect our game birds, but were really made in the interest of our city sportsmen and gun clubs. The *law* forbids the farmers hooting partridge on *his own farm*, during certain seasons of the year, even if they are destroying the buds on his fruit trees. It also forbids the farmer's boy from trapping or snaring this bird during *any* season of the year. But when this law is "*off*," the city sportsmen can take their dogs and scour the country for miles, allowing them to chase the farmers' sheep and *cleaning* out all the birds the law is supposed to protect. No wonder there is such a scarcity of all kinds of birds. Every thing seems to be against them. We should teach the young to love and protect all of God's creatures from the smallest to the greatest. After we have created a healthy sentiment in that direction, then will come a change, and not till then. All consistent students of ornithology and oology should do their best to bring about this change for the better protection of our birds.

THE HAWKEYE
ORNITHOLOGIST & OOLOGIST

EDITED AND PUBLISHED BY

E. B. WEBSTER.   F. D. MEAD.

CRESCO, - - IOWA.

A MONTHLY MAGAZINE
DEVOTED TO ORNITHOLOGY, KINDRED SUBJECTS, AND GEOLOGY.

TERMS OF SUBSCRIPTION.
Per year, - - - - - 50 cents.
Per year to foreign countries, - - 65 cents.
Single copies, - - - 5 cents.
Remittances for subscriptions must be made by postal note—stamps will be returned.

TERMS OF ADVERTISING.
1 line, 1 insertion, - - - - $ .10
1 inch, " - - - - 1.00
2 inches, " - - - - 1.75
½ column, " - - - - 2.50
1 column, " - - - - 5.00
1 page, " - - - - 10.00

A large discount on standing ads. Special rates can sometimes be given.

GENERAL AGENT.—Ph. Heinsberger, 184 Ludlow St., and 89 Delancey St., New York.

All books, periodicals, specimens, etc., sent us will be reviewed.

Correspondence and items of interest relating to the several departments solicited from all. All matter for publication must be in by the last of each month in order to insure insertion in the next number.

Entered at the postoffice at Cresco, Iowa, as second class matter.

NOTES.

During the recent cold weather at San Francisco, the city was visited by thousands of snow birds of a kind never seen there before.

Mr E. L. Brown, a well-known taxidermist of Durand, Wis., informs us that he has just returned from an extended expedition after Moose and Elk in Northern Minnesota.

The remaining copies of the second edition of Oliver Davie's "Nests and Eggs" are so few that he is about to issue a third edition. It will probably be ready by the 1st of April.

Owing to a rush of outside work the present month we were necessarily compelled to limit this issue to twenty-two pages, thus crowding out several valuable articles. Especially do we regret having to hold one on the "Care of Minerals" by W. S. Beekman, Ph. C., of West Medford, Mass.

We publish this month in the space usually devoted to the protection of birds from useless destruction, a condensation of an able speech delivered by W. F. Langdon, before the Society of Natural History of Cincinnati and published in one of the daily papers of that place. While we do not wish it to be understood that our views coincide entirely with those of Mr. Langdon, still we think a careful reading will furnish all with much food for reflection.

Mr. Austin C. Stemple, of Fort Madison, Iowa, informs us of the discovery at that place, sometime during last June, of a large tooth, supposed to be that of the mastodon. It was found by a colored workman, about twenty feet below the surface of the water, while work was in progress on the piers of the C. S. T.—Cal., bridge which crosses the river there. The workman gave it to the firm by which he was employed and it is said that they sent it to some museum. As Mr. Stemple was reporting for the daily paper of that city at the time, he had the pleasure of seeing the tooth, which he judged to weigh upward of six pounds, and to be eight inches in length by four and a half in width. This is the second tooth of the mastodon that has been found in that locality.

KIND WORDS.

So many of our friends have, during the past two months, complimented us on the character and contents of our magazine that we have been induced to present brief extracts from a few of the letters, trusting that they may be of interest to others.

COLUMBUS, OHIO, Jan. 10, 1888.
WEBSTER & MEAD.
Gentlemen:—Your magazine came duly to hand. I am highly pleased with it in every particular; its general style etc., ought to insure you success in its future numbers. You certainly understand the publishing business which, I can see, will aid you wonderfully in the undertaking.
Very Truly,
OLIVER DAVIE.

LISTOWEL, ONTARIO, Jan. 9, 1888.
MESSRS. WEBSTER & MEAD.
Friends:—Your letter and No. 1 of the Hawkeye O. and O. have come to hand and read with interest. As to the magazine, I am much pleased with its general appearance, form, type, and general contents. I wish it success, and hope it will at once become the standard organ of all the ornithologists of the Mississippi valley.........Wishing you success I remain,
Very Respectfully Yours,
WM. L. KELLS.

THREE RIVERS, MASS., Jan. 9, 1888.
WEBSTER & MEAD,
CRESCO, IOWA
Gentlemen:-Your magazine received. I am *well pleased* with its general appearance, and compliment you on the *general arrangement and style of the subject matter.* It will recommend itself to all *live* ornithologists; it is *just* what is needed at the present time, and I can cheerfully recommend it to *any* and *all* of my friends. ....I anticipate much pleasure in reading your magazine the coming season.
Yours Fraternally,
E. G. WARD.

WAYNESBURG, PA., Jan. 31, 1888.
MESSRS. WEBSTER & MEAD,
CRESCO, IOWA.
Dear Sirs:—Copy of the "H. O. and O." to hand and well pleased with it. ....To my eye it is a neat magazine and is full of interesting articles. Wishing you abundant success, I remain
Oologically Yours,
J. WARREN JACOBS.

BURR OAK, IA., Jan. 12, 1888.
EDITORS HAWKEYE O. AND O,
Dear Sirs:—Received the first number of the O. and O. last week and it is fully as good as I expected—excellent for the money. Such a magazine should work up a good subscription list, and I hope you may be fully successful.
Respectfully Yours,
HERMAN F. HEGNER.

ST. PAUL, MINN., Jan, 9, 1888.
MESSRS. WEBSTER & MEAD.
Gentlemen:—I received a sample Copy of your Hawkeye O. and O., which Mr. Davis of North Granville kindly sent me. It is needless to say that I am extremely pleased with it, and so subscribe for it. It is a useful as well as pleasant reading magazine, full of useful information; a magazine which was largely needed, one that devotes itself to the study of ornithology and oology. I will gladly give my service and time to record the bird migration of this place.........and allow me here to ask if any reader of the O. and O. knows if the indigo bunting (*Passerina cyanea*) inhabits this part of the country—southern Minnesota. I have noticed a bird of the description which leads me to believe it to be an indigo bunting.
Respectfully,
C. J. SONNEN.

HICKMAN, KY., Jan. 12, 1888.
Dear Sirs:—The Hawkeye O. and O. at hand some time ago. I am very much pleased with it. It exceeds my expectations.
Your Friend,
L. O. PINDAR.

NORTH GRANVILLE, N. Y., Jan. 8, 1888
W. & M..
Gents:—Paper came to hand a few days ago, also extra copies for which accept thanks..........It is neat in appearance and looks, and should think it ought to have a good support from the ornithological world.
Yours truly,
H. W. DAVIS.

TORONTO, CANADA, Jan. 6, 1888.
MESSRS. WEBSTER & MEAD,
Dear Sirs:—I duly received a copy of your new journal, and wish it great success, please enter my name as a subscriber......I have been an enthusiastic ornithologist for twelve years; most of the time being devoted to British Ornithology. I have only been in this country two years. I was a member of the Yorkshire (England) Naturalist Society and the Leeds Naturalist's Club..........During the past four years I have been at much expense in employing my own private collectors in Iceland, Holland, Turkey, in Asia and other places.........My collection of eggs, consisting of some 15,000 specimens, is almost as complete as I can make it.......
Yours Truly,
W. RAINE.

A monument is to be erected in Lincoln Park, Chicago, to the great naturalist, Linnæus. This monument will be modeled after the one erected to him in Stockholm, by King Charles XIV.

GEOLOGY & MINERALOGY.

For the Hawkeye O. and O.

THE SCIENTIST.

BY H. F. HEGNER, DECORAH, IOWA.

For the scientist all the works of nature are beautiful or sublime. First they come to him clothed in the cerements of finitude, and he loves to study them in this form, again, he studies them in the infinite and boundless expanse of the firmament above, and the sublimity of the laws that guide the planets through the realms of space is fully realized by him.

The works of nature are like a mirror of truth for the glory of the scientist; and in this mirror is imaged the unity and beauty of God's creation. He sees the image; tis more than an image, a blessed reality, dear to him in that he cannot comprehend, though he may apprehend it.

Nature is the mother of the Universe, and he loves her. That delicacy of expression which has beautified her work, even from the beginning builded on the stepping stones of animalization, has reached its ideal genius in the rational mind of man. Beauty decorates all objects, and man is the finishing touch, destined to turn the works of nature to glory, and finish them with a grandeur that will defy the misty fingers of time.

The mind of the scientist is one that cannot be idle. Natural phenomena constantly furnish food for study, and his observing and investigating spirit always finds something new to enrich the mind—the hills are his friends, the flowers and trees his companions, the merry songsters of the woodland his glory.

The bird he knows even by its song, and he marks its flight with an interest that is a perfect index to his mind. He is in his element and consequently happy. If his mind is susceptable of deeper impressions, he is more than happy.

Being inspired by the beauty of what he sees, the woodland's winged orchestra in harmony with the music of his soul, he leads an envious life indeed.

Nature has a language for him which is at once beautiful and grand, while a deeper sense of the beauty of his world is awakened by scientific study. How grand, how sublime are his conceptions of nature! She is his inspiration and he loves her. He loves her as the queen of a kingdom pendent in self, and a companion in his greatness. He loves to converse with her, and many a pleasant hour he spends in her felicity. Neither conspiracy nor usurpation can corrupt in his kingdom. Strangers are they, and nature is the Queen of his Soul. Even those changes of countenance that beautify her face from time to time, the sunny face of the golden day, the clouded face of the darkened day, the tempestuous voice and electrical eyes of the storm and the golden face of the sunset, inspire his mind with grand thoughts, and demonstrate daily the laws of gravitation, molecular forces and optics.

In the mountains among the buttresses and pinnacles, he finds another, a richer, field for study. Far above, towering alone in an aged silence, with countenance wrinkled by long years of storm, the noble mountain has dropped the tempest, and lifts his hoary head in eternal sunshine, while far away chiseling a way through his canons, lies the Colorado with his three thousand feet of prison wall on either side. Many years have passed away since he carved the rugged columns and barren precipices of the mountain side, and still though his chisel is dulled and his strength feeble, he continues his work. Ceaseless toil!—that carved these rugged peaks from the broad backs of the ancient mountains, and perfected this world of crags and columns in an awful grandeur!· Sublimity the student loves and a deepseated appreciation of this grandeur is his. He studies the sculptor Erosion.

[TO BE CONTINUED.]

TERTIARY FOSSILS IN THE BAD LANDS OF DAKOTA.

BY L. W. STILWELL, DEADWOOD, D. T.

The Bad Lands of Dakota along the Cheyenne and White rivers have attracted the attention of such scientists as Profs. Marsh, Leidy, Cope, Agassiz, Dana, Crosby, and others and very much time has been given by these eminent men to the study of fossil remains found in this region. Probably the most complete collections of specimens from these noted Miocene and Pliocene beds, are in the possession of Yale College and Smithsonian Institute. Collectors from these Institutes have spent much time and labor collecting skulls, teeth and skeletons of the strange animals left buried or bleaching in these dessiccated post-tertiary, lake bottoms. These fossil beds appear like a scar upon the face of old earth and the soil is indeed *bad land*; yet time and chemical action of the elements may transform this sterile land into fertile and productive soil. Unproducing soils have frequently yielded up their riches in this far western country to the tickling plow share of the new settlers.

It would be a long story to go over discoveries and descriptions of the mammalia which have been unearthed here. I have space only to mention a few of the forms. The tooth, a cut of which is here given, is a medium

sized molar of the Brontotherium. There are eight or nine molars upon each side of the upper jaw. The back molar is 3 to 3¾ inches square upon the crown, and each one from back to front of mouth is smaller in a graduating scale until a conical-shaped tooth, a sort of a tusk, is reached. The teeth are great, handsome and most wonderful specimens, with perfectly preserved enamel. The skull of this animal at full size is about three feet long and twenty inches wide. The concaved curved maxilary bone bore two great horns. The animal is said to have attained a length of 28 feet and a height of 9 feet.

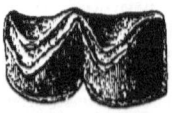

The second cut is an inferior one and imperfectly represents the tooth, perhaps of the same animal. The lower jaw containing this form of tooth and the upper jaw containing the former tooth have been found paired together in one complete head. Yet we call the former Brontotherium and the latter Titanotherium both belonging to the family called Brontotheridæ.

The "Titanotherium" back molar has three crests and is 4½ to 5 inches long by 2 inches wide, and the next tooth towards the front has but two crests. The outer edge of these crests of both species are sharp cutting edges, the inner points are rounded.

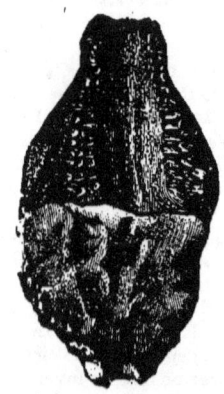

The third cut here shown represents a skull and upper teeth of an Oreodon Gracilis. These teeth are keen, sharp, jagged cutters, and appear as having three rows of crests. They are very interesting specimens. The head and body are about the size of a dog. We obtain some heads showing all the teeth in places in upper and lower jaws clashed together, excepting the front incisors.

The Miohippus, or three toed horse, is found here. The teeth are unlike those of any other animal discovered, and cannot be clearly described here. They must be seen to be appreciated. The animal had three divisions to each foot and a small hoof to each division, and is said to be one of the developing progenitors of our modern horse.

The Hyracodon (a tertiary Rhinocerous) teeth found are nearly square with zigzag edges on the crown. They are about ⅜ inches square, generally. The Phenocodus teeth, are rarely found. These have four rounded tubercles interior to the surface of the crown that give the teeth a very handsome appearance.

The remains of the Mastodon (an Elephant) Beaver, Wolf, Tapir, etc., are also found in this wonderful region.

ADVERTISEMENTS.

"He who by his biz would rise must either burst or advertise."

EVERYONE
SHOULD HAVE IT!

Write and receive a large sheet of printed explanations regarding our new and easy process of preserving birds, etc.

EMBALMING

Easy to learn; scarcely any expense; no time or money wasted; few tools required, and those made at home; simple and effective; no difficult complicados to dishearten the amateur or beginner; satisfaction guaranted.

ALWAYS SEND 2c STAMP FOR REPLY!

Eggs, Skins, etc., to exchange.

Wanted—All kinds of Natural History Specimens, also Indian Relics.

R. M. GIBBS,
KALAMAZOO, MICH.

Europe.   Established 1853   America

Ph. HEINSBERGER,

133 Ludlow St. and 89 Delancey St.,

NEW YORK, U. S. A.

International Gen. Agency.

Advertising, collecting, patents, addresses furnished in all parts of the world. Stamp Directories $1. U. S. and Foreign stamp papers, 10 papers $1. Postage and Revenue of all countries for sale. 1000 assorted European postage stamps $1. 100 postage stamps of South and Central America, West India Islands $1. 100 different postage stamps of Asia and Australia $5, 10 asst. Confederate notes $1. 400 gummed hinges $1. Mercantile agency, news depot, printer. Circulars sent on application with enclosed postage. Correspondence in English, German, French, Dutch and Spanish.

Agent for the Hawkeye Ornithologist and Oologist.

BIRDS' EGGS.

Any of the following first-class sets with full data will be sent by return mail at prices named. Safe delivery guaranteed.

No.	Name	Sets of	Per egg
55	Brown Creeper	5 to 7	$ 40
394	Am. Barn Owl	5	35
396	Short-eared Owl	4 to 6	50
407	Am. Hawk Owl	4 to 7	1 00
414	Am. Peregrine Falcon	2 to 4	1 50
433	Am. Gos Hawk	2 to 3	60
619	Barrow's Golden Eye	8 to 12	50
720	Am. Golden Eye	9 to 10	40

Address
HENRY W. DAVIS,
NORTH GRANVILLE, N. Y.

-BIRDS'-EGGS-AND-SKINS-
At reasonable prices. Send stamp for price list.
J. A. SINGLEY, GIDDINGS, TEXAS.

BIRDS' EGGS:

Eggs are all first class, one hole side blown and can be furnished either in sets with data or single,

A. O. U. No.	Name	Price each.
80	Black Skimmer	.08
294a	Cal. Valley Patridge	.10
378	Burrowing Owl	.15
385	Road Runner	.15
448	Cassin's Kingbird	.20
500	Tricolored Blackbird	.10
508	Bullock's Oriole	.08
510	Brewer's Blackbird	.04
519a	Crimson House Finch	.04
591b	Cal. Brown Towhee	.05
620	Phainopepla	.25
622 1	White-rumped Shrike	.04
703	Mockingbird	.04
713	Cactus Wren	.08

ALL KINDS OF SPECIMENS, WHOLESALE AND RETAIL.

Bird, Animal and Rep'tleSkins, Eggs, Minerals, Fossils, Shells, Insects, Alcoholic and Botanical Specimens, Indian Relics, Sea Curiosities, Coins, Stamps, Supplies, General Curiosities, etc. Price Lists, 2 cents each.

E. M. HAIGHT,
RIVERSIDE, CALIFORNIA.

CHEAP BIRDS' EGGS.

During the past year my collectors in Iceland, Greenland, Northwest Canada, and other places have sent me more specimens than I anticipated and as my .... of 15,000 SPECIMENS is as complete as I wish to make it, I have no use for the eggs received in the past year. Up to date I have been supplying European and American dealers, wholesale, with eggs; and I now wish to notify all collectors that I am going to put them on an equal footing with dealers, and let them have first-class rare eggs at rock bottom prices. I am in correspondence with all the leading oologists of Europe and America, and can quote in some very rare species, sets, pairs or single specimens.

Bonapart's Warbler	$ 35
Golden Eagle	5 00
Duck Hawk	1 40
European	35
" Kestril	18
" Redpoll	17
White	6
" ...ark	7
" Skylark	5
" ......ar	7
Snow ... ting	40
...erson's Owl	80
European Hawk Owl	90
Fulmar Petrel	35
Stormy Petrel	55
Black Sea water	55
European Oyster-catcher	18
Ringed Plover	12
Snowy Plover	75
Snipe	75
Dunlin	18
Curlew	35
Wainbrel	25
Whistling Swan	1 45
King Eider	90
Kittiwake Gull	25
Glaucous Gull	80
White-winged Gull	90
Red-throated Diver	80
Great Auk	
Cassin's Auk	5 0
	1 75

and many other species. Send for list.

As I wish to dispose of my duplicate eggs before visiting Europe this spring, I make the following liberal offer: To every one ordering $4 worth of eggs from my new list just issued I will give free, a ticket entitling them to a chance to win I in mail some sets of Golden, Bald, and Gray Sea Eagle and other good prizes. Don't miss this but send five cents in stamps for price list and particulars.

WALTER RAINE,
6 WALTON ST., TORONTO, CANADA.

Gem arrow points from the Willamette river Oregon, in any quantity.
BRONTOTHERIUM
Titanotherium, Oreodon, Hyracodon, &c. teeth from the Tertiary Fossils of the Bad Lands of Dakota (described elsewhere in these columns.)
Fossil Fish, Green River, Missouri; Black Hill's Minerals; Sioux and Apache Indian Buckskin Relics.
Send for large Illustrated Catalogue
L. W. Stilwell, Deadwood, D. T.

CLOSING OUT SURPLUS STOCK

We are carrying many hundred more specimens than we can handle at present and will give all readers mentioning this paper 10 per cent discount on all orders received before April 20, 1888. All are in sets with proper data, well prepared and positively identified.

No.	Sets of	Per Egg.
589 Savannah Blackbird,	1-3-5	$ .15
1 7 American Hawk Owl,	5-7	1.00
62° European Kestril,	4-5-5	.15
4 0 Mexican Turkey,	9,10	.10
619 Barrow's Golden Eye,	6 to 2	.45
710 Red-throated Diver,	2	.15

and 25 others equally as rare and cheap

Our prices can not be duplicated by any dealer in the United States and we will not be undersold.

Give us a trial and be convinced.

SCINDLER & SELOVER,
Lake City, Minn.

The Collectors' ILLUSTRATED MAGAZINE

Is a neatly printed monthly, consisting of twenty pages or more each month, filled with fine illustrations, and choice reading matter, written expressly for it by the best writers on all branches of

NATURAL HISTORY, ARCHEOLOGY, NUMISMATICS, PHILATELY, ETC.

It also contains an EXCHANGE DEPARTMENT, which is open free to all subscribers. Advertising Rates, 50 cents per inch. Subscription Price 50 cents per annum in the United States and Canada; foreign countries, 85 cents per annum. Single copies, 5 cents.

ALL KINDS OF SPECIMENS WHOLESALE AND RETAIL.

Bird, Animal and Reptile Skins, Eggs, Minerals, Fossils, Shells, Insects, Alcoholic and Botanical specimens, Indian Relics, Sea Curiosities, Coins stamps, Supplies, General Curiosities, etc. Price Lists 2 cents each.

E. M. HAIGHT,
RIVERSIDE, CALIFORNIA.

THE HAWKEYE ORNITHOLOGIST AND OOLOGIST

EDITED AND PUBLISHED BY
WEBSTER AND MEAD
CRESCO, : IOWA.

Contents For April

An Eclipse Among the Alps — — — — — H. F. Hegner
Oologists vs. "Rage Collectors" — — — — — — W. Hull.
Bird Destruction — — — — — — — — Jos. M. Wade.
The Wood Thrush, — — — — — — — — Jas. B. Purdy.
Canadian Flycatchers, — — — — — — Wm. L. Kells.
Bird Nesting in The North of England — — — — Walter Raine.
Notes on Some of the Passeres of Fulton Co., Kentucky — L. O. Pindar.
Death of Prof. Charles Linden — — — — Correspondence.
The Largest of Its Species — — — — — — New York Sun.
Oological Correspondence — — — — — — Jas C. Jay.
Suggestions for Properly Forming Collections of Birds' Eggs
Smithsonian Bulletin.
Notes.
Migration Notes.
How to Collect and Prepare Conchological Specimens — J. A. Singley.
The Scietist — — — — — — — — — H. F. Hegner.
Care of Minerals — — — — — — — — W. S. Beekman.

R. E. RACHFORD & SON,
COLLECTING NATURALISTS
—— AND WHOLESALE DEALERS IN ——
BIRD SKINS AND EGGS,
BEAUMONT, - - TEXAS.

The Hawkeye Ornithologist & Oologist.

"Better to search the fields for health unbought,
Than fee the doctor for a nauseous draught.
The wise for health on exercise depend,
God never made his work for man to mend."

VOL. 1.   CRESCO, IA., APRIL, '88.   NO. 4.

AN ECLIPSE AMONG THE ALPS.

BY H. F. HEGNER, DECORAH, IOWA.

Far along the frozen glaciers
  Where the milky waters leap,
Through the fresh and quiet valleys,
  Down the gorges wild and deep.

Creeps the night: The stars are shining
  In the twilight and the gloom:
Drifting through the Alpine heavens,
  Gently shines the rising moon.

Now she's climbing upward; shadows
  Dropping from the summit's crest,
Wrap the valleys in the darkness,
  Slumber on the mountain's breast.

But the earth has trailed her shadow
  Far out into empty space;
And the moon walks through the shadow
  With earth's image on her face.

Oh, how often has that journey
  By a human soul been made;
Passing through this world of trouble,
  Into sunshine—out of shade!

Long I watch her evening journey
  Far above the mountain's reach:
Her sad face is almost human,
  With an eloquence of speech.

For my soul is ever climbing,
  Through an Alpine world of thought;
Giant BLANCS to be surmounted
  Icy battles to be fought.
              —*Dubuque Herald*.

OOLOGISTS VS. "RAGE" COLLECTORS.

BY W. HULL.

By a "Rage" Collector is meant one who is suddenly seized with the idea that he is deeply interested in oology, and must get together a collection of eggs as soon as possible. Some are inspired by reading oological papers, others become interested by associating with those who are at the height of excitement.

A great many persons are seized with a greater or less desire to collect stamps, coins, etc. These can be identified at any time, but eggs cannot.

A true oologist collects with a scientific purpose, actuated by a true love of nature, and an egg is of no value to him unless its identity is certain. Some collectors have a large collection, but know little or nothing about the parent birds. This would not be the case if they really cared for the eggs, but they simply keep them to gaze upon in blank admiration and boast that they have so many more eggs than some one else who may or may not collect with real interest.

I have on my tongue's end the names of at least two dozen collectors of this class, those that collect merely for the number of eggs. These collectors can truly be called "Great American Egg Hogs." Unrefined as this expression is, nevertheless it is to the point.

This class of collectors number many hundred throughout the United States and Canada. The excuse is "that egg collecting is a healthful and innocent pastime." Healthful it is, if one collects the eggs himself (which is not the case with the majority) but as to the innocence, that is due to the fact that it is not taken under a full view, and as long as it is healthful and no serious results are immediately visible, it is taken for granted to be innocent. This is a matter which the American Ornithologist's Union is acting upon, and appeals to the true oologists, for their assistance in discouraging these "naturalists"(?) in their wild career.—*Milwaukee Naturalist.*

BIRD DESTRUCTION.

BY JOS. M. WADE.

Twenty to thirty years ago, it was not an unusual sight to see even the scarlet tanager, a bright red bird with black wings and tail, flitting from tree to tree in the heart of our cities like a fiery meteor in the sun-light, and to find their nests, built very lightly of straws and similar material on the horizontal limbs of our shade trees. But they were killed or driven off long before the advent of bird millinery as a fashion. They were, indeed, a "shining mark," and every body wanted a specimen, or thought they did, until at the present time the scarlet tanager is really a very rare bird throughout the New England States.

The Baltimore oriole, so named because the colors of the bird, black and yellow, resembled those of Lord Baltimore, has almost met the same fate, as it has done duty in ornamenting thousands of ladies' bonnets within the past five years. Four years ago this bird was quite plenty on the elms of Boston and suburbs. The hanging nests, made of hemp, old twine, etc., were quite common. But the past season showed a great change. These birds have been shot so ruthlessly, both while here and at the South, and during the migration, that hardly a pair could be found during the breeding season of 1886.

* * * * * *

Scientific American.

ORNITHOLOGY.

For The Hawkeye O. and O.

THE WOOD THRUSH.

COMPOSED BY JAMES B. PURDY.

The wood thrush is singing from the depth of
    the glen,
His clear, bell-like music, so pleasing to me
In the fair month of May, when all nature
    looks gay;
They vie with each other from briar and
    tree.
In a deep shaded nook, where the woodbine
    twine,
And the dark gloomy forest conceals them
    from view;
By a clear, winding brooklet, o'er tangled
    with vines,
His dear mate is guarding her treasures of
    blue.
Though dark be the weather and gloomy the
    morn,
And all other birds in the forest are still,
And the sad face of Nature, all dreary, for-
    lorn,
His clear, mellow notes through the drip-
    ping woods thrill.
In the evening, when nature is seeking repose,
And his dear little mate has repaired to her
    nest,
And the last golden sunbeams are kissing the
    rose,
It is then that his song is the sweetest and
    best.
Oh, then man why repine, be downcast on
    your way,
As through the long years you are jour-
    neying on;
For the sadder the morning and gloomier the
    day,
The happier and sweeter is the wood
    thrushe's song.

For The Hawkeye O. and O.

CANADIAN FLYCATCHERS.

BY WM. L. KELLS, LISTOWEL, ONTARIO.

TRAILL'S FLYCATCHER.
(*Empidonax pusillus Trailli.*)

In size and general appearance, this species closely resembles the wood pewee; but its habitat and mode of nesting are much different. It does not frequent the back-woods nor the high timbered places; and not until a thick second-growth of low underwood succeeds the original forest in low swampy places does it make its appearance in the central districts of Ontario. Then it is so shy and wary, darting off into the deepest concealment whenever its haunts are invaded by the presence of human kind, that were it not for its noisy notes, it would scarcely be known to exist.

It arrives in this vicinity toward the end of May, when its haunts are being clothed with the emerald foliage of summer, and when it can the more easily conceal itself from observation, which it appears to dread. Then, however, the rapidly repeated "wick-we-o" of the male, as he perches on some elevated, but shady branch, intimate its presence, and that his mate has probably chosen the neighboring thicket for her summer home, while should this be penetrated, her sharp "twick," repeated in a repellant tone, gives the intruder to understand that she is there, and that his presence is not welcome.

It is very active in its movements, and darts through the shrubbery with the rapidity of a flash. It appears to subsist chiefly on insects, many of which it captures on the wing after the manner of its family. It is only in recent years that this species has become a summer resident of this vicinity; and in the particular places where it chooses to reside, it seems yearly to be more common. In the manner and position of its nest, it differs from all the other Canadian flycatchers. This is placed in deep concealment among the thick foliage of the particular shrub, bush or underwood in which it is built, and if the first efforts at brood raising are successful, it does not appear to nest again that season, but if otherwise, it will try again. Its first nest may be found the early part of June, but its efforts at reproduction appear to cease after the month of July, and it becomes silent as August advances.

On the 19th of July, 1885, my boys reported to me they had found the nest of a new kind of bird in a piece of low woods on the farm opposite Wildwood. They stated that the bird was nearly as large as a hermit thrush, but more like a flycatcher; that the nest—placed in a low blue beech—was like an indigo bird's, but that the three eggs which it contained, were like those of a vireo. Eager to ascertain what this new discovery might be, I returned with the boys to the nesting place, and though the owner was absent, I saw at a glance that it was a discovery new to me. The nest was placed in the fork of a small blue beech, three feet off the ground, well concealed among the leaves and surrounding raspberry vines. It was composed externally of wool and coarse grasses; and lined with fine dry grass and some horse-hair. The three eggs were of a whitish-yellow hue, with a few reddish dots toward the large end. Now, anxious to see the owner of this nest, I took a ramble through the wood, where I heard and saw the male bird, and when I returned the female flushed off the nest and darted into the neighboring thicket, and for some time I supposed this species to be the olive-sided flycatcher, but learning my mistake, I became certain that it was the *Trailli*, and have since been confirmed in this identification. The next summer, about the 20th day of June, within a few yards of the above mentioned place, I found in the forks of a small swamp elm, about four feet off the ground, another nest of the same species; much the same in composition, and containing three fresh eggs, similar in hue and markings. And on the same day, a few rods further in the wood, another nest of this species, containing three young a few days old. This nest, however, was in the forks of a red-maple sapling about nine feet off the ground, and some of the coarse grass stalks of which it was composed hung down nearly a foot from the bottom of the nest. Last season I failed to discover any nests of this species, though I found the birds in several other places.

THE LEAST FLYCATCHER.
(*Empidonax minimus.*)

This species, in general appearance and place of habitat, much resembles the wood pewee, but it is smaller in size, and its mode of nesting is quite different.

Its scolding notes are the repetition of a simple "chip"; but these are seldom heard except when its nest or young are approached. Its song, if such it may be called, resembles the word "chebeck" repeated in a clear tone, may often be heard, especially for some weeks after its arrival

Its advent here usually occurs in the latter part of May; and it leaves Canada for more southern latitudes in the early part of September.

Its usual habitat is the high, rolling, hard-wood timbered lands; and for the hilly margins of gravel-bottomed creeks, it seems to have a decided partiality.

In the dry season it feeds occasionally on small fish, which it easily captures, as they wriggle in the shallow water, though in general it feeds on small insects and their progeny in various stages of development.

This little creature is quite pugilistic, and in the pairing season two males often indulge in a free and fierce fight, which probably influences the female in her decision of accepting the victor as her future partner.

The nest of this species is placed in the upright fork of a small tree, or where some small branches project from a larger stem. It is a neat, compact structure, much like that of the redstarts, composed chiefly of the fibrous matter that forms between the bark and wood of decayed trees, lined with fine hair. The set of eggs, numbering from two to five, are of a clear white hue. It does not appear to nest more than once during the season.

[FINIS.]

For The Hawkeye O. and O.
BIRD NESTING IN THE NORTH OF ENGLAND.

BY WALTER RAINE, TORONTO, CANADA.

Crossing the stream above Thornton Force, we ascend a hill; and on reaching the top a splendid panorama opens before us. Towards the west, the river Lune wends its way for nearly twenty miles, and after passing through the town of Lancaster, empties itself into Morcambe Bay. The sun is shining on the sea, which is twenty miles away, although it does not appear half that distance. The atmosphere is very clear in this region, and taking out our field glass we plainly see several ships and steamers sailing in the Irish Sea. Towards the north are the mountain peaks of Cumberland and Westmoland, standing out boldly; to the east stands Ingleborough mountain, towards the foot of which we make our way. We soon cross another stream which runs over Beezley Falls and down through another fairy gorge called Crina Bottom, which is similar to the one we have just traversed, with numerous cascades, and where more water ouzels, wagtails and redpolls breed; but we have not time to stay here, wishing to get on to the moors to find some plover's eggs.

Crossing some fields we find a nest of the skylark with four eggs. The mate is soaring high in the air and pouring out his joyous strains; it reminds us of the old German hymn: "Hark! Hark! the Lark at Heaven's gate sings." He is truly a wonderful songster. Immediately on leaving the ground, he begins to pour out his song, and soaring upward and upward, until he is a mere speck in the sky, when he begins to descend and does not cease singing until he reaches the earth again.

The titlark is one of the commonest birds of this district and we come across several nests, by the birds starting from in front of our feet. Their nests are always on the ground, made of dried grass, lined with hair; and contain from four to six eggs of a dusky brown, mottled over with darker brown, some having black hair lines around the egg.

A wheatear flying from out of some stones attracts our notice; and here is a nest made of grass and rabbit's fur, containing six pale blue eggs, not unlike the American blue-birds. This wheatear is called stonechat in America, though it must not be confounded with the English stonechat which is a different species.

We now reach the moors and are soon up to the knees in heather. Bird life here is very numerous. Lapwing plovers fly over our heads, crying "pewit, pewit" in a plaintive note; long-billed curlews are screaming loudly; golden plovers are whistling; red grouse are crowing; ring ouzel are calling; and above all can be heard the welcome cry of the cuckoo. High in the air, several snipes are drumming. This noise is caused by the bird's wings as it rapidly descends in the air. Nothing is more delightful than a ramble over a Yorkshire moor, where the purple heather grows in place of grass, relieved here and there with stretches of bracken, gray rocks and boulders. A lapwing rises some distance in front, and marking down the spot, we soon stand gazing upon its nest and four eggs with their points inward, meeting in the center, after the fashion of all plover's eggs. The nest is simply a slight hollow in the ground, lined with bits of grass. The eggs have a dark olive ground, abundantly blotched with brown and black; average size 2.00x1.50. These eggs are much sought after as delicacies for the table; and are offered for sale in the markets at three pence and four pence each. We look around and soon find several more nests and eggs; and in less than twenty minutes we have taken some two dozen eggs, and as we don't wish to carry them along with us, we hide them beneath a rock from carrion crows until we return.

Jumping over a little brook, a snipe darts away from a tuft of grass. In the center are snugly laid four richly marked eggs of a greenish-olive hue, blotched and spotted with two or three shades of brown. A large series show the eggs to differ much in ground color and markings. This bird is numerous in Yorkshire; I have found it breeding in all parts of the county.

Only two species of duck nest in the moors, near the lagoons, the common mallard and the teal.

The mallard usually lays from seven to twelve pale olive-green tinted eggs in a nest of grass, lined with down; size about 2.25x1.60.

The teal builds a nest of vegetable substances, lined with down and feathers. Six to twelve eggs are laid of a buffy white; size, 1.75x1.25.

The short-eared owl is found nesting here; its nest is always on the ground, a simple structure of sticks, grass and heather, upon which it lays four or five white elliptical eggs, averaging in size 1.55x1.25.

Three other species of owls nest in this district: the barn owl, the tawny owl and the long-eared owl.

The latter generally selects some old crow or magpie's nest; and lays from four to six eggs, not so round as those of the short-eared species.

Tramping over the moors for a mile or so, a bird rises from the hillside before us and dashes away at a great rate. Marking down the spot, we find a stone surrounded by bird's feathers and insects' wings, and pick up a titlark which is still warm. This is the shambles of a merlin hawk who was just going to dine off the titlark when we disturbed him. We set about to look around for its nest, when my brother cried out "Here it is with four splendid eggs." In a few seconds I was there, gazing on the treasures with delight and admiration. The nest was a mixed mass of twigs, heather and brakens, raised a few inches high; and the four eggs resting in a slight hollow in the center. Their ground color was a dark, crimson brown, speckled all over with dark brown and black. Some varieties resemble eggs of the kestril hawk, but a series of fifty eggs before me do not show such varieties in color as the eggs of the kestril do. As a rule, they are smaller than the kestril's eggs and not so round, nor so boldly marked. We blow the eggs and pack them away with care, and proceed farther on.

[TO BE CONTINUED.]

FOR THE HAWKEYE O. AND O.

NOTES ON SOME OF THE PASSERES OF FULTON CO., KY.

THIRD PAPER, BY L. O, PINDAR, PRES. Y. O. A., HICKMAN, KY.

Following the family *Corvidæ*,

comes the family *Icteridæ*. The commoner species of this family in this part of Kentucky are the red-winged blackbird, the meadow lark, the Baltimore oriole and the purple grackle. The orchard oriole and the rusty blackbird are also found; but over two years of study and careful searching in our woods and fields has failed to detect the bobolink and cowbird.

I purpose to devote this paper to the meadow lark and the Baltimore oriole.

First come; first served. The meadow or field lark is a common resident here and seems to collect in colonies. I know of two fields where I can always find them, while in other, seemingly just as favored meadows, I have failed to see them.

Early in the spring, I think, of '87, I shot at one of these birds and came very near making a clear miss as only one shot struck him and that cut off his leg. I picked him up and was going to kill him when the thought came across my mind to make a pet of him. Accordingly, on reaching home, I put him in a cage and fed him corn meal, which he ate greedily. He also relished a few wheat grains which I let him have. He grew very tame shortly, and on several occasions woke me up in the morning by his clear, rich whistling; but one day I left a lot of meal by the cage and he killed himself eating it. I would have supposed he would have known when he had enough, but he didn't.

Mr. J. B. Richards, Sec'y. Y. O. A., writes me that he has known a wild bobolink to kill itself by eating too much, and he lost a pet bobolink in the same way.

The meadow lark is accused by some writers of murdering and devouring, not only its own, but other birds' nestlings, and of being an egg-sucker; but I have nothing to offer on that point myself.

The nest of the meadow lark is made of grass, etc., built on the ground, often arched over, and sometimes at the foot of a bush or weed.

The eggs are four to six in number; crystal white, more or less marked with reddish-brown dots; average size, 1.10x.80.

And now, having called the bird a "lark" all through the article, let me say that it is not a lark at all, but a starling. The old name is, however, too firmly established to permit of a change.

The Baltimore oriole is a summer resident and quite common. The males arrive about the middle of April, and the females about ten days later. In 1887; the males arrived on the 13th, the females on the 23d. On the 30th, I found a nest nearly finished; and May 7th it contained five fresh eggs. Unfortunately the boy who tried to secure them broke the whole set.

The oriole is one of our most brilliantly plumaged birds, and on that account is much persecuted. I have heard that they stand captivity well, but as yet I have had no opportunity to try.

But it is in the nest that the chief interest in the study of this species centers. It is a closely woven pouch of various substances, grass, wool, thread, string, hair, lace, ribbons, rags, paper, leaves—all these and many more have been found in their nests. I have one by me now which is composed entirely of horsehair, with the exception of a white string around the rim to bind the hairs together; and I was shown one in Fulton, Kentucky, made entirely of long blades of grass.

I made a careful examination of the nest mentioned in the first part of the sketch. The foundation was made entirely of white wrapping twine, lined with dried grass; and as if to render it less conspicuous, it was covered with green locust leaves—it was in a locust tree—and suspended as it was, among a bunch of leaves, it was next to impossible to see it. I discovered it by watching the bird. One string in the nest was over five feet long. It was wrapped again and again around a limb, then to the nest, woven down one side under the bottom and up the other side to the rim where it was securely fastened.

The eggs are white, with blackish spots and scrawls irregularly distributed over the surface, especially toward the larger end. The average size is 1.00x.65, according to Coues; .92x.65 according to Davie. I consider the latter more correct so far as it applies to eggs taken here.

The bird is known by the various names of fire-bird, golden robin, hang nest, etc., besides the one given above.

DEATH OF PROF. CHAS. LINDEN.
Correspondence by Ph. Heinsberger.

Prof. Charles Linden, instructor in natural history at the Buffalo High School, died in that city, of acute mania on Feb. 3.

Prof. Linden came to America from Breslau, Germany, twenty-five years ago as a sailor, and was engaged as a seaman on the great lakes when his knowledge of natural history became known and the charge of the collections of the Society of Natural Sciences was given him, after which he took his position in the High School.

The Society sent him abroad every summer, visiting in turn Brazil, where he secured many valuable birds, South America, Hayti, and the Southern States. In 1879, while exploring the coast of Labrador, he was shipwrecked and put ashore by a rescuing vessel. It was his custom to send everything new to him to the Harvard Museum. He was an authority on ornithology, and a writer of many valuable articles on that subject.

THE LARGEST OF ITS SPECIES

A HINT TO OUR GOVERNMENT.

The biggest American eagle in the United States roosts in the state house in this city. It is the property of Maj. E. J. Anderson, the state comptroller, and its roosting place is on an imitation rock in the window of his private office. The bird measures seven feet and eleven inches from tip to tip of its wings, and it is so tall that if it were alive and standing on the ground it could pick off a man's waistcoat buttons without getting on tiptoe. The profusion of little fluffy feathers on the under sides of the wings, the peculiar markings of the breast, and the depression in the top of the beak are evidences of the great age to which the bird had attained before it was killed. Those skilled in such matters estimate that it must have been at least 75 years old. It is a genuine Washington or American eagle, and probably its only rival in the country, dead or alive, is at the Smithsonian Institute at Washington, but the specimen there is smaller.

The graceful yet powerful pose of this bird and the magnificent sweep of its wings show clearly how great a libel upon the bird of freedom is the atrocious figure that attempts to soar over the bundle of sticks on the back of the buzzard dollars of the present day. If the government will send an artist to Trenton it can obtain a model from which it can make a dollar that will not bring the blush of shame to the cheek of every American who has to spend it.

Maj. Anderson's eagle was shot in Hunterdon county, in this state. The bird is one of the most rare in the country, and it is scarcely ever even seen near the haunts of civilization. It is supposed that advanced age had made this bird unable to successfully pursue and capture the game of the wilderness, and that therefore it had ventured into settled regions for tamer prey. It was found near a farmer's barn, and the farmer filled it full of lead from a shotgun and a revolver without killing it, and finally captured it alive, having disabled it by wounds in the wing. It was taken to the village station, and lived there on exhibition a day or two before it died. It was then given to Maj. Anderson, who had it stuffed and mounted, and guards it now with the tenderness and pride of a young father. He has refused for it offers running well into the hundreds of dollars.—Trenton Cor. New York Sun.

✳OOLOGY.✳

Lalloyt. Henry Co., Ia., Mch. 10, '88.
MESSRS. WEBSTER & MEAD,

Dear Sirs:—March number of the H. O. AND O. at hand, and must say it is a daisy. I am an oologist, and on January last I found a nest of the great horned owl, with two fresh eggs, which is the earliest I ever knew it to breed here. The nest was in an old snag, about ten feet from the ground. The owl could be plainly seen and I could almost see the eggs while standing on the ground. I had frequently noticed her on the snag, but thought she was roosting there through the day. At the time I found the nest, the snow was on an average of two feet deep. This is the second nest of this species that I have ever found.

Red-tailed hawks are plenty here. I found eight nests in one season; they nest here in February and June, raising two broods. They always use the same nests each year unless they are disturbed. I once found a nest in which they had only laid one egg, so I went away, leaving it until they had finished the set. I visited the nest four days afterward, but that egg was gone and they never used that nest again. I have never found a nest yet of the red-tailed hawk but what it was in a tall tree, and *always leaning* over a ravine. They trouble the farmers' fowls a great deal, often killing the largest hens. I once set a steel trap by a hen which they had killed and next morning I had the male.

Yours truly,
JAMES C. JAY.

SUGGESTIONS FOR PROPERLY FORMING COLLECTIONS OF BIRDS' EGGS.

If the identification has been effected only by obtaining a good view of the birds, the fact should be stated thus: "Bird well seen," "Bird seen," or "Bd. sn.," as the case may be. For eggs not taken by the collector himself, but brought in by natives, or persons not having a knowledge of ornithology, the *local name* or the *name applied by the finder* should *only* be used, unless indeed it requires interpretation, when the scientific name may be added, but *always within* brackets thus: "'Toogle-aiah (*Squatarole helvetica*);" the necessary particulars relating to the capture and identification being added. Eggs found by the collector, and *not* identified by him, but the origin of which he has reason to think he knows, may be inscribed with the common English name of the species to which he refers them; or if it has no appellation, then the scientific name may be used, but in that case *always with a note of interrogation* (?) after it, *or else* the words "Not identified." If the collector prefers it, many of these particulars may be inscribed symbolically or in short-hand, but *never unless* the system used has previously been agreed upon with persons at home, and it be known that they have a key to it. *Each specimen should bear an inscription;* those from the same nest may be inscribed; but different nests, especially of the same or nearly allied species, should never be so marked that confusion can possibly arise. It is desirable to mark temporarily with a *pencil* each egg as it is obtained; but the permanent inscription, which should always be ink, should be deferred until after the egg has been emptied. The number terminating the inscription in all cases referring to the page of the collector's note-book, wherein full details may be found, and the words or letters preceding the number serving to distinguish between different collectors, no two of whom ought to employ the same. (The initial letter of the collector's name, prefixed to the number, will often be sufficient.)

PREPARATION OF SPECIMENS.

Eggs are emptied, with the least amount of trouble, at *one* hole, which should be drilled in the *side* with an instrument called the egg-drill. The hole should, of course, be proportioned to the size of the egg and the amount of incubation it has undergone. Eggs that are hard sat upon are more easily blown by being kept a few days, but the operation must not be deferred too long, or they are apt to burst violently immediately upon being punctured, though this may be avoided by holding them under water while the first incision is made. The hole being drilled, the lining membrane should be cleared away from the orifice with a small penknife, by which means not only is the removal of the contents, but the subsequent cleansing of the specimen facilitated. The small end of a blowpipe should then be introduced, while the other extremity is applied to the mouth and blown through, *at first very gently*. If the embryo is found to be moderately developed, a stream of water should be introduced by means of a syringe, and the egg then gently shaken, after which the blowpipe may again be resorted to, until by the ultimate use of both instruments, aided by scissors, hooks, knives and forceps, the contents are completely emptied. After this the egg should be filled with water from the syringe, shaken, and blown out, which process is to be repeated until its interior is completely cleansed, when it should be laid upon a pad of blotting paper or fine cloth, with the hole downwards, its position on the pad or cloth being occasionally changed, until it is perfectly dry. During this time it should be kept as much as possible from the light, especially from the sunshine, as the colors are then more liable to fade than at any subsequent time. In the case of very small eggs, when fresh, the contents may be sucked out by means of a bulbed tube, and the interior afterwards rinsed out as before. It is always advisable, as far as possible, to avoid wetting the outside of the shell as the action of water is apt to remove the "bloom," affect the color, and in some cases alter the crystalization of the shell. Consequently dirt stains or dung spots should never be removed. While emptying the contents, it is well to hold the egg over a basin of water, to avoid breakage in case of its slipping from the fingers. Eggs that are very hard sat upon, of whatever size they may be, should be treated in the manner detailed in "Concluding Observations," in next issue, which is a method superior to any other known at present to the writer for preventing injury arising to them. Should the yolk of the egg be dried up, a small portion of *carbonate of soda* may be introduced (but with great care that it does not touch the outer surface of the shell, in which case the color is likely to be affected) and then the egg filled with water from the syringe, and left to stand a few hours with the hole uppermost, after which the contents are found to be soluble and are easily removed by the blowpipe, assisted by one of the hooks. It is almost unnecessary to add, except for the benefit of beginners, that the manipulation of the different instruments requires extreme caution, but a few trials will give the collector the practice necessary for success. Those who may still prefer to blow eggs by means of *two* holes are *particularly requested not to make them at the ends of the eggs, nor on opposite sides,* but on the same side. In this case the hole nearest the smaller end of the egg should be the smallest and the contents blown out at the other. If the holes are made at the *ends* of the eggs, it not only very much injures their appearance as cabinet specimens, but also prevents their exact dimensions from being ascertained accurately; and if they are made at *opposite* sides, the extent of the "show surface" is thereby lessened.

[TO BE CONTINUED.]

THE HAWKEYE
ORNITHOLOGIST&OOLOGIST

EDITED AND PUBLISHED BY
E. B. WEBSTER,   F. D. MEAD,
CRESCO,   IOWA.

A MONTHLY MAGAZINE
DEVOTED TO ORNITHOLOGY,
KINDRED SUBJECTS,
AND GEOLOGY.

TERMS OF SUBSCRIPTION.
Per year, - - - - - - 50 cents
Per year to foreign countries, - 65 cents
Single copies, - - - - - 5 cents

Remittances for subscriptions must be made by postal note—stamps will be returned.

TERMS OF ADVERTISING.
1 line, 1 insertion,	- - - -	$ .10
1 inch,	" - - - -	1.00
2 inches,	" - - - -	1.75
½ column,	" - - - -	2.50
1 column,	" - - - -	5.00
1 page,	" - - - -	10.00

A large discount on standing ads. Special rates can sometimes be given.

GENERAL AGENT.—PH. Heinsberger, 181 Ludlow St., and 89 Delancy St., New York.

All books, periodicals, specimens, etc., sent us will be reviewed.

Correspondence and items of interest relating to the several departments solicited from all. All matter for publication must be in by the last of each month in order to insure insertion in the next number.

Entered at the postoffice at Cresco, Iowa, as second class matter.

NOTES.

A neat appearing monthly devoted chiefly to philately, hails us from Mexico, N. Y., under the somewhat peculiar name of "Common Sense;" F. A. Thomas, editor. "May it live long and prosper."

Mr. Oliver Davie has in preparation an article on the golden-crowned thrush, which we expect to publish in a month or so. This is, in his opinion, one of his best efforts, as the bird is an especial favorite with him.

We notice that the *Bay State Oologist* appears in an improved though "condensed" form this month. Success.

Datas, 5x8, neatly printed, good paper, bound in lots of fifty, with flexible cardboard covers, 50 cents each in exchange.

The *Calmar Exchange*, published by our friend S. C. Scott, of Calmar, Iowa, comes to our table bright and fresh in its eight-page form and new dress. Those interested in the subjects of which it treats will find it an excellent paper at a small price.

Every person sending me 50 cents for one year's subscription to the HAWKEYE ORNITHOLOGIST AND OOLOGIST will receive free six varieties of rare Iowa minerals, labeled. Send postal note.   JAMES C. JAY.
LaHoyt, Henry Co., Iowa.

Among other fine specimens recently received from Messrs. Schindler & Selover, of Lake City, Minn., was one of the large, showy eggs of the Egyptian vulture, collected in Spain, which they are selling at the very low price of $1.25 each. We can take pleasure in recommending this firm as being thoroughly reliable, and as their rates are so extremely low, we bespeak for them a most liberal patronage.

The last number of the *Collector's Illustrated Magazine*, published by E. M. Haight of Riverside, Calif., which, by the way, is our finest exchange, contains, among its many valuable articles, the first installment of a series on Vireos, by Wm. L. Kells, written in his customary interesting manner; also fine articles on "Natural History" by Chas. L. Mason; "Wonderful Mica" by J. J. Alton; and "The Cliff Dwellers of Southwestern Colorado."

Our readers will notice that in this issue we commence the publication of a valuable article on Conchology, by J. A. Singley of Giddings, Texas. If a person has a hobby, he generally rides it well; therefore we make no hesitancy in saying that Mr. Singley's article will prove of much value and interest to the conchological student.

HOW'S THIS?

We would respectfully call the attention of the *Bay State Oologist* to the following:

Columbus, O., Nov. 17, 1888.
WEBSTER & MEAD,
Gentlemen:— * * * * *
* * I have copies left of the present edition (a copy of which I send you by to-day's mail) which you may have at ——per cent off. *
* * OLIVER DAVIE.

March 8, 1888.
WEBSTER & MEAD,
Gentlemen:— * * * *
I note what Mr. Foote says in regard to my "Nests and Eggs." When I sent you the copies they were all I had in stock- at least I thought so, for it was all I could find in the closet where I kept them. In turning over a large number of ornithological books for reference, I found a package of eight copies, one of which I sent Mr. Foote and quoted prices, but he did not take them and I sent them to Mr. Lattin who was entirely out of them and wanted them and 500 more if he could get them at once. Mr. Foote has not *purchased a single copy of the work from me.* I *now am entirely out until* the *third* edition appears. I have notified Mr. Foote to that effect. * * *

Yours truly,
OLIVER DAVIE.

Mr. Foote's article, which you have probably all seen, was decidedly ungentlemanly, to say the least.

MIGRATION NOTES.

BERNADOTTE, ILLINOIS.
BY DR. W. S. STRODE.

NAME	FIRST SEEN	NO. SEEN	NEXT SEEN	WHEN COM.
Cedar Waxwing	2— 3	2		
B.-throated Bunting	2— 5	7		2—13
Am. R.-legged Hawk	2— 7	2		
Red-tailed "	2— 7	1		
Mourning Dove*	2—11	1		
Wild Geese	2 -18	7		
Bluebirds	2 —19	23		3— 5
Brown Creepert	2—26	1		
Ducks—on river	3— 1			
Robin	3 - 1	1		3—11
Killdeer	3— 1	3		
Ducks—Old Squaw	3 - 3	11		
Flicker	3— 3	1		
Red-w. Blackbird	3— 4	12		
Meadow Lark	3— 8	3		
Cooper's Hawk	3—11	2		
Pileated Woodpecker	3—14	2		
Purple Grackle	3 -15	7		
Phoebe	3 -18	1	3—19	
Am. Sheldrake‡	3 -18			
Sparrow Hawk	3—19	3		
House Wren	3—19	2		

*In company with a large number of Juncos and Song Sparrows; and near some straw sheds had probably been left during the fall migration.

†Found dead at foot of a tree, in very poor condition.

‡Numerous on the river; a friend shot three.

Great-horned Owl—found first nest February 8, containing three eggs.

Red-tailed Hawk—took first eggs, ½, on March 3.

Crows—counted 206 flying northwest to roost eight miles away, on March 5; on the 17th found new and finished nest.

I have made no mention of our winter residents, such as Junco, B. C. Chickadee, Tufted Titmouse, Song Sparrow, Am. Goldfinch, Crows, Jays, Hairy, Downy and Red-bellied Woodpeckers, Cardinals, etc., for scarcely a day of the period covered by this record has passed in which I have not observed more or less of all of them; and also have seen nearly every day, in my twenty to forty miles ride, more or less of some of the following more rare permanent residents: Great Horned, Barred and Screech owls, Am. Rough-legged and Red-tailed Hawks, Prairie Hens, Ruffed Grouse and Bobwhite, and occasionally a wild Turkey would cross my path.

CRESCO, IOWA.

Downy Woodpecker	2—23	1	3— 4
Horned Lark	2—23	7	3— 4
W.-breasted Nuthatch			3— 5
Red Crossbill	3— 2	1	
Red-h. Woodpecker	3— 3	1	
Bluebird	3—15	1	3—18
Chipping Sparrow	3—15	2	3—16
Robin	3—16	2	3—17
Red-tailed Hawk	—17	1	3—18
Pewee	3—17	1	

MEDINA, N. Y.
BY N. F. POSSON.

Snow Bunting	1— 1
Am. Robin	1— 1
Black-c. Chickadee	1— 4
White-b. Nuthatch	1— 7
Brown Creeper	1— 7
Downy Woodpecker	1— 7
Hairy "	1— 7
Red-h. "	1— 7
Shore Lark	1—28
Gt. Northern Shrike	2— 2
Bluebird	2—24
Pine Grosbeak	2—25

CHICAGO.
BY W. E. PRATT.

Am. Herring Gull*	2— 4	20	2— 5	2— 4
Hooded Sheldrake	2—18	4		
Red Crossbill	2—15	2		
White-r. Shrike	2—18	1		
Shore Lark	2—18	10†	2—22	2—18
Bluebird	2—22	12†	2—24	
Sparrow Hawk?	2—22	4		
Red-tailed "	2—22	1		

*A winter resident here when the lake (Michigan) is free of ice.
†All males.

The Red-breasted Sheldrake and Black-capped Chickadee, winter residents, were also observed.

Those interested in bird migration will, we hope, read our "Notes" with interest. We wish to thank those who forwarded reports for their aid; and would be pleased to receive reports from all. Those wishing to aid us in this department and sending us their address will have the necessary blanks sent them.

Our home reports are meager, owing to the extreme lateness of spring.

To secure insertion, the reports should be sent not later than the 15th of each month.

CONCHOLOGY.

For The Hawkeye O. and O.

HOW TO COLLECT AND PREPARE CONCHOLOGICAL SPECIMENS.

BY J. A. SINGLEY.

The editors having given me permission to ride my "hobby," I intend to give brief but full instructions on the above as well as make a few remarks on matters connected with a collection. There are many collectors who can profit by what I write, but these notes are intended mainly for the class to which I belonged about 23 years ago, i. e.; the young collector and the beginner. Had I had these instructions then, it would have saved me many a false step aside from doing some things that, while not very serious mistakes, might be called "verdant."

I want, in the first place, to point out the advantages of collecting shells. Collecting can be done all the year round in many localities; and on the sea-shore there is no intermission. There is no climbing of trees as in egg collecting, and no danger of broken bones. Shells are not easily broken, are much handsomer than eggs; and, best of all, a shell always carries its name about with it, while you must take your correspondent's word for the egg. And tho' some oologists profess to be able to identify a species by the egg alone, I am bound to say that after several years of professional collecting in oology, that in the majority of cases a species can not be determined from the eggs.

The first thing a collector thinks of when a species of any kind is obtained is the identifying or determination. The Smithsonian Institution at Washington, D. C., or the Academy of Natural Sciences at Philadelphia, Pa., will always determine specimens sent them for that purpose.

In sending out specimens for naming be generous. Send all that you can spare—and perfect specimens too, as it is impossible to make a positive determination from weathered, worn or broken specimens. Don't ask that the specimens be returned to you, but present them to the institutions or individuals to whom you sent them for naming. Besides the institutions named above there are many of our prominent naturalists who make a specialty of conchology and will name any specimens sent to them for determination. One thing I wish to warn the beginner against is submitting his collections to an amateur and depending on his labeling. This was one of the "verdant" things of which I was guilty.

The beginner in land and freshwater shells will probably vote such a pursuit as "slow" when he first commences. After making a few exchanges and seeing the diversity of form, color, and sculpturing, he will become interested and begin making comparisons. He is then on the right road to knowlege, and as he adds species after species to his collection from land, river, or lake and sea, the hobby will grow on him and it will not be dropped when entering a business life as is the case with postage stamps and eggs, but the collection will be kept up and give many an hour's recreation when worried with the cares of life.

Another advantage of such a collection is that you don't offend those æsthetic people who are horrified at the idea of collecting birds and eggs and give us "fits" for "murdering" and "robbing" the poor birds. To tell the truth, after years of collecting and becoming "hardened" to it a guilty feeling sometimes comes over me when taking a set of eggs.

[TO BE CONTINUED.]

MINERALOGY.

For The Hawkeye O. and O.

THE SCIENTIST.

BY H. F. HEGNER, DECORAH, IOWA.

But now he stands upon the sandy beach with the breakers in sight, his eyes attracted to the sea weeds and pearly shells at his feet. He is interested, and examines them carefully. Some of the shells he finds inhabited, and, as he is a naturalist, is soon acquainted with each specific form, and has a learned name for it. But he also finds a real architect in the delicate tinted coral branches at his feet. Around the head and mouth of this little creature, serving as arms for obtaining food, he finds a number of tentacles. "Nature has given you a goodly work to do, little architect," cries the naturalist, "and these tentacles are well adapted to your animal wants. *Polypus* is many armed, and henceforth, most scientifically, your name shall be polyp!"

And then he begins a pleasing study. Zoophytes he finds everywhere, spreading their beautiful architectural works along the continental borders.

He crosses the stormy Atlantic, weighing the mighty power that drives the storm. On, on through the quiet Indian ocean, the phosphorescent Indian ocean, naming and collecting myriad living forms, until he reaches the beautiful Polynesia, where, spread out in the tropical sun are the coral reefs—monuments of submerged islands—with an epitaph to the departed written in living characters around each placid lagoon.

The scientist, though, can read and understand; it is not beyond his conception; and bringing together these epitaphs, he forms a perfect image of those submerged lands. Vegetation and animalization, well defined, are as clear in his imagination as though, even now, the white sunlight were reflected from those ancient islands, forming a perfect image on the retina.

He studies hard, and his conclusions, builded on the material laws of nature, are reliable; and now he returns to civilization honored and respected, bringing the material of his researches to the civilized world.

There are other phenomena tho', fully as grand as coral islands and polyps, and he is soon in the field of work again. The gallant ship carries him through the wintry northern seas, with their ice mountains towering beneath an enfeebled sun, to the realms of perpetual snow. Past Greenland's milky glaciers that feed the Arctic main with ice mountains. Past the struggling crater of Mount Hecla, where, bound by the king of these ultimate realms, the Fire Demon struggles to be free, groaning out the essence of wrath from his fiery nostril in moulten rivers that are petrified by the rigid Ice King, and added to the adamantine chains with which he is bound; on, on to the north through a world of icebergs that moan and groan as though they were fettered in this desolate waste of frozen sea, to bar the explorer from the frosty Ice King's ultimate throne, the North Pole. But no; the scientific mind knows no defeat, and he toils on over the icy fields, while the sun, aweary with his long virgil, sinks further and further in the horizon, as though he could no longer banish the sleep from his eyes, when lo!—an open Polar-sea stretches away to the northward, breaking against a rocky, mountainous coast.

Filled with the joy of first discovery, the scientist voices the language of his soul in one grand apostrophe: "Oh restless Polar sea, that breaks upon this rock-bound coast, and spreads away, I know not where, ee'n as Eternity, had I but my gallant ship, I'd sail thy tossing main!"

Sadly he toils back to the south, and none to soon. Creaking and roaring the massive icebergs among, on comes the tempest, and the scientist is thankful for the much needed shelter. The sun, too, has deserted him, and the grand aurora borealis, like a flaming sword above the lost Eden, seems to guard the Arctic realms, while sparkling gems glitter on each icy pinnacle.

The Arctic winter, which but for the aurora borealis would be black as the inkiest night, passes slowly away. Oh, how cold and gloomy it is! How the explorer struggles and struggles with the rigid Ice King, eagerly waiting for the departed sun to return and rescue him, and at last his anxious watch is rewarded. The east puts on the blush of modesty, a sure prophesy of his majesty's return, and immediately his welcome face appears. As he comes up the way, the icebergs part to let him pass, and the gallant ship, freed from her rigid chains, sails onward to the south.

Thus, even thus it is that the scientist toils on and on in a masterly search for truth. Is it for glory or wealth that he dares this? No; the luxuries of civilization are even like contagion in his estimation, and with a Stoical spirit that is grand, he leads a purely intellectual life, drawing from Nature her richest treasures which she is only too glad to give. His wisdom is like a rich soil in which the seeds of knowledge and virtue germinate. He is a lover of truth, and in Nature he finds his ideal.

Natural phenomena become beautified before his studious mind, and the lower animal forms teach him objective lessons of wisdom, that, by their very simplicity, are deeply impressed on his memory.

Even in the profound laws of chemistry and astronomy he finds a beauty that is irresistable and studies them until he develops a giant intellect. He can see beauty in truth; he can see truth in Nature; and Nature becomes his inspiration.

For The Hawkeye O. and O.

CARE OF MINERALS.

BY W. S. BEEKMAN.

There seems to be difficulty in realizing a progress that is not in some manner dependant upon care. Care is exemplified at our several points of observation in the universe, and is realized in all things capable of advancement. Ourselves require care. Care for health, system, surroundings, character, and appearance. Among some of the many things, where, in its advancement, care greatly tends to produce a degree of perfection, equal to the amount bestowed, may be mentioned the various forms of accumulating objects for advancement. Among these forms, it will serve us at present to consider only that which has for its object-matter the accumulation of the natural chemical bodies for mineralogical study. Every one admires a prettily arranged series of rocks, and in our efforts to please both visual and intellectual senses, ever bear in mind that the direct results to be obtained are ever dependent upon the genuineness of the care bestowed.

Minerals are as much under the necessity of receiving care as is the delicate skin of an infant. Those hard and popularly considered imperishable bodies we do not exempt from the rulings of *care* as one would suppose. It is the first impulse that much govern our actions while working our specimens of the bed-rock. Specimens must be broken from their homes as carefully as one would exhume a mummy. Hammer and chisel must be deftly applied to the mother-rock, giving a nip here and a whack there, making every blow tell. After securing the specimen carefully protect all its friable or delicate parts. This can be done in many ways; often in emergencies where one does not care to utilize their handkercheifs, a handful of grass applied to a projecting crystal will insure its safety while trimming for cabinet use.

Before trimming your specimen very much, consider carefully all the objectionable parts you wish to remove. As in a game of chess—you must know the positions and the effects of every move. Many times one will in a hurry glance over a rock and say: "Well, now, if that was trimmed about so it would be a good thing." Whack goes the hammer, and crumble goes the specimen. Failing to see that there was a weak place of partial fracture of the rock, which, had it been seen, could have been protected, the specimen is destroyed, owing to the lack of care. In trimming a specimen consider what you want saved and what will be better off than on. See how it can be best shaped so as to stand easily and show what is to be admired mostly. In many instances applying the chisel to the surface in directing cleaveage planes will facilitate the improvement of the mineral at a less expense of battered material. A hard compact rock may be more easily broken by striking the stone while held in the hand, first protecting the hand by an old glove, than when laid on a hard surface. Where a stone is known to be quickly broken into fragments it may be found well to wrap the stone in stout paper, or cloth, before pounding. In this way the smaller fragments are easily obtained. Always trimming your specimens at the quarry your next attention should be the wrapping of each individual in soft paper, previous to being carried home.

[TO BE CONTINUED.]

ADVERTISEMENTS

"He that whoopeth up his business in the newspapers shall reap a bountiful harvest of golden sheckels."

⊰:BIRDS' EGGS:⊱

Eggs are all first class, one hole side blown and can be furnished either in se's with data or single,

A. O. U. No.	Name.	Price each.
80	Black Skimmer	.08
294a	Cal. Valley Patridge	.10
378	Burrowing Owl	.15
385	Road Runner	.15
448	Cassin's Kingbird	.20
500	Tricolored Blackbird	.10
508	Bullock's Oriole	.08
510	Brewer's Blackbird	.04
519a	Crimson House Finch	.04
591b	Cal. Brown Towhee	.05
020	Phainopepla	.35
022 t	White-rumped Shrike	.04
703	Mockingbird	.04
713	Cactus Wren	.08

ALL KINDS OF SPECIMENS, WHOLESALE AND RETAIL.

Bar 1, Animal and Rep le Skins, Eggs, Minerals, Fossils, Shells, Insects, Alcoholic and Botanical Specimens, Indian Relics, Sea Curiosities, Coins, Stamps, Supplies, General Curiosities, etc. Price Lists, 2 cents each.

E. M. HAIGHT.
RIVERSIDE, CALIFORNIA.

RUBBER STAMPS MADE
TO ORDER

One Line stamps, 25c.; extra lines 10c. each. Pocket stamp two lines, 40c. Pen and Pencil Stamp, two lines, 35c. Self inking stamp, 2¼x1¼ in., only $2.00. Single line dating stamp, good for 8 years, only $1.50. Self-inking pads, 30c., 2¼x3¾ in, 60c. 6x3¾ inches.
Special Attention to Mail Orders. Postage Extra. Cash With Order.

GREENE & CO.
65 High St., Fitchburg, Mass.

FOUR ✸ FOR ✸ A ✸ DOLLAR
ENGRAVED TIGER-EYE
Heads for Scarf Pins.
—WORTH A DOLLAR EACH—

Closing Out A Vast Assortment of
MINERALS, GEMS, AND CURIOS.
Send Stamp Stating Your Wants.

W. S. BEEKMAN,
Box 108. West Medford, Mass.
Mention this Magazine!

NOTICE TO OOLOGISTS.

It is my intention to visit Europe this coming Spring, and as I desire to dispose of all my duplicate Bird's Eggs before leaving early in May, I make the following liberal offers:—
To everyone sending me an order for $4.00 worth of eggs, I will give, free of charge, a ticket entitling them to a chance of winning one of the following prizes. Orders of $8.00 will receive two tickets, and so on, one ticket for every $4.00 invested.
Young collectors who are not able to send $4.00 at one time, order $2.00 worth now, and another before May 1st. On this date the prizes will be drawn by disinterested parties and the results published in the HAWK-EYE O. AND O., and several Oological papers.
1st prize, set of 2 Golden Eagles, $15.
2nd prize set of 2 Bald Eagles, 8.
3rd prize set of 2 Sea Eagles, 5.
Other prizes will be given, the value of which will depend upon the number of orders received.

WALTER RAINE,
Walton Street,
TORONTO, CANADA

—BIRDS'-EGGS-AND-SKINS—
At reasonable prices. Send stamp for price list.

J. A. SINGLEY, GIDDINGS, TEXAS.

COLLECTORS' ILLUSTRATED MAGAZINE.

Is a neatly printed monthly, consisting of twenty pages or more each month, filled with fine illustrations and choice reading matter, written expressly for it by the best writers on all branches of

NATURAL HISTORY, ARCHÆOLOGY, NUMISMATICS, PHILATELY, ETC.

It also contains an EXCHANGE DEPARTMENT which is open free to all subscribers. Advertising Rates 50 cents per inch. Subscription Price 50 cents per annum in the United States and Canada; foreign countries, 65 cents per annum. Single copies, 5 cents.

ALL KINDS OF SPECIMENS, WHOLESALE AND RETAIL.

Bird, Animal and Reptile Skins, Eggs, Minerals, Fossils, Shells, Insects, Alcoholic and Botanical specimens, Indian Relics, Sea Curiosities, Coins, Stamps, Supplies, General Curiosities, etc. Price Lists 2 cents each.

E. M. HAIGHT,
RIVERSIDE, - - CALIFORNIA.

Embalming Taught Free

Send $1.00 cash and receive a pound of Gibbs' CELEBRATED COMPOUND,

Full instructions sent Free with powder. We have been charging $2.00 for this process and receipt of compound, but we now make this

GRAND REDUCTION

being assured that we will sell a large amount of our Compound, and teach many the process of Embalming.

This Grand Reduction offer is only open for next 60 days. Address, with stamp,

R. M. Gibbs, Kalamazoo, Michigan.

MINERALS.

All the leading minerals of the Black Hills, Cretaceous and Tertiary Fossils from the Bad Lands of Dakota, 100 varieties of Buckskin and War Relics of the Sioux, Apache and Pueblos. Western and Eastern Stone Relics in great variety. Send for large illustrated catalogue, wholesale and retail.

L. W. Stilwell, Deadwood, D. T.

BIRDS' EGGS & SUPPLIES.

New Price List and 3 Eggs only 20c post free.

∴FINE MINERALS∴

Send 50c for List and 10 Specimens, size 1x1 in.

I. C. GREENE & CO., - - 65 HIGH ST.,
Fitchburg, Mass.

THE GEOLOGIST'S GAZETTE.

Commenced in the February No. a series of articles on Geology which are illustrated by cuts made expressly for this purpose. 8 pages of latest geological news, exchange column, etc. Send us 25 cents and we will enter your name on our subscription books for one year, dating from February No., and send a fine premium. Address, GEOLOGIST'S GAZETTE,
337 Seneca St.,
Wichita, Kansas.

$1.00 GIVEN AWAY

By means of our "TRIAL ORDER CERTIFICATE." Send 5 cents in stamps for CERTIFICATE and 20 pp. catalogue of BIRD'S EGGS, SHELLS, MINERALS, INSTRUMENTS, etc., at prices that will astonish you.

*⁎*Natural History papers insert this and above three months, send marked copies and bill payable in anything we advertise.

DICKINSON & DURKEE, SHARON, WIS.

EXCHANGE NOTICES.

Notices under this heading inserted for one half cent per word, but no notice will be inserted for less than 25 cents.

Birds' skins, and eggs in sets and single to exchange for skins, and eggs in sets.
CARLETON GILBERT,
No. 116 Wildwood Ave.,
Jackson, Michigan.

WANTED—First-class eggs of Swallow-tailed Kite, Prairie Falcon, Pigeon Hawk, American Bittern, Wilson's Snipe, Solitary Sandpiper, Bartram's Sandpiper, Baldpate, Blue and Green-winged Teal, Hooded Sheldrake, Noddy and Sooty Terns. I can offer sets of Golden Eagle, Iceland Falcon, Iceland Gulls, Skua Gulls, and other eggs from the Arctic regions.
W. RAINE, Walton St.,
Toronto, Canada.

VOL. I, No. 5.   MAY, 1888.

H-O-O!

PUBLISHED BY
WEBSTER & MEAD,
CRESCO, IOWA.

Contents for May.

What the Birds Accomplish	Golden Days.
A Superstitious Sailor	Golden Days.
Canadian Sparrows	Wm. L. Kells
Bird Philanthropists	Golden Days
American Woodcock	Will C. Brownell
Bird Nesting in the North of England	Walter Raine.
A Few Suggestions to Ornithologists and Oologists.	"Scolopax."
Correspondence	N. F. Posson.
Migration Reports.	
How to Collect and Prepare Conchological Specimens	J. A. Singley.
Care of Minerals	W. S. Beekman.
Editorial.	

THE HAWKEYE
ORNITHOLOGIST AND OOLOGIST.
WEBSTER & MEAD, EDITORS AND PUBLISHERS.

A MONTHLY MAGAZINE DEVOTED TO ORNITHOLOGY, OOLOGY, TAXIDERMY, CONCHOLOGY, MINERALOGY AND NATURAL HISTORY.

STAFF OF CONTRIBUTORS.

Oliver Davie, Columbus, O.; Wm. L. Kells, Listowel, Ontario; W. Raine, Toronto, Canada; Rev. S. A. Noble, Spiceland, Indiana; "Scolopax"; J. A. Singley, Giddings, Texas; Dr. W. S. Strode, Bernadotte, Ill.; J. T. Emile Bonnet, Montpelier, France; L. O. Pindar, Pres. Y. O. A., Hickman, Ky.; Prof. E. G. Ward, Three Rivers, Mass.; Will C. Brownell, Ann Arbor, Michigan; Chas. B. Wilson, Waterville, Me.; Arthur H. Lockett, Exeter, N. H.; T. H. Neulis, St. Louis, Mo.; Frank A. Patton, Roswell, Dakota; Chas. H. Marsh, Dulzura, Calif.; James B. Purdy, Plymouth, Mich.; J. Warren Jacobs, Waynesburg, Pa.; Neil F. Posson, Medina, N. Y.; E. L. Brown, Durand, Wis., Frank L. Burns, Berwyn, Pa.; Carleton Gilbert, Jackson, Mich.; W. E. Pratt, Chicago, Ill.; Chas. Sonnen, St. Paul, Minn.; Charles Mason, Cincinnati, Ohio, W. S. Beekman Ph. C., West Medford Mass.; H. F. Hegner, Burr Oak, Iowa; L. W. Stilwell, Deadwood, Dakota; S. Shick, Sea Isle City, N. J.

SUBSCRIPTION RATES.	ADVERTISING RATES
Per Annum. 50 cts. Foreign countries 65 cts. Single copies 5 cts.	Made known on Application. Send for estimate. They will pay.

ADDRESS,

WEBSTER & MEAD, : : CRESCO, IOWA.

The Hawkeye Ornithologist and Oologist.

WHAT THE BIRDS ACCOMPLISH.

THE swallow, swift and nighthawk are the guardians of the atmosphere. They check the increase of insects that otherwise would overload it. Woodpeckers, creepers and chickadees are the guardians of the trunks of trees. Warblers and flycatchers protect the foliage. Blackbirds, crows, thrushes and larks protect the surface of the soil. Snipe and woodcock protect the soil under the surrface.

Each tribe has its respective duties to perform in the economy of nature, and it is an undoubted fact that if the birds were swept off the face of the earth man could not live upon it. Vegetation would wither and die. Insects would become so numerous that no living thing could withstand their attacks. The wholesale destruction occasioned by grasshoppers, which have lately devastated the West, is undoubtedly caused by the thinning of the birds, such as grouse, prairie-hens and the like, which feed upon them.

The great and inestimable service done to the farmer, gardener and florist by the birds is only becoming known by sad experience. Spare the birds and save your fruit. The little corn and fruit taken by them is more than compensated by the quantities of noxious insects they destroy. The long-persecuted crow has been found by actual experience, to do more good by the vast quantities of grubs and insects he devours than the harm he does in the few grains of corn he pulls up. He is one of the farmers' best friends.—*Golden Days.*

A SUPERSTITIOUS SAILOR.

MANY sailors are superstitious, and believe in bird omens. Not long ago the Norwegian barque Ellen picked up forty nine men, the passengers and crew of the steamer Central American, wrecked in mid-ocean. Says the captain of the Ellen: "About six o'clock one afternoon I was standing on the quarter deck, there being near me the man at the helm and two others of the crew. Suddenly a bird grazed my right shoulder, and flew around me. Afterward it flew around the vessel. Then it began again to fly around my face when I caught it. The bird was utterly unlike any I have ever seen. The color of the feathers was a dark iron-gray. The body was a foot and a half in length, with wings three and a half feet from tip to tip. In capturing the bird, it gave me a bite on the thumb. Two of the crew who assisted in tying its legs were also bitten. As it tried to bite everybody, I had its head cut off, and the body was thrown overboard. When the bird flew to the ship we were headed a little east of northeast. I regarded the appearance of the bird as an omen, and an indication that I must change my course. I accordingly steered to the eastward direct. I should not have deviated from my course had not the bird visited the ship, and had it not been for this change of course I should not have fallen in with the forty-nine persons whom I saved from death." So much for superstition; whether the bird was an omen or not, it will always remain as such in the captain's mind.—*Golden Days.*

CANADIAN SPARROWS.
Family: Fringillidæ.

BY WM. L. KELLS.

THIS is the largest family of birds found in North America and is represented among the birds of Canada by over twenty species. This family consists more especially of those species which in the Cuvierian system of arrangement was known as the *Conirostres*, on account on the general cone-shaped form of the bill. In the general form of the body, and many of the habits, there is also much resemblance, tho' there is much variation in size, plumage and migratory movements. They all feed more or less upon grain, various kinds of seeds, buds and berries, and most of them also feed largely on insects, especially when their young require assistance.

In this family are also included, besides the sparrows proper, finches, grosbeaks, buntings, crossbills, juncos and snowflakes; but it is not our intention in these sketches to mention the particular genus to which each species belongs, but will speak of them here as common members of the same great family.

In the nesting habits of this family are wide variations; for while some nest upon the ground; others prefer sites in bushes or cavities for that purpose; while others, again, select high situations in trees for the cradle of their progeny.

The eggs of the majority of sparrows are more or less spotted, and the young of all are hatched out naked and only capable of opening their bills for food, but towards the young the greatest care is exercised by the parent birds. Incubation lasts about two weeks.

All of them are more or less gifted with the power of song.

THE SWAMP SPARROW.
(*Melospiza Georgiana*.)

This species is a summer resident of Ontario, as well as various other parts of the Canadian Provinces, including Labrador and Newfoundland. Though noticed in most sections of these countries, it does not appear to be abundant or even common anywhere, yet, owing to its love of deep concealment, the wet places that it frequents and its unnoticeable song, it may be more numerous than is now generally known. It is seldom ever seen near the habitations of man, or in the open fields; but haunts low, marshy grounds and the margins of slow-running creeks, where there is a thick growth of willows and other low bushes and fallen brush-wood. Water-ponds where there are tall flags and grass in which it can readily conceal itself undisturbed by the approach of human kind, or other creatures that it may regard as foes, especially birds of prey, that often sweep with murderous intentions over its home. But though it may conceal itself and nest from the eyes of marauding birds and the collector, yet doubtless it is often robbed by some of the various species of wild animals which also frequent those places that it choses for its summer home.

Its common notes, when its nest is approached, or it is otherwise alarmed, are a series of sharp "chicks" and its song much resembles those of the slate-colored junco and chipping sparrow, though perhaps a little louder; but this is seldom heard except in the early days of summer, or perhaps at the nesting period.

It feeds on the seeds of the grasses, and such insects as it can procure in the particular places it frequents, and its partiality for such food-stuffs no doubt induces it to haunt such out of the way places as are seldom frequented by other members of its family.

Its nest is placed upon the ground among the grass or low bushes, and chiefly formed of fine, dry grass.

The eggs, four or five in number, are of a grayish or bluish hue, spotted variously with light reddish brown.

In size and general plumage it much resembles the song sparrow, but it has a bay or chestnut patch on the crown of the head, and by this and its manner of flight, and notes, it can easily be distinguished at a considerable distance.

THE TREE SPARROW.

(*Spizella Monticula.*)

This species is more an irregular spring and autumn visitant than a summer or a winter resident, in central Ontario, though it is more often seen in the winter months than in the summer season. Some springs it makes its appearance in this vicinity early in March, and during the month of April becomes quite numerous, when its pleasing song notes are for a time among the most conspicuous heard in the orchard, grove, or by the wood-land side. Again, other springs, it is quite scarce, and its stay short, as it seems in a hurry to pass onward to its summer home in more northern regions. It does not nest in this Province, but as it has been observed on the lower St. Lawrence, and in Labrador, during the summer months, it is supposed to rear its young in those regions. It is also numerous in the western territories of the Dominion as well as Alaska, where its nest and eggs have been noticed.

Its nest is usually placed in low bushes or in tufts of grass, formed of fibers of bark, grasses, hair and feathers.

The eggs are four to six in the set, and are of a light greenish hue, marked with brownish spots.

It feeds on many species of insects, and various kinds of seeds.

In length the Tree Sparrow is about six inches. The plumage on the upper parts is variously marked with brownish, black and bay, the wings having two conspicuous cross bars; the lower parts are grayish white; the breast has a dusky blotch, and the crown a chestnut patch.

Its range extends from the borders of the Arctic ocean in summer to the southern states, and eastern Kansas in the winter season.

[TO BE CONTINUED.]

BIRD PHILANTHROPISTS.

SOME birds are very charitable, it seems. At Dayton, on the Carson river, Nevada, a pair of robins built their nest on a fence, near which stood a bush containing a nest that belonged to a pair of cat-birds. The young were hatched about the same time, and all went well for several days. But, in their eagerness to feed the young, the cat-birds tried to steal some bees. The result was that the bee-keeper shot both the old cat-birds. In a little while it became evident to a boy who had been watching the little comedies and tragedies of bird life, that the young cat-birds were in danger of starving. But they did not starve, for the neighboring robins discovered the orphans in the bush and began to feed them. Not only did they take many worms to the young cat-birds, but at night the male robin sat on the nest, his mate hovering over the nest that contained the young robins. In this way both broods were reared, the catbirds growing to be as strong as though cared for by their own parents. For a long while the young robins and cat-birds flocked together; but, when full grown, they separated.—*Golden Days.*

AMERICAN WOODCOCK.

(*Philohela minor* (*Gmel.*))

BY WILL O. BROWNELL.

THE Woodcock is spread pretty generally over the eastern part of the United States, inhabiting, during the greater part of its sojourn, the wet, low-lying marsh lands where the soft, spongy nature of the earth renders it easily penetrated by the long, slender bill as it is thrust into the soil in quest of the worms upon which the bird mainly subsists.

Later, in August, when the summer rains have driven to the surface the well-known anglers or fish-worm, the Woodcock may be found in the uplands, in the cornfields, where the full grown stalks of corn answer the same purpose as do the alders and willows in the swale.

Although tolerably plentiful in certain localities it may be classed as one of our rare birds, and were it not for its fame as a game bird, it would remain in more or less obscurity to the casual observer.

During the breeding season, which occurs shortly after their arrival from the South early in April, when the puss-willows and the mild, warm winds first foretell the approach of coming summer, they resort to borders of swamps and marshes where the sloping bank, thickly over-grown with black-briar and alders, offers protection from foes and the elements,

The nest is a very simple affair, merely a few dead leaves of the fern or native heather arranged in any natural depression where the brush is the thickest, or at the foot of some favorite tussock of dead grass.

The finding of a Woodcock's nest is a very delicate undertaking and will tax the patience of the collector greatly. So exactly does the sitting bird resemble the brown, dead leaves that surround her, that the unpracticed eye will fail to discover anything bird-like. The bird, so confident is she of remaining unseen, will often allow you to touch her, only leaving the nest and her eggs when forced by the hand of the intruder.

Usually four eggs are laid of a peculiar shiny, oily appearance which characterizes the eggs of some species of the waders. The ground work is pale blue, spotted and splashed with darker brown and lavender and other tints less marked. The markings are scattered generally over the surface of the shell, being somewhat smaller at the pointed end.

Invariably, they are arranged in the nest with the small end pointing inward, forming a cross. But one brood is raised in a season.

Whether the male takes part in incubating or not, I am unable to say from observation—some writers affirm that they do.

After the breeding season, during the hot months of summer, the plumage of both sexes is much lighter in color than in the spring, and I am confident that the bird moults before migrating northward as their plumage is richest in color upon their arrival with us.

Lying close before the dog, they become an easy victim to the sportsman, who can mercilessly destroy in a few minutes the whole colony that were reared with so much patient toil, only to succumb to the sportsman's gun.

Late in November, when the cold winds have cut the last remaining leaves from the forest trees, the frosts have rendered the ground too hard to be probed, the Woodcock disappears only to return with the soft winds and sunny skies of another spring.

BIRD NESTING IN THE NORTH OF ENGLAND.

BY WALTER RAINE, TORONTO, CANADA.

YONDER is Pennyghent, the fourth highest mountain in Yorkshire. It is seven miles away but appears as if it were not more than four miles off. Among those crags facing us the Peregrine Falcon has its nest. The last time I visited Pennyghent, the birds had young, and, as I approached the front of the cliff, they grew very bold, darting over my head and screaming fiercely. The nest is built of sticks and heather, half way down the cliff on a ledge of rock, and can only be got at by being lowered with ropes from above. Two or three pairs of Peregrines also nest at Sedberg, although much persecuted by the gamekeepers. There is one nest usually occupied by a pair of Ravens early in March, and, as soon as the young have left, a pair of Peregrines take possession and lay their eggs early in May. A friend of mine has a set of Raven's eggs and another of Peregrine Falcon's, both taken from the same nest in one season. How beautiful are the eggs of the Falcon! Four sets in my collection vary somewhat in color and markings; the ground color of some is creamy white, others pinky, richly spotted and blotched with reddish brown and chocolate, whilst other specimens are like large eggs of the Kestril Hawk, of an uniform rich brown, mottled at the larger end with dark chocolate brown. The handsomest set I ever saw were the four eggs that were taken from the Raven's nest before mentioned. The ground color was a pale, pinky red, capped at the larger end of the eggs with rich, crimson brown. The number of eggs is three or four; average size, 2.10x1.70. Both the Peregrine and Raven will soon cease to exist in Yorkshire, as they are shot and trapped by the gamekeepers because they kill a few grouse, a most heinous offence in their sight and those by whom they are employed.

The Common European Buzzard is becoming scarce, but still a few pairs may be found nesting among the limestone cliffs. Their nests are made of sticks and heather, and in this district seldom contain more than two eggs, which are similar in size and color to the eggs of the Red-shouldered Hawk. This species is more plentiful among the Cumberland Hills a few miles away.

But to proceed along our journey over the moors, we arrive at Gaping Ghyll Hole, also called Devil's Hole, a vertical cavern of unknown depth. A courageous young man was once lowered three hundred feet down this awful pit, but, owing to the water pouring into it from all sides, he was compelled to be drawn up again without adding any more information as to its depth. The mouth of this pit is some twenty feet in diameter and reminds one of the center of some volcano. We collected some large stones, and, throwing them into the pit, we hear them bound from ledge to ledge in their descent, each time growing fainter, until the sound is lost and we exclaim, "What a fearful depth it must be," and shudder at the thoughts of falling into this place, out of which we could not be taken dead or alive.

Our watches tell us it is noon, so we sit down and partake of some refreshments brought along with us, to which we do justice after our long tramp over the heather clad hills.

Down in the valley below lies Clapham, with its wonderful cave three miles long; and while we are at rest, I will tell you of a visit I made to this cave with a church choir party a few years ago. On entering the mouth of the cave, the two guides gave a candle to each man, and as there were twenty-five of us, we made a good light which illuminated the deepest recesses in the cave. We were at once amazed with the sights before us; stalactites were hanging like icicles from the roof of the cave. In some places there are huge chambers of considerable heighth; in one of these we all collected and sung several hymns, which had an imposing effect upon all present. Around and above us were hanging hundreds of glittering stalactites of all sizes and shapes. They have a musical sound on being struck gently with a stick; and at the place called the organ, a guide played several tunes. A stream winds its way through the cave, and in several places wooden bridges are built across to enable visitors to travel through without wetting their feet. Many ladies visit this place, and the way through has been made as easy of access as possible. At the end of the cave is a small waterfall, behind which the guides go, taking as many lights as they can carry and thus illuminate the falls from behind.

This limestone district is full of caves and natural wonders. Two miles away is Yorda's Cave; and five miles away up Chapel-le-Dale at the foot of Whernside mountain is Weathercote Cave, worthy of a visit. This place reminds one of a large limestone quarry, down to the bottom of which we descend by a natural stairway. A large waterfall 60 feet high comes pouring through a hole near the top of one side of the cave, across which is jammed a stone coffin. The water thunders down before us and enters into the bowels of the earth. This waterfall is supposed to run along under the ground for two miles when it appears from a hole at the base of a cliff and joins Kingsdale Beck.

My brother was packing up his boxes when he suddenly sprung to his feet alarmed, and I soon found the cause, for, just where he had been sitting, there was a viper hissing away like a demon. We soon laid hold of our sticks and stepped forward to give him a settling, but he turned around and darted through the heather, and, although we searched the spot, we found no trace of him. The viper, or adder, is the only poisonous British snake. The other two species, called the grass-snake and slow-worm, are not poisonous.

It is now time to move away from this spot; and as many Longbilled Curlews are screaming away on our left, we make in that direction. Taking advantage of any slight elevation, up which we might crawl on our hands and feet and then show ourselves at the top, we soon startled a Curlew down the slope before us. Marking down the spot, we advance eagerly and here we are lucky in falling in with a nest and four large, spotted eggs. The nest was eight inches in diameter, and consisted of a hollow in the ground lined with heather. The eggs were of a greenish-olive ground, well spotted with umber brown of various shades and obscure shell markings; average size, 2.70x1.85. This we considered a good addition to our day's work. Having prepared and packed the eggs, we proceed. But surely there must be many nests around this quarter for many Curlews are flying about whistling, but so wary are the birds that it is difficult to find their nests. At last another bird rises in what we call a skulking manner, flying close to the ground in a suspicious sort of way. We again mark down the spot, some sixty yards ahead, but arriving there found no signs of any nest. We knew it had one by the way it left the spot, and looked around for some time and then retired some distance behind a rock. In ten minutes we again advance; showing ourselves, the Curlew rises again and we carefully mark the spot down, and running forward soon found its nest containing three eggs a little smaller in size than the set previously found. The nest materials were the same.

[TO BE CONCLUDED IN JUNE NUMBER.]

A FEW SUGGESTIONS TO ORNITHOLOGISTS AND OOLOGISTS.

BY "SCOLOPAX."

THE writer of this article has seriously thought for some time of writing a few suggestions to the many readers of the O. AND O. These thoughts may not be appreciated by the large majority; and many will say that it is not our right to give directions to collectors, and that they are quite capable of collecting according to their own rules. Did you ever think what a man's rules or methods of collecting and forming a cabinet are? Let us discuss this point. A boy, and the readers of the O. AND O. are largely boys I doubt not, is sure to collect just as he sees fit; and will often go on destroying specimens, killing unnecessarily, doing many foolish and even bad acts year after year; whereas, if he had proper instruction, he would be a success as a collector as well as, in all probability, a thorough ornithologist, capable of advancing the science.

All the sciences have advanced wonderfully within the last few decades; and now, with improved facilities, all classes of specimens are preserved with a much more natural appearance than formerly. Taxidermy and the preparation of eggs have become perfections in the hands of many; yet the large majority of skins, taking them as a whole are worthless. This results, not as generally supposed, from the inability of a man to make a good skin, but rather from lack of energy. People do not stick to it long enough to learn; and further, many skins are make when a collector is very busy and only puts a limited time on each bird. This is all wrong; no one has any business or right to ruthlessly slaughter our innocent birds unless he is amply provided with means of preservation, and has time to attend to them fully

I killed birds and many other animals thoughtlessly when first beginning the study; they were never killed maliciously—the thought was abhorrent to me. I have never cared to associate with those who kill everything for the mere sport of killing and burning powder. I have seen sportsmen who, in order to test a gun's quality, would kill a large number of little birds, laughing as they fell, forgetting where they dropped the next minute; the brutal gunner passes on, remarking how he knocked them over. A man of this nature belongs to that class who see no beauty in our feathered friends, and only consider them in the line of sport. Verily, the line of demarcation is wide if drawn between what should be a thorough, high standing ornithologist and many of our so-called sportsmen. They had better be classed as sporting men and stand rank and file with pugilists, cock fighters, and others of that ilk.

Boys, kill what birds you need and can make good use of—there cease, Let your cabinets contain good evidence of hard work and thoughtful study. Spend time on each skin, time without limit if necessary, and you will never be sorry, for "a thing of beauty is a joy forever." If your skins are a poor lot, when you see a neat cabinet you will become disgusted with your own specimens and perhaps lose all interest, and it will be well if you do unless you strike out for a grand improvement. Do not throw away your old skins however, but save for study as a reminder of your early efforts. The writer committed many indiscretions when first collecting, and was a most stupid fellow in regard to bird skinning, but ambition to succeed and plenty of birds to skin carried us through; and now, after years of practice, some fair skins may be found in my cabinet. Readers, you may laugh, but we are through trying to skin five birds an hour, and limit ourselves to ten birds a day, even in the busiest season. Who wants a bird skinned so one cannot tell from where the legs proceed, or the breast from the back? Many collectors say "I do not care how my specimens look," and their cabinets are truthful, miserable proofs of what they say. This class of so-called ornithologists are the utterly shiftless ones; look out for them.

When a boy, Audubon's life was read and re-read many times, and every chapter and incident noted, There I learned that his apartments were festooned with eggs on strings. What more natural than a collection to be formed, each with two holes? Now there is not a boy in the country, particularly readers of the O. AND O., who is not conversant with egg drills and blow-pipes, and could, therefore, give Audubon and Wilson many points on the preparation of eggs. I know a man who has been to Florida twice collecting and he invariably blows his eggs with two holes. He is perfectly satisfied, and therefore it is not my business to say anything; but I have and it did no good. Here is one of those cases I spoke of at the beginning of this article; and it is for that class that this advice is given. I wish that the advantages resulting from a paper like the O. AND O., were apparent when I was a boy, and many errors and indiscretions would not have occurred; many end blown eggs and scrub skins would not remorsefully appeal to me, and cause me to feel that had there been a proper mentor in my neighborhood, many precious birds would have continued their sweet songs and gracefully gamboled in their happy retreats.

One more point, boys; when you are collecting, do not confine yourselves to birds, eggs, or any other branch of natural history. Keep your eyes open and you will see many rare specimens in various departments of the great study of nature that you never dreamed of. Examine the trees, flowers and insects; it is easy to pick up a few stones which are often rare, fossils and shells, found by industrious research. The article in the April number of the O. AND O. by W. Hull was a timely warning, and should be heeded. Don't be rage collectors, boys.

I notice with regret that the various papers published in the U. S., devoted, as their names would imply, to birds and eggs, are almost entirely filled with topics relating to eggs, and very little space devoted to birds. This is not the fault of the publishers, but demonstrates the taste of the readers.

CORRESPONDENCE.

MEDINA, N. Y., March 24, 1888.
MESSRS. WEBSTER & MEAD,

Gentlemen:—In May, 1886, a Robin built a nest in a fruit tree in my garden. When the nest was completed, a piece of twine some two feet in length was left swinging in the air. One day while the Robin was setting upon her eggs, a Cedar Waxwing appeared upon the scene and began tugging at the twine. The Robin remained quietly upon her nest, and, after a prolonged struggle, succeeded in flying away with the twine; the whole occurrence seemingly to be but barely noticed by the Robin.

I would like to ask if any readers of the H. O. AND O. have ever found Cowbird's eggs in the nest of a Meadow Lark. In the season of 1885 I found a nest of the Meadow Lark containing three eggs of the owner and one of the Cowbird; also a nest of the Kingbird containing three eggs of the owner and one of the Cowbird.

NEIL F. POSSON.

MIGRATION REPORTS.

CRESCO, IOWA.

NAME.	FIRST SEEN.	NO. SEEN.	NEXT SEEN.	WHEN COM.
Y.-shafted Flicker	4- 1	1	4- 2	4- 8
Bronzed Grackle	4- 1	23	4- 3	4- 4
Tree Sparrow	4- 1	2		
Meadow Lark	4- 1	1	4- 3	4- 4
Red-s. Blackbird	4- 1	1	4- 4	
Brown Creeper	4- 2	1	4- 3	
Purple Martin	4- 2	2	4- 3	4- 6
Kildeer	4- 2	1	4- 4	
Gt. Blue Heron	4- 2	1	4- 3	
Pigeon Hawk	4- 3	2	4- 4	
Mallard Ducks	4- 3	9		
White Cranes	4- 3	7		
Robin			4- 4	
Bluebird			4- 4	
Cardinal Grosbeak	4- 4	12		
Grass Finch	4- 4	2	4-12	
Song Sparrow	4- 7			4- 7
Hooded Merganser	4- 7	1		
Pintail Ducks	4- 8	9		
Mourning Dove	4- 9	1	4-12	
Geese	4-10	15		
Blue-bill Ducks	4-12			
Bufflehead "	4-12			
Teal "	4-12			
Sparrow Hawk	4-15	1		
Y.-crowned Warbler	4-19	1	4-22	
Whipporwill	4-14	1	4-15	
Chewink	4-17	1		
Brown Thrasher	4-20	1		
Lesser Yellowlegs	4-18	2		
Ruby-c. Kinglet	4-17	6		
Chestnut-s. Warbler	4-22	14		
White-r. Shrike	4-22	1		
Kingbird	4 25	1		

Eggs of the Crow and Horned Lark were first found on the 15th.

The Crows of this section are more or less migratory, though many remain here during winter. During the recent migration, an albino specimen was frequently noticed in the outskirts of the city; but as he was very careful to keep well out of rifle range, he had the pleasure of leaving unharmed.

On the 26th day of April a Robin was seen to begin building her nest.

ST. PAUL, MINNESOTA.

REPORTED BY CHARLES SONNEN.

Am. Goldfinch	3- 7	5	3- 8	
Shore Lark	3- 7	10	3-11	
Crow	3-11	1	3-18	
Blue Jay	3-11	1	3-16	
Robin	4- 1	6	4- 8	4-13
Red-tailed Hawk	4- 1	1	4- 6	
Chipping Sparrow	4- 4	10	4- 5	4-10
Red-w. Blackbird	4- 4	80	4- 6	4-10
Field Sparrow*	4- 5	25	4- 6	4-10
Bluebird	4- 7	1	4- 8	4-12
Flicker	4- 8	1	4- 9	4-14
Cardinal Grosbeak†	4 8	1	4-10	
White-b. Swallow	4- 9	3	4-14	
Red-b. Nuthatch	4- 9	1		
Purple Grackle	4-10	1	4-13	
Purple Martin	4-10	15	4-13	4-14
Meadow Lark	4-10	1	4-13	
Wood Pewee	4-10	2	4-12	
House Wren	4 11	3		
Sheldrake	4-11	4	4-12	
Loon	4-11	2		4-15
Am. Widgeon	4-12	9	4-13	4-15
Swamp Sparrow	4-12	8	4-13	
Orange-c. Warbler	4-14	1‡		
Rose-b. Grosbeak	4-15	1‡		
Pine Finch	4-15	3		

Having seen but two each of the Crows and Blue Jays during the winter, and as they were very common by the last of March, I am confident that the intensity of the cold drives them southward.

*In company with a lot of Chipping Sparrows and Snowbirds.

†With a lot of Chipping and Field Sparrows and Snowbirds.

‡Males.

Ending April 15.

WAYNESBURG, PENNSYLVANIA.

REPORTED BY J. W. JACOBS.

Bluebird	2-10		2-19
Red-h. Woodpecker	2- 3		2-17
Am. Crow	2- 5		2-19
Am. Robin	2-10	8	2-19
Mourning Dove			2-16
Grass Sparrow	2-17		2-27
Meadow Lark	2-22		3-28
Kildeer	3- 2		3-30
Purple Grackle	3- 3	8	3 28
Song Sparrow	3- 3		3- 5
Pewee	3-15		3-20
Wood Thrush	3-24		
Kingfisher	3-30		
Flicker	3-20		3-30
Red-w. Blackbird	3-30		

CHICAGO, ILLINOIS.

REPORTED BY W. E. PRATT.

Species				
Lapland Longspur	3- 3	1	3-10	3-10
Canada Goose	3- 3	8	3-10	3-30
Pintail	3-10	7	3-30	3-30
Mallard	3-10	3	3-30	
Robin	3-17	*	3-24	
Song Sparrow	3-17	*	3-24	
Red-w. Blackbird	3-17	*	3-30	
Meadow Lark	3-17	2	3-24	3-24
Bronze Grackle	3-17	*		
Passenger Pigeon	3-17	1	3-30	
Chewink	3-20	1		
Black Snowbird	3-20	6	3 30	
Pewee	3-21	1		
Flicker	3-21	6	3-20	
Savannah Sparrow	3-21	4		
Fox Sparrow	3-21	*		
Field Sparrow	3-21	*		
Barn Swallow	3-30	1		
Grass Finch	3-30	*		
White-c. Sparrow	3-30	6		
Mourning Dove	3-30	2		
Hawks--Red-tailed, Red-shouldered, Broad-winged, Rough-legged, Sharp-shinned, Cooper's, Pigeon, Sparrow,				
Black Vulture (?)	3-30	*		
Long-eared Owl	3 30	1		
Jack Snipe	3-30	1	4- 3	4 14
Killdeer	3-30	*		
Butterball Duck	3-30	6		
Bluebill "	3-30	*	4- 7	
Green-w. Teal	3-30	2		
Red-head Duck	3-31	1		4- 7
Prairie Hen†	3-31	1		
Great Blue Heron	2-31	2		
Hermit Thrush	4- 5	2		
Golden-c. "	4- 5	2		
Brown Creeper	4- 5	6		4 6
Blue-winged Teal	4- 5	6	4- 7	
Swamp Sparrow	4- 5	4	4- 7	
Brown Thrush	4- 5	1		
Y.-bellied Woodpecker	4- 5	2	4- 6	
Olive-backed Thrush	4- 5			4- 7
Rusty Grackle	4- 6	6		
Canvass-back Duck	4- 7	30		
Ring-bill "	4- 7	*		
Common Coot	4- 7	*		
Florida Galinule	4- 7	6		
Bald-faces	4- 7	*		
Spoon-bill	4- 7	*		
Black Brant	4- 7	62		
Snow "	4- 7	1		
White Pelican	4- 7	3		
White-b. Swallow	4- 7	12		
Cliff "	4- 7	4		
Purple Martin	4- 7	2	4-11	4-14
Partridge	4- 7	1		
Loon	4- 7	2		
Whistling (?) Swan	4- 7	1		
Lesser Yellowlegs	4-11	50	4-14	4-14
Greater "	4-11	1		
Pied-billed Grebe	4-14			4-14
Short-eared Owl	4-14	1		
Whistle-wing Ducks	4-14	30		

*Numerous.
†Very rare here now.

The observations were chiefly made at Normal Park and Grass Lake.
Ending April 16th.

JACKSON, MICHIGAN.

REPORTED BY CARLETON GILBERT.

Species				
Robin	3- 3	1	3- 8	3-18
Am. Crow	3- 1	100	3- 2	3-15
R. and b.-s. Blackbird	3- 8	12	3- 9	3-15
Bluebird	3- 9	2	3-12	3-19
Meadow Lark	3- 8	3	3-13	3-24
Mourning Dove	3-19	1	3-20	4-10
Killdeer	3-19	3	3 20	4- 8
Song Sparrow	3- 9	1	3-15	3-27
Chipping "	3-19	2	3-29	4- 7
Purple Grackle	3-20	18	3-25	4- 4
Towhee	3-19	1	3-27	3-30
Y.-shafted Flicker	3-14	1	3-19	4- 6
Y.-bellied Woodpecker	3-19	1	4- 4	4- 6
Herring Gull	3-29	1	3-31	
W.-bellied Swallow	3-29	1	3-31	4- 7
Cowbird	4- 2	3		
Summer Yellowbird	4- 2	4	4- 6	
Ruby-c. Kinglet	4- 2	1	4- 5	4- 7
Brown Thrasher	4-14	1		

BERNADOTTE, ILLINOIS.

REPORTED BY DR. W. S. STRODE.

Species		
Chewink	3-20	3
Purple Grackle	3-20	*
Pileated Woodpecker	3-23	3
Fox Sparrow†	3-25	*
Red-w. Blackbird	3-25	20
Mallard Duck	3-25	*
Old Squaw "	3-25	*
Killdeer	3-25	12
Little Black Duck	3-26	*
Merganser	3-26	*
Mourning Dove	3-30	5

Barn Swallow	3-30	20
Whooping Crane	3-30	*
Kingfisher	4- 1	2
Green Heron	4- 2	8
Brants	4- 3	
Great Blue Heron	4- 3	2
Am. Woodcock‡	4- 3	3
Crow Blackbirds	4- 3	*
Whippoorwill	4- 7	
Brown Thrasher	4- 7	*
Gt. Northern Diver	4-12	1
Double-c. Cormorant	4-12	4
Turkey Buzzard	4-13	3
Wood Thrush	4-15	1
Ruby-c. Kinglet	4 16	*
Song Sparrow	4 16	*

*More or less numerous.
†Shot two.
‡Shot a female.

Of the Brants a large flock containing a few white ones was seen going north; shot one for skinning and identification.

At this date the Horned Larks which have been numerous since Feby. 5th have about all departed for their breeding grounds further north.

Could you not have mistaken the Red-headed Woodpecker for the Red-bellied, reported seen at Cresco. The Red-bellied much resembles the Red-headed, and is a winter resident, while the Red-headed is not. It has not yet appeared here.

Mr. Pratt's four Sparrow Hawks of Feb. 22 must have been something else. They did not appear here, 200 miles further south, till nearly a month later.

My Black-throated Bunting in April H. O. AND O. should have been Horned Lark.

MEDINA, NEW YORK.

REPORTED BY NEIL F. POSSON.

Pine Goldfinch*	3-11	5		
Common Redpoll*	3-18	†		
Bluebird	2-24	1		3-18
Song Sparrow	3-21	†		3-21
American Goldfinch	3-21			
Meadow Lark	3-24	2		3 30
Mourning Dove	3-24	1	4- 4	
Cedar Waxwing	3-25	5		
R. and b.-s. Blackbird	3-26	1		3-30
Purple Grackle	3-27	2		3-29
Y.-shafted Flicker	3-30	1		3-31
Red-tailed Hawk	3-31	1	4- 5	
Grass Finch	3- 3	2		4- 4
Field Sparrow	4- 4	1		4- 4
Killdeer	4- 4	2		
White-r. Shrike	4- 4	1	4- 6	
Purple Finch	4- 5	1		4- 6
Chipping Sparrow	4- 6	1		
Cowbird	4- 6	3		4- 7
Marsh Hawk	4- 6			
Black Snowbird	4- 7	†	4- 8	4- 7
Pewee	4- 7	1		4- 7
Chewink*	4- 7			
Ruffed Grouse	4- 7	1		
Hermit Thrush*	4- 7	1		
Canada Goose	4- 8	6		

*Rare visitants here. †Numerous.

HOW TO COLLECT AND PREPARE CONCHOLOGICAL SPECIMENS.

BY J. A. SINGLEY.

AFTER this digression, I return to my subject. A cabinet for specimens is a necessity. The handiest thing I know of —and cheap—is the thread cabinets of the dry goods stores. They can be had everywhere and will hold any but a few of the largest shells. A specimen large enough can have the label pasted on it and be laid in the drawer. The smaller species—and these comprise three-fourths of a collection —can be put in pill boxes of various sizes and the label put in the box with the shell. A little experience will soon teach you the best method of arranging your collection.

The North American land shells, or snails, live mostly in the forest, sheltered under the trunks of fallen trees, layers of dead leaves and in the soil; from this hint the collector will know where to look for them.

The *Helices* are the largest family, the majority of them being large, and some of them very beautiful shells. After collecting, the larger species as well as small ones with a large aperture should be boiled for two or three minutes; when the animal can be removed with a pin or piece of wire, and the shell washed off with a soft brush, rinsed out and laid away to dry.

The aperture of nearly all species has a thickened peristome, or lip, when mature, often armed with denticles, or teeth; and after the beginner learns to differentiate between immature specimens of the species that assume the thicked lip with maturity and those that do not have the thickened lip at any stage of their existence, he should not collect the former until the lip is perfect. Dead shells that are weathered or bleached are not admissable under any circumstances, and sending out such or poorly prepared specimens of any kind stamps one as a slovenly collector.

A good time to collect *Helices*—and in fact any of the land shells—is during and after a warm rain, when they will be found crawling about. The sun will at once drive them to their retreat under logs, etc.

The *Zonites* are generally small, fragile, glassy looking shells, although some of the species attain a large size. They are very partial to moisture, and, this will have to be the collector's cue.

[TO BE CONTINUED.]

CARE OF MINERALS.

BY W. S. BEEKMAN.

THE habit of carefully and closely scrutinizing what you bring home can not, by any means, be overdone. It is a bad habit to place before yourself a collection of specimens when sitting down for a short investigation. The eye and attention becomes distracted, and the mind runs from one prominent point of interest to another without becoming, as it should, concentrated upon a given object from which it should not divert until there was nothing about the specimen that has not been seen and commented upon. No matter how certain you feel that there is nothing about the specimen you have not seen with your eye just as well as you think you would have with a glass, you should make it a point, every time, to examine the surface with the aid of a good lens. Making this a constant habit, in the long course of events you will find that you have acquired a goodly number of valuable points that were derived from that little habit, and without which you would surely feel the loss.

Having now trimmed and examined our specimen to the best of our ability; the next move will be towards cleaning or improving at points which have suggested themselves during our examination.

Water of course is the universal cleanser. But even with this abundant agent, that substance that, "So delicate might lave an infant's cheek without injuring it; so limpid that the finest thread of gossamer might divide it and sustain no harm" must be used with caution. There are many minerals that can not even stand a bath. It is not long since that I saw a large specimen of pink pearl-spar that I had sold to a party on account of the hairy millerite upon it, lying on its label, prettier than ever, but minus the millerite. Some of the finer crystalized Aragonites that won't stand even running water can be cleaned by immersing in water for a few moments and then gently swished back and forth in the water. There are others to which the stiff brush and soapy water may be freely applied without injury. One must exercise a little common sense.

[TO BE CONTINUED.]

EDITORIAL.

In the circular sent out with our first number, we promised to let the support be shown by the magazine; and, owing to the generous support given us by the enterprising ornithologists and oologists of Canada and the United States, we have changed the form of the H. O. AND O., which we think will be welcomed and appreciated by its many readers. It will be our earnest endeavor to improve it further and make it one of the leading magazines of its kind.

A great number of valuable articles are crowded out this month, and others shortened more than we like to see, on account of a lack of time.

BIRD'S EGGS AND SUPPLIES.

New Price List and Three Eggs only 20 cents post free.

---:FINE MINERALS.:---

Send 50 cents for List and Ten Specimens, size 1x1 inch.

I. C. GREENE & CO., : 65 HIGH ST.
FITCHBURG, MASSACHUSETTS.

FOUR FOR A DOLLAR.

FINE ENGRAVED TIGER-EYE
Heads for Scarf Pins.
—WORTH A DOLLAR EACH.—

Closing Out a Vast Assortment of
MINERALS, GEMS AND CURIOS.
Send Stamp Stating Your Wants.

W. S BEEKMAN,
Box 108, West Medford, Mass.
Mention this Magazine!

BIRDS'—EGGS—AND—SKINS.
At Reasonable Prices. Send Stamp For Price Lists.
J. A. Singley, Giddings. Texas.

Embalming Caught Frgs.

Send $1.00 cash and receive a pound of Gibbs' CELEBRATED COMPOUND.
Full instructions sent Free with powder. We have been charging $2.00 for this process and receipt of Compound, but we now make this
—EXTRAORDINARY REDUCTION—
Being assured that we will sell a large amount of our Compound, and teach many the process of Embalming.
This Grand Reduction Offer is only open for next sixty days. Address, with stamp,
R. M. Gibbs. Kalamazoo. Mich.

MINERALS.

All the leading minerals of the Black Hills, Cretaceous and Tertiary Fossils from the Bad Lands of Dakota. 100 varieties of Buckskin and War Relics of the Sioux, Apache and Pueblos. Western and Eastern Stone Relics in great variety. Send for large ilustrated catalogue; wholesale and retail.
L. W. Stillwell, Deadwood, D. T.

LOON'S EGG sent to any address for 75c. postal note. List of curiosities 5c.
N. E. CARTER, Delevan, Wis

The OLD CURIOSITY SHOP for May,
A Mammmoth Twenty-Page Quarto.
Price, 15 cents. Ads., 10 cents a line.
Address, C. R. ORCUTT,
San Diego, California.

$1.00 GIVEN AWAY.

By means of our "Trial Order Certificate." Send 5 cents in stamps for Certificate and 20 pp. catalogue of Bird's Eggs, Shells, Minerals, Instruments, etc., at prices that will astonish you.
*.*Natural History papers insert this and above three months, send marked copies and bill payable in anything we advertise.
Dickinson & Durkee, Sharon, Wisconsin.

R. E. RACHFORD & SON.

COLLECTING NATURALISTS,
AND WHOLESALE DEALERS IN

BIRD*SKINS*AND*EGGS,

BEAUMONT, : : TEXAS.

RUBBER STAMPS
MADE TO ANY ORDER

One line stamps, 25c.; extra lines 2c. each. Pocket st mp, two lines, 40c. Pen and Pencil stamp, two lines, 35c. Self-inking stamp, 2¼x1¼ in., only $2.00. Single line dating stamp, good for 8 years, only $1.50. Self inking pads, 30c., 2¼x9¾ in.. 60c., 6x9¼ in.
Special Attention to Mail Orders.
Postage Extra. Cash with Order.
GREENE & CO.
65 High St., Fitchburg, Mass

EXCHANGE NOTICES.

Notices under this heading inserted for one-half cent per word, but no notice will be inserted for less than 25 cents.

TO EXCHANGE—Birds' eggs in sets with full data for sets and nests as I may want.
HENRY W. DAVIS, North Granville.

WANTED—A set of 2, 375a, Western Horned Owl; a set of 2, Sandhill Crane; and following sets with nests: Cal. Bluebird, American Redstart, Chimney Swift, Short-billed Marsh Wren, Long-tailed Chat, and Orchard Oriole. Also send list of any sets you may have with nests. Will give good exchange for above.
HENRY W. DAVIS, North Granville, N. Y.

Vol. I, No. 6.   JUNE, 1888.

H-O-O!

PUBLISHED BY
WEBSTER & MEAD,
CRESCO, IOWA.

Entered at the Cresco P. O. as Second-class Mail Matter.

Contents for June.

Bird Nesting in the North of England	Walter Raine
Canadian Sparrows	Wm. L. Kells
Personal Observations on the Decrease of Familiar Birds.	
Foot Movements in Birds	R. M. Gibbs, M. D
Notes on Some of the Passeres of Fulton Co., Ky.	L. O. Pindar.
Migration Reports	
Editorial	
How to Collect and Prepare Conchological Specimens	J. A. Singley

THE HAWKEYE
ORNITHOLOGIST AND OOLOGIST.

WEBSTER & MEAD, EDITORS AND PUBLISHERS.

A MONTHLY MAGAZINE DEVOTED TO ORNITHOLOGY, OOLOGY, TAXIDERMY CONCHOLOGY, MINERALOGY AND NATURAL HISTORY

STAFF OF CONTRIBUTORS.

Oliver Davie, Columbus, O.; Wm. L. Kells, Listowel, Ontario; W. Raine, Toronto, Canada; Rev. S. A Noble, Spiceland, Indiana; "Scolopax"; J. A. Singley, Giddings, Texas; Dr. W. S. Strode, Bernadotte, Ill.; J. T. Emile Bonnet, Montpelier, France; L. O. Pindar, Pres. Y. O. A., Hickman, Ky.; Prof. E. G. Ward, Three Rivers, Mass.; Will C. Brownell, Ann Arbor, Michigan; Chas. B. Wilson, Waterville, Me.; Arthur H. Lockett, Exeter, N. H.; T. H. Nealis, St. Louis, Mo.; Frank A. Patton, Roswell, Dakota; Chas. H. Marsh, Dulzura, Calif.; James B. Purdy, Plymouth, Mich.; J. Warren Jacobs, Waynesburg, Pa.; Neil F. Posson, Medina, N. Y.; E. L. Brown, Durand, Wis., Frank L. Burns, Berwyn, Pa.; Carleton Gilbert, Jackson, Mich.; W. E. Pratt, Chicago, Ill.; Chas. Sonnen, St. Paul, Minn.; Charles Mason, Cincinnati, Ohio, W. S. Beekman Ph. C., West Medford Mass.; H. F. Hegner, Burr Oak, Iowa; L. W. Stilwell, Deadwood, Dakota; C. S. Shick, Sea Isle City, N. J.

SUBSCRIPTION RATES.	ADVERTISING RATES
Per Annum, 50 cts. Foreign countries 65 cts. Single copies 5 cts.	Made known on Application. Send for estimate. They will pay.

ADDRESS

WEBSTER & MEAD, : : CRESCO, IOWA.

BIRD NESTING IN THE NORTH OF ENGLAND.

BY WALTER RAINE, TORONTO, CANADA.

WE are now half way up Ingleborough Mountain, but as we begin to feel tired, and it is three o'clock and the sun is making round to the west, we do not ascend to the summit, although it is worth the climb, for a more magnificent panorama is not to be seen anywhere in England than from the summit of Ingleborough. Here in olden times beacon fires were lit to warn the surrounding country that enemies were advancing. It is many years since the beacon fires were wont to send their vivid flames into the air; but last year fires were again heaped upon these summits, not as a token that the Danes were over-running the country, but in commemoration of the Queen's Jubilee. We now turn round and make our way toward Ingleborough village.

This side of Ingleborough is very stony, and huge boulders impede our way. Here the Dunlin nests somewhat sparingly. The birds look like mice, running in and out between the stones. Their nests are so small they cannot be found without one actually flushes the bird from under his very nose. The nest is a slight hollow about three inches in diameter, lined with bits of grass, and most usually contains three or four pointed eggs. In beauty of coloring and elegance of form the eggs of the Dunlin are unrivaled. A series of forty eggs before me show a great variety; the ground color of some specimens is a clear, light green, in others, bluish white, whilst some have a yellow stone color; some are speckled all over with brown, other specimens are boldly blotched at the larger end with rich brown, but all are very beautiful.

We now begin to descend the mountain slopes, when a large bird flew from the ground from under my very feet, and I almost trod upon her. She exposed to our gaze three handsome eggs of the Golden Plover. The nest was simply a slight depression in the ground lined with a few blades of grass. The eggs proved to be partly incubated, which accounted for the bird remaining on the nest so long. The eggs are very large for the bird, and are the handsomest of all the plovers eggs; they are of a warm, yellow stone color, well blotched, chiefly at the larger end, with brown and black, in some specimens the ground color is a pale green; size about 2.10x1.40.

A Red Grouse startles us both as she flies with a loud whir from the heather just before us, and here we found her nest of ten eggs. They were very beautiful and richly colored, differing much in ground color and markings. But it is a risky job taking the eggs of this bird; they are game and protected by law, and a heavy fine is imposed upon any one found taking the eggs. These Grouse moors are famous, and the nobility from the south come up here every season, and on the 12th of August parties are out at break of day and work and fire away until sunset. Next day the newspapers give long accounts of the day's sport, and how many brace of

Grouse Lord or Earl So-and-So bagged, and before the end of the week the poulterer's shops are full of Grouse. The Red Grouse is found nowhere except on the British Islands, and, like the Bald Eagle of the United States, their national emblem, so should be the Red Grouse the national emblem of Great Britain.

We found several Lapwing's nests, and one nest of the English Snipe, but as we had already taken several sets of both species, and our boxes were too crowded already, we did not take these.

A half hour's walk brings us to the place where we hid the plover's eggs we collected in the early part of the day, but it was some time before we struck the exact spot. "Oh, here they are!" my brother exclaimed, but how shall we carry them, our boxes are full, the only way left is to put them in our hats, cover them with our handkerchiefs, and carry them on our heads. We now leave the moors, and begin to descend into the valley. The village is only a mile off, and on our way through the valley we each collect a large bouquet of wild-flowers, lillies of the valley, primroses and forgetmenots, for the fair ones at h me.

A pair of European Woodcocks usually nest in this valley. Their nest is very slight, seldom more than a hole in the ground with bits of grass and moss for a lining. The four eggs are very similar to those of Bartram's Sandpiper.

The sun is fast setting behind the Lancashire Hills, and the birds are singing their evening songs before going to rest. We soon reach the village and make for the New Inn, and, while supper is being prepared, we throw off all encumbrances and go in for a good, refreshing wash. After our ravenous appetites are somewhat satisfied, we tramp to the station with burning faces and light hearts. Jumping into the eight o'clock train, we are soon rattling along on our way home to Leeds, having spent a most enjoyable and exceedingly profitable day.

Five years ago the region I have just tried to picture to my readers was unknown except to a few artists, naturalists and geologists, but of late the railway companies are waking up, and now, during the summer months, excursion trains bring many people from the large manufacturing towns of Yorkshire and Lancashire, and before long this district will become as popular as the Scottish or Welsh scenery.

[FINIS.]

CANADIAN SPARROWS.

BY WM. L. KELLS.

THE SONG SPARROW.
(*Melospiza Fasciata.*)

THIS species is among the most common and melodious of our song birds. In the morning of the early summer time, when the dew is heavy on the vegetation, and the cool air is laden with the odor of herbs and flowers, while the majority of the human family are still wrapt in slumber and a calm stillness pervades the atmosphere, long before the orb of day has made its appearance in the eastern sky, and while yet but few of the feathered tenants of our woods and fields have begun to utter their varied notes, it is then that the most charming lays of the Song Sparrow seems to greet the student of nature, as the singer, occupying some elevated position near where his companion has chosen her nesting place, makes his best efforts to tell her of his love and cheer her weary hours, or greet the spring-day morning in tones of joy and gladness. Soon, as the dawn progresses into day, a rivalry of song notes are heard, and from all parts of the farm, the orchard, and the deep, wild woods, other of its species answer, while the robin, the wood and hermit thrushes, have already been wide awake and greeting the new-born day with their soul-inspiring melodies; but in the open fields, though the solos of other species are not to be despised, the Song Sparrow is the master musician.

And this bird is not only a pleasing songster, but also a hardy and adventurous ranger; some of its species generally returning to this country while the ground is still deep in the garb of winter, and the watercourses locked in bands of ice. And no sooner does the pioneer penetrate the backwoods, erect his rude shanty, and begins to clear the surrounding forest, than from the brush-piles or the newly cut stump, this little companion of civilization greets and cheers him with its song which must ever recall, to the thoughtful mind, the days of youth, forever gone, when we wandered o'er the homestead or played round the dwelling called by the endearing name of 'home;' and not until the night frosts and stormy winds of autumn herald the approach of winter, does this songster cease its lays, forsake its Canadian home, and begin its flight toward the sunny South. Its arrival in Central Ontario, of course, depends much upon the weather, but generally in the last week of March, sometimes by the 20th of that month the appearance of some of the more adventurous of these birds may be looked for; and by the middle of April, the great body have probably all arrived and dispersed over the country where they make their homes for the season.

As soon as the weather becomes sufficiently temperate, they begin to select their nesting sites, usually in the first week of May. In the early part of the season, the nesting place is usually found to be in the side of a bank, the root of a fallen tree, under a log or stump, or in a bunch of grass or stubble; but, later in the season, they will nest wherever they can find sufficient shelter, whether in the grass or grain field, the garden, the newly chopped fallow, or the margins of the woods. Sometimes they will build in the thickest parts of an evergreen or a thorn-bush, several feet from the ground; again, their nests may be found in a hollow stump or old log, or sunk in a hole in the ground. On one occasion I saw a nest of this species, with three fresh eggs, on the 6th of August, in a shock of fall wheat that had been set up six days before, and often in the pea harvest, I have seen their nests among the long, tangled vines; and on several occasions I have found their nest in tufts of water grass deep in the woods, and also in brush-piles. The nest is formed of any soft materials that come in the birds' way; stalks of weeds, vines, grass, dry leaves, and hair of either horses, cattle or other animals, are commonly used, and neatly placed in a form that can generally be distinguished from any other species.

The set of eggs in the early part of the season is always four or five; but later, three, and sometimes two form the clutch. The eggs of this species vary much in color and markings, having a greyish, whitish, greenish or bluish hue, sometimes clay-color; spotted and blotched with varying shades of brown. It nests several times in a season.

It feeds occasionally on grain, seeds and small fruits, but its principal food appears to be insects and their products, as well as the lower forms of animal life, of which it destroys vast numbers.

When mated, these birds appear to be strongly attached to each other, and their affection for their young is very great.

The Song Sparrow is over six inches in length. The plumage on the upper parts is marked with brown, bay and ash white, the breast and sides are streaked with dark lines, and the lower parts are whitish; the crown is dull bay with fine black lines. Both sexes are alike in color and size.

[TO BE CONTINUED.]

PERSONAL OBSERVATIONS ON THE DECREASE OF FAMILIAR BIRDS.

BIRD destruction, owing to the efforts of the Eastern societies organized for their protection, has come to be a topic of general interest in the newspapers, particularly those of the Eastern states, and every effort is being made to introduce the most stringent laws forbidding the killing of birds and disturbance of their nests, for other than scientifical purposes, and the use of their plumage for ornamentation. That birds are suffering a notable decrease in numbers cannot be doubted; but, to a great extent, the case is represented to be worse than it really is. The protectionists cite a long array of figures on the wholesale slaughter of sea coast birds and mention numerous instances of different species becoming wholly or partially extinct during the past few decades, and using this as a basis for argument apply the results directly to the thrushes, warblers, sparrows and other beneficial birds of the interior. A careful comparison of the circulars issued by the Audubon Society and the speech delivered by Dr. Langdon (published in our March number) brings out these facts with great clearness.

Throughout the Western States, the more common species of birds are very plentiful, and hence the agriculturist sees but little, if any, need for their protection. In the East, it is different; year by year the birds have become scarcer until now, comparitively speaking, there are but few left. Our correspondents frequently mention the rareness of certain species which were once common and even the dissapearance of some of the brighter colored rarer birds, while ornithological friends on a visit to the West frequently express their astonishment at their abundance.

Locally considered, however, the cause of protection is one of much interest to all, and becoming a topic of general conversation, particularly with the ladies, who frequently mention the fact that the robins, catbirds and other songsters are gradually becoming scarcer. We have often been asked what should cause the scarcity of the robin, why it is that his song is not as frequently heard in the evening as of old. We can give but one reason—the broken bark on so many of our trees. It speaks so plainly that he who runs may read. The robin commences to breed in the early months of spring, long before the leaves have put in an appearance, and as he usually chooses a convenient fork in an open maple or oak for a site, the nest is a prominent object and from the time the first straws are carried the small boy gives it his personal supervision. Nest after nest is harried, dozens, yes, even hundreds, of eggs broken for sport or "collected" for "science." During the present spring we have frequently seen the blue eggs broken on the sidewalks and we could locate at least a dozen nests in the very heart of our city which are empty—forsaken. This is not the work of one or two, but of many, who go by evening in gangs of three or four, carefully examining every promising tree, or visiting the nests marked down during the day, until it is almost impossible for a bird to hatch the first set of eggs. Of course they build another nest and lay again, and again if necessary, until finally the craze dies out or the small boy, seeing a few lucky young birds, concludes with regret that the days for robbery are past.

It is here that the true reason for the robin's disappearance lies; he finds that his friends in the city will not protect him and he moves further to the outskirts until at last he is forced to take refuge in the borders of the larger groves. Here his chances are better; and, as he returns each year to the same locality to breed, the people of the cities must miss his song. In support of this comes the observation that there are ten robins breeding in the edges of the groves, where a few years ago there was one. But even here they are far from being safe, for, although the nests are not so easily found, they are confronted by another enemy in the shape of a shot gun. During a recent evenings stroll, we saw, in one small grove and surrounding underbrush, three parties of boys busily hunting. The smallest of these gangs, consisting of two about fourteen years of age (each being armed with a revolver) had succeeded in securing a chipmunk, the remaining two parties were doing fairly well among the smaller birds, and, judging from the incessant firing on the opposite side of the grove, several others were having immense luck. We merely mention this as a common occurrence—six days in the week.

And even this is not all; there are other scarcely less important influences, one of which, the "bird-minder," requires special mention. He is usually an old man (boys are too impatient) who spends the greater portion of the small fruit season in exterminating the smaller birds in his vicinity. As a particular instance of this, we might mention one, a retired minister, well thought of by our people in general, but at heart so mean and stingy that he could not spare the orioles a few peas from his bountiful supply. Of what value is a half peck of peas worth 20 cents, compared to two pairs of orioles? Ask his neighbors, in whose trees their nests were built and young left to the slow tortures of starvation.

It is not, as one would imagine, the children of the poorer people of the town who commit the most wholesale robbery, but those of the wealthy business men—men who should know that they are responsible for every bird killed and every nest disturbed in violation of law. Yes, we have laws but they are never enforced. The gentleman before mentioned rendered himself liable to fines for violating two distinct laws every time he shot a bird, and yet we suppose he considers himself a thorough Christian.

But to return to the original subject; one might enquire, "What do they do with the eggs?" Some get them to throw at each other; the majority collect them for a pastime—such smash a hole in each end, put them on strings and preserve them as an Indian would scalps—usually breaking them when tired of them, and then get a new lot the next spring; others collect them as you would shells or fossils, the more the better; quantity is the only thing taken into account, each one trying to get a larger collection than his friend has. That this is the case is evinced by the frequent inquiries as to the number of eggs we have. "Don't know as we ever knew; never counted them," is the only answer that can be given. We began collecting one or two eggs of a species; and our cabinet contains the same two robin's eggs that it did eight years ago, and no more. As the eggs of the different species were gradually added, we have had to travel farther and farther in search of new species, until a ten mile walk has become a short mornings stroll, affording excellent opportunities for the study of habits and song, and but seldom giving occasion for the blackening of gun barrels.

FOOT MOVEMENTS IN BIRDS.

BY R. M. GIBBS, M. D.

SOME one has said: "Let me see a person walk and I will give you many points in his character without further introduction." To those who have carefully studied the peculiarities of different individuals in their manner of moving the lower extremeties, we doubt not conclusions may often be drawn; and that the dispositions and general make-up may be understood, we will not attempt to deny. We are all more or less apt to form an opinion of a person from watching his style of locomotion; and it is a common occurrence to remark on the good business ability of a passing pedestrian if we observe a quick, prompt step, or to censure as a sluggard the man who drags his feet, and dallies on his way to work. To a limited extent we are charitable to the man who hobbles by on crutches, for we know only too well that an imposition is often pressed upon our sight by one too lazy to work and yet smart enough to attempt to enlist our sympathies. We fully sympathize, however, if the man is really maimed by paralysis or loss of limb, and our remark generally is, "How hard to go through life in such a plight."

In the lower animals we will find that greater variation exists in the styles of moving about than even between the six day pedestrian, who draws a house to see his wonderful feat of endurance and speed in walking, and the slow-poke who wearily drags his cumbersome feet after him, and who is known as the lazy man of the neighborhood. That the lazy man is equally entitled to a living with the rapid walker is evident from the fact that he still lives; and the principle of the "survival of the fittest" evidently favors the sluggard, for does he not often, aye usually, outlive the active man? In the economy of nature we will also see that, among the lower animals, those of slow movements evidently have a place to fill in Nature's great thoroughfare; and that the active and strong have no better chance of life than the slow and weak. The remarkable activity of the lizard known as the swift, in no way better provides for his wants than do the clumsy movements of the toad. And further, if we carefully observe the dull creature which we frequently spurn from our path, impatient from its slow locomotion, we will find that the celerity with which the toad picks up a fly or ant with its agile, well trained tongue, is fully equal to the quicker, general movement of its lizard relative. Now may we not say, with reason, that not infrequently the lazy man who lives in a higher scale of existence, although many would not like to acknowledge it, and who is usually a diplomat to the extent of his wants, really often surpasses his more active neighbor in the fulfillment of his desires.

Among the birds a great variation of movement exists, and perhaps in no department, unless we except the insects, shall we find so many interesting features and opportunities for study of locomotion. It may be said that the locomotion of birds is mainly by flight, and it is natural that the suggestion should arise; but, from the fact that as a class we consider birds as fliers, it does not follow that we are to classify them from their aerial movements, or look on them as entirely confined to their wings either in traveling or seeking their food. On the contrary, many species never leave the ground, many others are but indifferent fliers, while others even use their wings as propellers or fins in swimming. We will study a few forms of bird movement on the ground, comparing various orders and species. If we attempt classification of birds on a whole, from their manner of walking, the entire system in vogue would be sadly entangled, and therefore a scientific basis will not be drawn.

Beginning with the *Passeres*, and speaking only of those species which we have observed, we start in with the Robin. Here we have a veritable, undignified hopper, or more properly jumper, for he invariably rises from the ground and strikes on both feet in moving about, whether feeding or playing with his mate. The movements are executed with great regularity and precision, and under all cases appear to be the result of mature deliberation. Our Robin does not hop, or jump—which ever you please—until he has thoroughly considered it. You see him standing proudly on a tussock, or dead fallen limb, his form is erect, his head well up, and the broad, beautiful breast strained out in front. In this position he frequently stands five minutes; and then, with his cheery chirp, uttered a few times, he lowers his head somewhat, directs it toward a point ten feet or more away, and hop-hop-hop he goes toward it. These hops are almost invariably in a straight line, and I doubt if the hopper could turn aside until the last hop had occurred. I have seen the attempt made, and a sorry effort it was, much like the attempt of a drunkard to suddenly turn about; the bird wobbled about and nearly fell. In almost every case, the Robin hops his two, three, or up to ten hops, in a direct line; and then it is a common thing for him to jig back on almost the same course, or off at right angles. In this way we have seen them tack, about a lawn, recently freshened by an April shower, until almost every part had been covered and few, if any, earth-worms were left exposed. It is interesting to note an occasional sudden stop made by Robin, while he is on one of his five or six hops; he fairly tumbles over on his head in his effort to suddenly seize a worm while hopping. In these attempts he usually takes a step or two with each foot separately, not hopping as is his usually wont. However, the Robin, and all the other thrushes are like him, is very undignified in his manner of getting over the ground; and if he were not an old acquaintance, we would laugh at his odd movements. The Robin usually hops a distance of a foot or fifteen inches at each attempt, and generally makes a distance of eight to twelve feet before discontinuing his movements; whereupon he looks about for worms or food, and again hops. In the trees the Robin often performs the same movements, when the limbs and twigs are placed to his liking. When the limbs are rather too far apart, he often spreads his wings, and occasionally striking his feet, looks as if he were half flying, half hopping, which is the case. The Catbird and Brown Thrush also have this habit. The Thrasher is a strong hopper and frequently makes jumps of two feet or more, but his jumps rarely number over three or four in succession. He is a very accurate jumper, much more so than the Robin. We have seen a Brown Thrush repeatedly leap through a small space scarcely large enough to admit his body. It is amusing to see one jump between the rails of a fence, with the long tail streaming after. The Hermit and Wilson's Thrushes are also hoppers; in fact, we have never seen a member of this family walk or even use their feet separately, except in feeding, rarely, and in covering their nests or young, when they stand first on one foot—then on the other, before setting.

The Bluebird is a hopper also, but will frequently take a few steps when crowded; and often clings to the excavation entrance in which is his nest, first with one foot—then with the other, meantime fluttering his wings and gratifying us with his delightful warble. He is not nearly so much of a ground bird as the Thrushes, and secures much of his prey from dead limbs and stumps, or even picking it from the ground as he hovers just above it, without touching his feet.

[The above article was read before the R O. C. at Chicago; and would have been published in their Bulletin had not the Club been discontinued.]

[TO BE CONTINUED.]

NOTES ON SOME OF THE PASSERES OF FULTON COUNTY, KENTUCKY.

FOURTH PAPER, BY L. O. PINDAR, PRES. Y. O. A., HICKMAN, KENTUCKY.

AND now we come to the large family *Fringillidæ* which is the largest family we have, comprising about one-seventh of the birds of N. America, according to Dr. Coues. If we have counted aright the A. O. U. Check List places 133 species in this family, which includes the Grosbeaks, Finches, Redpolls, Goldfinches, Longspurs, the various Sparrows, Juncos, Towhees, Cardinals, Buntings, etc.

We will be compelled to devote two papers to this family; and will first take up the Am. Goldfinch (*Spinus tristis*) as I have had many opportunities of observing it. It is a common resident here, though this is perhaps one of their most Southern breeding grounds; and, like the Meadow Lark, is extremely local in its distribution. Six miles south of Hickman, just over the line, in Obion Co., Tenn., they are very abundant; but right at Hickman we rarely find them except in winter, when they come around the houses and barns.

I have often noticed them feeding on the seeds of the sweet gum tree in winter; and this habit drew the following remarkable sentence from a boy who spoke of them as "Them 'ere little black and yeller birds what eats sweet-gum seeds." Ought not that description puzzle anyone as to what it meant. This bird has many local names, Wild Canary, Flaxbird, Thistlebird, Lettucebird, etc. being most common, all being received, as will be seen, from its habits of feeding on thistle tops, wild flax, lettuce seed, etc.

This bird enjoys the distinction of being about the latest nester we have, usually commencing its domestic care in July, sometimes not till August. The probable reason for this is that the various seeds fed to the young are not to be found in their greatest abundance till this time, for the birds always nest earlier if we have an early spring and *vice versa*.

The nest is saddled on a limb, something after the manner of that of the Wood Thrush, though of course so dainty a bird could never be imagined to use mud in its nest. Instead, it weaves together the soft inner bark of the grape vine, slender blades of grass, fine moss, and small leaves, lined with an exquisite carpet of felted thistle down.

When their home is at last completed, four to six white eggs, delicately tinged with green and sharply pointed at one end, are laid. The above is the normal color, but occasionally a set is found with black spots, and again they may be bluish white. They measure about .65x.50.

The Chipping Sparrow (*Spizella socialis*) is another common bird here, being most common in summer though many generally remain through the winter. Last winter, '87-'88, however, contrary to their usual habits, they all left late in the fall, returning early in April.

The Chippy, Hair-bird, or Social Sparrow, is one of our best known birds, probably on account of its abundance and the trust it reposes in man, nearly always nesting near buildings, and also on account of its extended habitat, reaching west to the Rocky Mts., and south to Mexico.

The nest is said by some to be generally placed in shrubbery, etc., but we do not find this to be the case. Our first nest was in a mulberry tree, and about 12 feet from the ground.

The nest is not an exceptionally neat structure; it is composed of leaves, dried grass, fine twigs, and with always enough horsehair in its make up to justify the popular appellation of Hair-bird.

The eggs are four to five in number, bluish green, speckled with blackish brown, and measure, according to Mr. Davie, who gives the average of 30 specimens, .69x.48.

MIGRATION REPORTS.

CHICAGO, ILLINOIS.
REPORTED BY W. E. PRATT.

NAME.	FIRST SEEN.	NO. SEEN.	NEXT SEEN.	WHEN COM.
Pectoral Sandpiper	4-16	*		
Horned Lark†				
Am. Bittern	4-21	1	4-23	4-25
Virginia Rail	4-21	2	4-25	5- 1
Carolina "	4-21	5	4-23	4-30
Cowbird	4-21	*		
Bobolink	4-21	*		
Kingfisher	4-21	1	4-25	5- 3
Golden-c. Kinglet	4-23	*		
Ruby-c. "	4-23	*		
Y.-headed Blackbird	4-24	6	4-26	4-28
Cat bird	4-24	2	4-25	5- 5
Ruddy Duck	4-24	2		
Black-c. Nightheron	4-24	*		
Golden Plover	4-22	*		
Chipping Sparrow	4-25	*		
Swamp "				4-25
Duck Hawk‡	4-25	1		
Osprey	4-25	1		
Bonaparte Gull	4-25	20		4-26
Black Tern	4-26	1		5-12
Spotted Sandpiper	4-26	1		4 30
Bartram's Sandpiper	4-27	1	4-30	5- 2
Kingbird	4-28	8	5- 1	5- 4
Horned Grebe	5- 1	9		
Green Heron	5- 1	*		
Baltimore Oriole	5- 1	1	5- 3	5- 4
Chimney Swift	5- 1	2	5- 3	5- 4
Summer Yellowbird	5- 3	1	5- 4	5-12
Bl'h-t. Blue Warbler	5 4	*		
Black and Y. "	5 4	*		
Redstart	5- 4	2	5- 5	5-12
Chestnut-s. Warbler	5- 4	1		5-12
Least Flycatcher	5- 4	3		5-12
Blackburnian Warler	5- 4	5		5-12
Nashville "	5- 5	1		
Woodcock	5- 5	1		
Wood Thrush	5- 9	1		5-12
Short-b. Water Th'sh	5-12	5		
Long-b. " "	5-12	1		
Warblers—Golden-w.				
Yellow-rumped				
Blue Yellow-backed				
Black-throated Green				
Tennessee				
Palm				
Can. Flycatching				
Wilson's Black-capped				
B. & W. Creeping	5-12	*		
Maryland Y.-throat	5 12	*		

Bl'e Gr'y Gnat-catcher	5-12	3		
Scarlet Tanager	5-12	*		
Bank Swallow	5-12	*		
Forester's Tern	5-12	*		
Least Bittern	5-12	1		
Wood Pewee	5-12	*		
Acadian Flycatcher	5 12	3		
Whippoorwill	5-12	2		

*Numerous.
†Two half-fledged young ones found, 4-21.
‡A very large, long-winged Hawk, a very swift flier. Saw him kill four Mud Hens on the wing in about ten minutes.
The observations were made at Grass Lake and Grand Crossing.

JACKSON, MICHIGAN.
REPORTED BY CARLETON GILBERT.

Barn Swallow	4 10	4	4-20	4-23
Chimney Swift	4 20	3	4-22	4-24
Scarlet Tanager	4 25	1	4-30	5-14
Golden-c. Thrush	4 15	1	4-26	5- 5
Purple Martin	4- 3	2	4- 6	4-22
House Wren	4 29	1	4-30	5-10
Baltimore Oriole	4 29	2	4-30	5-15
Catbird	4 20	1	4-28	5-13
Parula Warbler	5- 4	1		
White-t. Sparrow	5 1	10	5 2	5-16
Bl'k and W. Creeper	5- 2	1	5- 3	5-10
Vesper Sparrow	4 26	3	4-30	
Pine Grosbeak	5- 2	1		
Mourning Warbler	5- 4	1		5-12
Y.-rumped "	5- 4	1	5-10	5-16
Maryland Y.-throat	5- 4	1		
Blackburnian Warb.	5 14	1	5-18	5 21
Black-t. Green "	5 13	1	5 17	
" Blue "	5 19	4		
Bl'e Gr'y Gnatcatcher	5 10	3	5 16	5 20
Gt. C'st'd Flycatcher	5 12	2	5 18	
Rose-b. Grosbeak	5 12	6	5 15	5-21
Whippoorwill	5 12	1	5-18	
Nighthawk	5 10	1		
Orchard Oriole	5-12	2	5-13	5-20
White-c. Sparrow	5 14	7	5-15	5-17
Chestnut-s. Warbler	5 12	1		
Golden-w. "	5-15	3	5.17	5-19
Black-billed Cuckoo	5-15	1	5-19	
Y.-bellied Flycatcher	5 11	5	5-15	5-20
Redstart	5-12	8	5 14	5-15
Red.-h. Woodpecker	5- 1	6	5-13	5-18
Field Sparrow	5 12	3	5 16	5-18
Swamp Sparrow	5-13	2	5 15	5-19
Bobolink	5 12	1	5-16	5 20
Indigo Bunting	5-21	1		
Least Flycatcher	5-18	1		

ST. PAUL, MINNESOTA.

REPORTED BY C. J. SONNEN.

Species				
Geese	4-15	8	4-17	
Woodcock	4-17	4	4-18	
English Snipe	4-18	1	5- 6	5-10
Passenger Pigeon	4-20	1		
Kingfisher	4-21	2	4-22	4-30
Chewink	4-21	*		
Sand Martin	4-21	*		
Wood Pewee				4-21
Orange-c. Warbler			4-21	4-30
Mud Hen	4-21	1	5-10	
Chimney Swallow	4-24	*		
Purple Grackle				4-25
Marsh Hawk	4-25	2	5- 4	
Brown Thrush	4-25	*		4-26
Snow Brant	4-25	11		
Am. Bittern	4-25	1	5- 1	5 15
Kingbird	5- 5	1	5- 5	
Sparrow Hawk	5- 5	1	5-12	
Horned Lark	5- 5	2	5- 6	5-12
Spotted Sandpiper	5- 7	1		
Rose-b. Grosbeak			5 10	5-12
Baltimore Oriole	5 11	2	5-12	
Catbird	5-12	*		5-15
Summer Redbird	5 12	1†		
Bobolink	5 15	2		

*Numerous. †Rare visitant here.

MEDINA, NEW YORK.

REPORTED BY NEIL F. POSSON.

Species				
Tree Sparrow	4-13	4	4-20	4 21
Golden-c. Kinglet	4-14	5	4-15	4-14
Savannah Sparrow	4-10	1	4-19	4-19
Purple Martin	4-19	1	4 20	4-19
Wood Thrush	4-21	1		
Chimney Swift	4-23	1	4-24	4-23
W.-bellied Swallow	4-26	1		4-26
Belted Kingfisher	4-26	3		4-26
Yellow Warbler	4-28	1		
Barn Swallow	4-28	2	4-29	4-30
Least Flycatcher	4-29	1	4-30	
Baltimore Oriole	5- 1	1	5- 4	5- 5
Spotted Sandpiper	5- 5	5		5- 5
Bobolink	5- 5	1		
B. & W. Cr'p'g Warb.	5- 5	3		5- 5
Golden-w. "	5- 5	1		
W.-crowned Sparrow	5- 5	1		

WAYNESBURG, PENNSYLVANIA.

REPORTED BY J. WARREN JACOBS.

Species				
Cowbird	4- 1	3	4- 4	4-12
Chewink	4- 1	4	4- 8	4- 8
Red-w. Blackbird	4- 1	2		4-15
Wood Thrush	4- 1	2		
Kingfisher	4 1	1		
Purple Martin	4- 4	3	4- 6	4 12
Bobolink	4 3	2	4- 9	
Green Heron	4-14	1	4-20	4 20
Bank Swallow	4-14	2	4-18	4 20
Spotted Sandpiper	4 14	1	4-20	4-20
Bl'e Gr'y Gnatcatcher	4-15	1	4-17	4-23
Redstart	4-15	1	4-20	4 28
Wilson's Thrush	4-15	1	4-15	
Long-b. Wat'r Thr'sh	4-15	2	4-22	
Catbird	4-15		4-16	4 20
Barn Swallow	4 16			4-20
Yellow Warbler	4-22			4-30
Acadian Flycatcher	4-22	1		4-30
Warbling Vireo	4 23	1		4 30
Baltimore Oriole	4 26	1		4-28
Y.-breasted Chat	4-28	1		5 1
Scarlet Tanager	4 28	1	4-30	5- 2
Gt. C'st'd Flycatcher	4-25	1	4-30	5- 3
Indigo Bunting	4-29			5 5
Red-eyed Vireo	4 29	1		
Kingbird	4 29	2	5- 3	5- 3
Orchard Oriole	4 30		5- 1	5 5
Wood Pewee	5- 5	1	5- 6	
Ruby-t. Hummingbird	5- 7	3	5 12	5-12

CRESCO, IOWA.

Species				
Long-b. Curlew	4-15	2		
Golden Plover	4-16	50	4-19	
Am. Bittern	4-15	1		
Brown Thrasher	4-30	2		
Green Heron	5- 1	1		
Spotted Sandpiper	5- 1	1		
Scarlet Tanager	5 4	3	5- 5	
Indigo Bunting	5- 4	1		
Wood Thrush	5- 4	1	5 6	
Wilson's "	5 4	2	5 5	
Catbird	5 4	1	5 8	
Am. Redstart	5 0	1	5 10	
Y.-bellied Woodpecker	5 5	1		
Maryland Yellow-t.	5 6	1	5 9	
Bobolink	5 6	8	5 7	
Rose-b. Grosbeak	5 6	2		
Am. Woodcock	5 6	2		
Lesser Yellowlegs			5 9	
Baltimore Oriole	5 12	1		
Least Flycatcher	5 12	1		
Bank Swallow	5 13	2		
Cerulean Warbler	5 20	1		
B. and W. Creeper	5 12	2		

EDITORIAL.

Correspondents all speak appreciatingly of our change in form.

Mr. F. A. Patton of Roswell, Dakota, promises us some interesting articles on the birds of that section in the near future.

Chas. F. Carr of Madison, Wisconsin, who has one of the finest collections in the State, writes us that he intends furnishing us with several articles before long. They will surely be interesting.

Just before the close of the season, when oologists are anxious to make good exchanges, a new directory becomes a much valued article. This year Mr. Taylor of Dunkirk. N. Y., intends to supply the want. As it will probably contain some fifteen hundred names, it bids fair to excel all previous efforts in this line, and should be in the hands of every working student.

We have received the first sixteen pages of Prof. Oliver Davie's "Nests and Eggs." The work is not nearly so condensed as formerly, giving numerous notes on the nesting habits of the species. Some idea of the improvement in the work may be had when we say that his article on the "Habits of Some American Grebes" in our April number was but a fair synopsis of the notes on these species given in the work.

Received since last issue: Agassiz Companion; Agassiz Record, Badger State Philatelist, Common Sense, Excelsior, Exchanger's Monthly, Garner, of London, Geolo' Gazette, Leisure Hour, Oologist, Oologist's Exchange, Our Dumb Animals, Scientist, United States Philatelist, World of N are; but the Bay State Oologist, "h where, oh where has it gone?" Why the whichness of this Mr. Foote?

Following are the lucky winners in the prize drawing of Walter Raine:
1st prize: ½ Golden Eagle, ticket 41, Mr. J. C. Sharp, Taunton, Mass.
2nd prize: ¼ Bald Eagle; ticket 13; Mr. W. C. Flint, San Francisco.
3d prize: ¼ Sea Eagle; ticket 31; Frank Lattin, Albion, N. Y.
4th prize: ¼ Merlin Hawk; ticket 2; Messrs. Webster & Mead, Cresco, Iowa.
5th prize: ¼ Rough-legged Hawk, ticket 35, Mr. G. Gregory, New Haven, Conn.
6th prize: ¼ European Buzzard; ticket 20 G. Dexter Gregory, New Haven, Conn.
7th prize: 1 Fulmar, 1 Puffin, ticket 21; Mr Frank Lattin.
8th prize: 1-7 European Coot, ticket 39; Mr. J. C. Sharp,
9th prize: 1 Egyptian Vulture; ticket 46; Wm. J. Parkes, Toronto, Canada.

We, the undersigned, declare that the above drawing was done in an upright and satisfactory manner to all parties concerned.

E. V. Rippon, 60 Scotland St.
Wm. J. Parker, 1 Darcy St.
Toronto.

HOW TO COLLECT AND PREPARE CONCHOLOGICAL SPECIMENS.

BY J. A. SINGLEY.

E must take everything he can see—no matter how small, as some of the species are almost microscopic in size. The larger specimens can be cleaned as directed for the *Helices*. The smaller specimens, as well as *all* small shells and those of a larger size where the aperture is contracted or filled with teeth, preventing us from extracting the animal, should be put into alcohol for 24 hours, taken out and washed and dried; these delicate shells require careful handling, as the sharp lip must not be chipped. In collecting these, it is best to have a wide-mouthed vial containing alcohol, so they can be dropped in as soon as collected. A pair of tweezers is indispensable in collecting small shells. Large shells can be put into an ordinary collecting box.

Vitrina. This genus resembles *Zonites*, and requires similar treatment.

Bulimulus and *Glandina* are Southern and Mexican genera. Mostly large and handsome species. They inhabit the same station as the *Helices*, and are treated like them.

Cylindrella. There are but two species of this genus found in the U. S. *Macroceramus*, of which also two species are found in this country, is related to this genus. They are elongated, slender, many-whorled shells, and must be treated with the alcohol bath.

Pupa and *Vertigo* are small cylindrical genera found everywhere in the U. S. No particular place can be given as their station, but some species are partial to wet meadows; and any chip, piece of bark, or accumulation of trash will richly reward the collector who investigates it. Other species will be found in damp moss. Look closely for these small species, as it is among them that the collector hopes of finding a species new to science may materialize. Treat these species with alcohol.

The *Succineas* are all fragile shells, not of a large size; but having a short spire and large body-whorl and aperture, the animal can be removed from them, making fine specimens.

The species of this genus are the nearest to being amphibious of any of the *Pulmonata*, and are found on the margins of lakes and streams crawling on the mud, and sometimes on sticks or logs projecting out of the water. They can also be found in wet bottom lands, not plenty of moisture being a necessity to them, there is not much use looking for them elsewhere. A simple scalding will loosen the animal so it can be removed and the shell cleaned. Being so fragile they require careful manipulation.

If the collector wishes to collect the naked Mollusks, Slugs, &c., they will require to be kept permanently in alcohol. While I have not enumerated all the genera of American terrestrials, I have given the most important ones; and all specimens can be prepared by some one of the methods given. The collector will rapidly gain experience in finding the best localities for the different species; and he will hardly find a barren locality.

The most important family of American fresh-water shells is the well known "river-mussel," or *Unionidæ*. Of the 1200 known species, more than one-half have been described from American waters. There is a wonderful diversity of form and other characters; and a complete collection of the American species alone would be worth a small fortune. There is scarcely a stream, lake or pond that will not have one or more representatives of this family; and as they are all interesting, and some very beautiful, they are much sought after, especially by foreign collectors. In collecting this family the collector can don an old suit and wade after them if the weather is warm and water shallow, or if he is afraid of a wetting he can use a rake with close-set teeth and dredge for them.

They are prepared for the cabinet by scalding, when the shell will gape open. With a sharp knife remove the animal; wash the shell thoroughly inside and outside; close the valves and tie a string about the shell, and it will dry closed. If you want your cabinet specimens to look just as they do when removed from the water, give them an application of glycerine on the outside, but don't drench them in it, a slight application will do. Be particular to label every specimen, giving the stream or lake where taken, county and state. This is necessary with all fresh-water shells. In land shells give the county and state on the label.

[CONCLUDED IN JULY NUMBER.]

A SKELETON

... ...ame of any structure upon which the main parts are t... ... li... ...nd this definition exactly agrees with a description of our ... ...r Outline Collection of Bird's Eggs. After much experience and ... ...t...l of the needs of both the student and collector, we have prepar... ... ...ollection of typical eggs, adapted to the requirements of ...h... ... ...ollectors and all others who desire to form a complete select... O... ... ...mens, but, from the costliness of many of the rarer eggs ... ...invest a large sum in purchasing a complete collection even f s ... ...sirable, preferring to secure a small cabinet and add thereto...

In ... ...se to be confounded with some miscellaneous gatherings, ...Cabinets, its specimens being selected from the best of ... ...of Birds' Eggs. The difference between the so-termed Amateur ... ...me other dealers, and our Cabinets is essentially one of ...teri... ... ...al, one representing *all natural families, classes and* or ...s as are required to form a rudimentary knowledge of ... ... which every well informed person is supposed to be acquainted... These cabinets have all been planned with a direct and ... ...d in collections of this kind, and NOT from what ... ...k, w...h..t thought as to w..t was needful. We think ... ...sulting the following series contained in our Skele...

... ...hat used in Ridgway's Nomenclature of N. A. Birds and ...st of the A. O. U. and the second column and names com... V...ties have the varietal name following the typical form. *Calius pleseardinensis*, Catbird. D... *Cinclus Mexicanus*, Am. Water Ouzel. ... *S...aiia Sialias*, Bluebird. ... *Phain..pepla nit...*, Black-crested Flycatcher. ...mber, which, for want of room we are compelled to omit, way ... ...ay be found by consulting the following No's. in Prof. ... 74, 10 k 17, 118, 120, 126, 124, 132, 182, 184, 186, 188, 201, 206, ... 300, 310 3.1, 316, 325, 360, 365, 388, 391, 412, 420, 423, 431, 444, 474, ... 621, 652, 6.1, 725, 728, 747, 735 712, 751 and 766. Ens.] ... ...ent Col. No. 1 embraces 60 specimens, and 57 families. ... ...ecurely packed, shipped and delivered at your freight depot ... ...pood, all risks assumed.

... ...ther collections arranged on the same plan, for sale at $5, $10 and ... ...ecured No. 1 where a collection that will *thoroughly* and ... ...d is desired. You may substitute any specimens in No.

... ...H... ... ...a *complete* collection of 800 varieties of N. A. Birds' ... ...annual or semi-annual, and give two or three years to pay for it. ... ...ollections of Bird's Eggs in the U. S. that are complete ... ...erently wish a collection of Birds' Eggs write for estimate ... A... ...ted in every county.

W. H. WINKLEY,
CLEARFIELD, IOWA.

SEND F...

BIRD'S EGGS AND SUPPLIES.

New Price List and Three Eggs only 20 cents post free.

FINE MINERALS.

Send 50 cents for List and Ten Specimens, size 1x1 inch.

**I. C. GREENE & CO., 65 HIGH ST.,
FITCHBURG, MASSACHUSETTS.**

FOUR FOR A DOLLAR.

FINE ENGRAVED TIGER-EYE

Heads for Scarf Pins.
—WORTH A DOLLAR EACH.

Closing Out a Vast Assortment of
MINERALS, GEMS AND CURIOS
Send Stamp Stating Your Wants.

**W. S BEEKMAN,
Box 108, West Medford, Mass.**
Mention this Magazine!

BIRDS' EGGS AND SKINS.

At Reasonable Prices. Send Stamp For Price Lists

J. A. Singley, Giddings. Texas

Embalming Taught Free.

Send $1.00 cash and receive a pound of Gibbs' CELEBRATED COMPOUND. Full instructions sent Free with powder. We have been charging $2.00 for this process and receipt of Compound, but we now make this

—EXTRAORDINARY REDUCTION

Being assured that we will sell a large amount of our Compound, and teach many the process of Embalming.

This Grand Reduction Offer is only open for next sixty days. Address with stamp.

R. M. Gibbs. Kalamazoo, Mich.

EXCHANGE NOTICES.

Notices under this heading inserted for one_ half cent per word, but no notice will be inserted for less than 25 cents.

TO EXCHANGE—Nice complete sets of Dakota birds' eggs, for other eggs in sets, or any good books on Ornithology. Wanted—Davie's Egg Check List, third edition.

F. A. PATTON, Roswell, Dakota.

WANTED—A full-fledged young Sparrow Hawk. Will pay your own price for a specimen in good condition.

E. B. WEBSTER, Cresco, Iowa.

$1.00 GIVEN AWAY.

By means of our "Prize Oological Card" Send 5 cents in stamps for Certificate and 30 pp. catalogue of Birds' Eggs, Skulls, Minerals, Instruments, etc., at prices that will astonish you.

. Natural History paper, insert this and above three months, send marked copies and bill payable in anything we advertise.

Dickinson & Durkee, Sharon, Wisconsin.

R. E. RACHFORD & SON.

COLLECTING NATURALISTS,
AND WHOLESALE DEALERS IN

**BIRD SKINS AND EGGS,
BEAUMONT. TEXAS.**

RUBBER STAMPS MADE TO ANY ORDER

One line stamps, 25c extra lines 2c each. Pocket stamp, two lines, 40. Pen and Pencil stamp, two lines, 35c. Self-inking stamp, 3 x 1½ in. only $2.00. Single line dating stamp, good for 8 years, only $1.70. Self inking pads, 50 2x3½ in., 60c 6x8½ in.

**Special Attention to Mail Orders.
Postage Extra. Cash with Order**

**GREENE & CO.
65 High St., Fitchburg, Mass.**

LOON'S EGG sent to any address for 75c, postal note. List of curiosities 5c.

N. E. CARTER, Delevan, Wis.

RARE EGGS.

(434)	Harris' Hawk.	$1.50 each
(441)	White-tailed Hawk	$2.00 each
(423)	Cara Cara.	$1.50 each

These eggs are first-class. Can furnish them in sets or singly, with full data.

Chas. F. Carr, 539 State St., Madison, Wis.
Taxidermist and Collector.

TAYLOR'S NEW DIRECTORY IS

BOOMING.

Send Ten cents and have your name inserted and secure a copy of first issue.

Will be issued the 1st of August

Advertisements, 10 cents per line.

Exchange notices one cent per word

Write for further particulars. Best of References furnished if they may be desired.

ZACH TAYLOR, DUNKIRK. N. Y.

Vol. II, No. 1.   JANUARY, 1889.

:!:-O-:!:

PUBLISHED BY
E. B. WEBSTER,
CRESCO, IOWA.

Entered at the Cresco P. O. as Second Class Mail Matter.

Contents for January

To a Golden-crested Kinglet,	Wm. L. Kells
Birds of Greenbrier Co., West Va.,	T. Surber
The Scarlet Tanager.	
Instinct or Reason?	Rev. S. L. Noble
Notes on the Passeres of Fulton Co., Ky.,	L. O. Pindar
Editorial Notes.	
The Scientists,	Dr. W. S. Strode
Noted Collections—No. 1,	F. R. Stearns

BOOKS - FOR - NATURALISTS.

Any of the following books will be sent postpaid on receipt of price:

BIRDS:

Ridgway's Manual of N. A. Birds,	$7.50
Coues' Key (third edition)	7.50
Langelles' "Our Birds and Their Haunts,"	3.00
Ridgway's Colors for Naturalists	4.00
Capen's "Oology of New England,"	8.65
Baird, Brewer & Ridgway's Water Birds of America—2 vols.	24.00
Baird, Brewer & Ridgway's Land Birds of America—3 vols.	30.00
Wilson & Bonapartes' Am. Ornithology	7.50
Vernon's Our Birds of Prey in Canada— 30 photo illustrations	10.00
Samuels' Our Northern Birds,	3.00
Bailey's Our Own Birds—col'd.	3.50
Adam's Humming Birds	1.40

A. A:

Three Kingdoms,	.75

TAXIDERMY:

Kinsley's Naturalists' Assistant,	1.50
Brown's Taxidermist's Manual	1.25
Maynard's Manual of Taxidermy,	1.25
Taxidermist,	1.60

INSECTS:

Packard's Guide to the Study of Insects,	5.00
" Insects of the West,	2.50
Rev. W. F. White's Ants and Their Ways,	2.00
Lubbock's Ants, Bees and Wasps,	2.00
Adams' Beautiful Shells,	1.75
Marvels of Pond Life,	1.50
Hogg on Microscope,	.85

NATURAL HISTORY:

Standard—6 vols., cloth,	36.00
" " half morocco,	48.00
White's Natural History of Selborne,	3.00

E. B. WEBSTER, Cresco, Iowa.

ARTIFICIAL - GLASS - EYES.

THOS. HURST, Mfr.

SIZE.	CTS. PER PAIR,	TEN PAIR.
1	3	.30
2	3	.30
3	4	.35
4	4	.35
5	5	.40
6	5	.45
7	6	.50
8	7	.60
9	8	.70
10	9	.90
11	11	1.00
12	12	1.10
13	14	1.30
14	16	1.50
15	18	1.70
16	22	2.00
17	23	2.20
18	20	2.50
19	32	3.00
20	36	3.50
21	40	3.80
22	50	4.80
23	60	5.30
24	65	6.40
25	75	7.00
26	90	8.50
27	1.00	9.50

Round black pupil; Nos 1 to 27, brown, hazel or flint iris; Nos. 1 to 22, yellow or straw; 1 to 18, carmine; 1 to 16, white, green, redbrown; 1 to 15, blue.

Can furnish Albino eyes, Nos. 1 to 17, at a slight advance.

Also eyes for Mammals, of middling and fine qualities. Reptiles and Fishes; clear Glass for painting and B'k.

Price l st furnished on application.

E. B. WEBSTER, Cresco, Iowa.

The Hawkeye Ornithologist and Oologist.

TO A GOLDEN-CRESTED KINGLET.

BY WM. L. KELLS.

Beautiful bird of the wilderness;
Oft I have wondered where might be thy nesting place.
Is it in the cedar or pine's airy shade?
Or in the top of the spruce is thy nursery made?
Is it in the north, by the Hudson Bay shore?
Or on Labrador's coast, where the wild billows roar?
Or on the ever green hills, whence the Ottawa comes,
Where the jay and the raven have their winter homes?
O tell me *satrapa* that I too may tell,
The place where in summer ye choose for to dwell,
For I know that in autumn, ye choose here to come;
And in our deep wildwoods make your winter home;
And active and cheery when snow closeth the ground,
And the chill blasts of winter are drifting around;
But when the winter's over, and spring comes again,
We miss for a season thy pleasing refrain;
Where then do you go with your bright golden crest,
To seek in seclusion a place for thy nest?
Then I wish I might see, when in summer I roam,
In some deep tangled wildwood the place of thy home,
And gaze on thy nest amid deep sheltered bowers.
Where the green garb of summer is mingled with flowers;
Where no voice of a foe, or dread sound of a gun,
May disturb thy retreat till thy purpose is done;
Come again to our woodlands when summer is gone,
And low in the south sinks the late autumn sun,
When the birds of our summer to the tropics have flown;
And the leaves of the forest are withered and gone;
When the white snow of winter lies deep on the ground;
And the cold Arctic breezes are blustering around;
While but few other birds will so cheerily sing,
Till our winter departs at the voice of the spring.

BIRDS OF GREENBRIER CO., WEST VA.

BY THADDEUS SURBER.

WHITE SUL. SPRINGS, WEST VA., Nov. 13, 1888.

MR. E. B. WEBSTER,
   CRESCO, IOWA.

Dear Sir:—By a careful study of Natural History for a number of years past, I have been enabled to prepare the following list of birds of Greenbrier Co., West Virginia. In the preparation of this list I have had to rely entirely on my own personal observation, therefore I am alone responsible for any mistakes made. Though incomplete, the list will give a pretty fair idea of the bird-life of this county. I will endeavor to add to it from time to time, as there are probably several species here which have not come beneath my notice. You will find in this list 121 species representing about 30 families. List numbered according to Ridgeway's Nomenclature. Additions and corrections solicited from all. Hoping this will be of some interest to the readers of the HAWKEYE ORNITHOLOGIST and OOLOGIST, I am very respectfully your humble servant, THADDEUS SURBER.

1. *Hylocichla mustelina.* Wood Thrush; "Swamp Robin." Common summer resident; breeds. Arrives first of May; departs in October. Food, insects.

2. *Hylocichla fuscescens.* Wilson's Thrush. Specimens secured; very rare.

5b. *Hylocichla unalascae pallasi.* Hermit Thrush. Common migrant.

7. *Merula migratoria.* American Robin; "Robin Red-Breast." Abundant summer resident; breeds. Arrives in March; departs in November; occasionally a few winter here. Food, insects and worms.

12. *Galeoscoptes carolinensis.* Catbird. Common summer resident; breeds. Arrives first of May; departs last of September. Food, seed, etc.

13. *Harporhynchus rufus.* Brown Thrasher; "Sandy Mockingbird." Common summer resident; breeds. Arrives in April; departs in September. Food, insects mainly.

22. *Sialia sialis.* Bluebird. Abundant; breeds. Arrives in February; departs in November. Food, insects.

27. *Polioptila caerulea.* Blue-gray Gnatcatcher. Rare summer resident; breeds. Arrives in May; departs in September. Insectivorous.

33. *Regulus satrapa.* Golden-crowned Kinglet. Common winter visitantt

36. *Lophophanes bicolor.* Tufted Titmouse; "Sugarbird." Common resident. breeds. Food, insects, nuts, etc.

41. *Parus atricapillus.* Black-capped Chickadee; "Tomtit." Common resident; breeds.

51. *Sitta carolinensis.* White-bellied Nuthatch. Common resident; breeds.

52. *Sitta canadensis.* Red-bellied Nuthatch. Occurs occasionally during winter; rare.

55. *Certhia familiaris rufa.* Brown Creeper. Common during immigrations. Insectivorous.

61. *Thryomaneo bewicki.* Bewick's Wren. Very rare summer resident; breeds.

63. *Troglodytes aedon.* House Wren; "Jenny Wren." Common summer resident; breeds. Arrives first of April; departs in October. Food, insects.

74. *Mniotilta varia.* Black-and-white Creeper. Summer resident; breeds (?) Arrives last of April; departs in October.

93. *Deudroeca aestiva,* Summer Yellow-bird; "Yellowbird." Common summer resident; breeds. Arrives in April; departs in September. Food, insects.

97. *Deudroeca maculosa.* Black-and-yellow Warbler. Common; migrant.

98. *Dendroeca caerulea.* Cerulean Warbler. Rare; migrant.

113a. *Dendroeca palmarum hypochrysea.* Yellow-Redpoll Warbler. Migrant; rare.

115. *Siurus auricapillus.* Golden-crowned Thrush; "Oven bird." Common summer resident; breeds. Arrives in April; departs in October. Food, insects, etc.

120. *Geothlypis philadelphia.* Mourning Warbler. Occasional migrant.

122. *Geothlypis trichas.* Maryland Yellow-throat. Summer resident; breeds.

123. *Icteria virens.* Yellow-breasted Chat. Common summer resident; breeds. Arrives in May; departs last of August. Food, insects, worms, etc.

135. *Vireosylvia olivacea.* Red-eyed Vireo. Common summer resident. breeds. Arrives in April; departs in October. Insectivorous.

139. *Vireosylvia gilva.* Warbling Vireo. Summer resident; breeds. Arrives and departs with *V. olivacea.*

148. *Lanius borealis.* Great Northern Shrikes; "Butcherbird." Specimen secured November 4, 1887.

151. *Ampelis cedrorum.* Cedar Wax-wing; "Cherry-bird" Abundant summer resident; breeds. Arrives first of May; departs in October. Food, insects and fruit.

152. *Progne subis.* Purple Martin. Common summer resident; dreeds. Arrives in April; departs in September. Insectivorous.

154. *Hirundo erythrogastra.* Barn Swallow. Common summer resident; breeds. Arrives in April; departs in September.

157 *Cotile riparia.* Bank Swallow. Common summer resident; breeds. Arrives in April; departs in September.

(*To be continued.*)

THE SCARLET TANAGER.

Pyranga rubra.

Every one should be familiar with the habits as well as the appearance of this elegant bird. His gracefully formed body, clothed in the most brilliant and glowing scarlet, and his wings and tail of jetty black, as he gambols among the thick foliage, presents one of the most lovely and attractive objects which our feathered world can afford. It is widely scattered over the United States during the summer months, seeming to have a decided preference for the deeply shaded woods.

The female presents an entirely different appearance from the male, being olive green above and greenish-yellow below; young resemble females very closely at first and presenting an admixture of yellow, red and black as they advance in age. It is generally supposed that the male (like the Bobolink) changes to the yellowish plumage of the female at the fall moults.

The song resembles that of the Rose-breasted Grosbeak to some extent; they also have a quickly uttered alarm note. Occasionally they may be seen in the neighborhood of a farm house or the outskirts of a village, but for the most part they are very shy. The bright contrast of their plumage with the sombre oak groves which they chiefly frequent renders them an attractive mark to the young sportsman; this, together with the demand for their skins for ornamental purposes, has been rapidly reducing their numbers until now, in most sections of the country, they are almost rare.

The nest is a very loosely woven structure, composed of roots, twigs and bark strips, lined with finer similiar substances, usually placed in the fork of a horizontal limb, and oftentimes so slight that the eggs can be seen readily from below. There are usually four in number, and of a greenish-blue cast; spotted with reddish-brown, usually forming a ring on the larger end.

INSTINCT OR REASON?

CARTHAGE, December 3, 1888.

I have long thought of writing to the O. AND O. some things of interest to all who love our birds. I have for years been a close observer of the many strange vagaries of these, our friends, who are so near us. I have arrived at the conclusion that no rule of conduct with regard to the building of nests or mode of life can be laid down as arbitrary. The observations of one summer will destroy all preconceived notions. There must be something beyond what we call instinct to guide in some of the strange things we see so often. I shall endeavor to give some of my own observations with regard to these things that prove to me that some grains of reason lurk in the small brains of these little busy bodies.

Years ago when, as a boy, I roamed through the woods and fields of Bremer county, Iowa, I gathered many fragments that may now interest the readers of the O. AND O. I well remember the year the Rose-breasted Grosbeaks built their nests in Bremer county. I cannot now give the date, but I know that that year the nests were in the low bushes and thin trees, where no such nests were to be found the year before. The consequence was many of the nests were taken by the omnipresent small boy. The next spring the nests of the Grosbeak were in the elm trees out of reach of any but skillful climbers, of which I never was one, and so saw but few eggs after that. Did instinct or reason teach the bird that a tall tree was a more safe place than a low bush.

Note the case of the Oriole as cited in *St. Nicholas* (The mistake was made of calling it an Orchard Oriole instead of a Baltimore, the nest of the Orchard Oriole being of grass instead of strings and tow like the Baltimore.) The nest was on some small twigs of which one was too slender, allowing the nest to sag to one side. Was it instinct or reason that taught the Oriole to take a string, weave it in one side of the nest and then carry it up and tie it in a knot over a limb. (This nest was found at Spiceland, where I live.)

A few years ago a friend of mine at Spiceland had some nests made to order by furnishing the material, tow, strings and carpet thrums. The Oriole seemed much pleased with the red, green and blue, but after much study chose the gray and brown. Did not reason teach her that the bright colors would reveal the nest to the eyes of boys?

I will give but one more curiosity of the working of the small mind. As I was passing the corner of a street in Waverly some years ago I saw a nest in a small maple tree that attracted my attention. On taking it down I found that a Sparrow had built a nest and laid some eggs; a Cowbird had left one egg in the nest; the Sparrow then built another nest above the first, laid some eggs, and the Cowbird again leaving an egg, she had built the third and in this were eggs of both; then she had given up the task.

These are only a few of the curious things I have seen among the birds in my years of watching. If these are of interest to the readers of the O. AND O., I will at some future time tell of some of the strange songs I have heard of Jay-bird and Magpie.

I remain yours for the birds,   S. L. NOBLE.

NOTES ON THE PASSERES OF FULTON CO., KY.

BY L. O. PINDAR, PRES. Y. O. A.

The *Vireonidae* are represented in Fulton county by the Red-eyed, Philadelphia, Warbling, White-eyed and Bell's Vireos. The last named is rarest; two were seen and one killed July 16, 1887. The Philadelphia and Warbling Vireos are rare fall migrants. The White-eyed is a common fall migrant. None of these have been seen in the spring.

The Red-eyed species is a common summer visitant, arriving about the middle of April.

The Vireo is one of my especial favorites among our feathered friends. Trim, slender and graceful, of modest colors, never forcing itself on our notice as is the case with some of our more brilliant birds, always keeping up its cheerful strain from the early dawn, the sultry noon and through the dusky eve till the stars shine on its sleeping form as it reposes in its delicate nest, keeping warm its eggs in which are wrapped up all its hopes. This bird has always possessed a peculiar attraction for me.

The nest matches the bird. Like those of all the Vireos it is a pensile cup in the forks of a horizontal branch. It is nearer the cup shape than almost any nest built in this locality. The foundation of the nest is usually the fine, dry inner bark of grapevines, a favorite substance with many birds. On the outside it is covered with shreds of a wasp's nest, and lined with fine bits of hay. The above is a description of a nest now before me. This particular nest was rather high for this species, being about thirty feet from the ground, while the usual distance is half that. It was on the end of such a slender limb that no one could have climbed to it, but I secured the empty nest by cutting the limb on which it was hung, with a rifle.

The eggs are pure white with a few dark brown spots, the marking thickest at the larger end. They are usually four in number and measure .80x.60.

The large family *Mniotiltidae* next comes under consideration. The beautiful Maryland Yellow-throat is the one which I have had the most and best chances to study. It may seem strange to pass over such a large and important family so hastily, but I am not going to have the leisure I hoped to have to finish these sketches and hope my readers will pardon me for qeing so cursory.

(*To be continued.*)

EDITORIAL.

With this month's issue, the first number of the second volume, the HAWKEYE appears in a new form. Greater convenience to the reader and a uniform size throughout future volumes, coupled with a desire to make the distinction between the first and second volumes as prominent as possible, have induced us to make the change. We have no apology to offer our readers for our share of the work connected with the volume just completed. The articles have, with but one or two exceptions, been written expressly for the HAWKEYE by the leading ornithological writers of the United States and Canada; nor has the geological department been neglected. In fact, though we have far from reached the goal we yet aim at, we feel that we have fulfilled our every promise and presented the ornithologists of the Central and Western States with a magazine, as frequent letters of encouragement show, they can well take pride.

But with regard to the mechanical execution, variance in size, and irregularity of date of issue, matters which were not under our control and which we could not stand responsible for, we can only look back and say, "It might have been."

Our support has been far better than we expected, fully ample to warrant continuance through coming years and we commence the second volume with the feeling that we can present the bird students of the Western States with more and better reading matter for the money than any other publisher.

Our subscription price will remain the same, 50c in advance; our advertising rates 50c per inch, $5.00 per page, payable cash in advance. When special contract is made otherwise, an advance of 50 per cent is always required. As the printing is now done by contract, all copy must reach us by the first of the month. Yours ——ologically,

E. B. WEBSTER.

THE SCIENTISTS.

The Fulton County (Ill.) Scientific Association held their monthly meeting on the evening of November 29th, at the Normal College Chapel, Lewiston. An appreciative audience of perhaps a hundred and fifty guests greeted them.

H. L. Roberts for Bureau of Zoology reported that he had a frog that had reversed all former precedent by swallowing a snake, a small puff adder. This phenomena was accounted for by a member who said that Prof. Roberts had neglected his frog, let it starve nearly to death, and that it had to swallow the snake or starve; a survival of the fittest.

Rev. George, from Bureau of History, reported that the Nile river for the first time since the days of Joseph had failed to overflow its banks, and it was believed that the Abyssinians from near its source had, as a war measure, diverted its chief tributary into the sea. The President reported that some engineer had made the discovery that the Nile's chief tributary was separated from the Indian Ocean by only a narrow strip of land, through which a canal could easily be dug.

Dr. Strode exhibited some rare eggs. Those of the Limkin, or Crying Bird, from St. John's river, Florida, attracting much attention from their peculiar color and markings.

Prof. T. R. Wilcoxson read the first paper on "Energy" and at its close illustrated his subject with some very pretty and interesting electrical and other experiments.

J. R. Rowlands paper on "An Answer to the Labor Question" was frequently applauded and at its close he was treated to a general handshaking.

H. L. Roberts' paper, "Evolution" was the most truly scientifical paper of the evening and Mr. R. was loudly applauded at its close.

The Fulton Democrat had this to say of this meeting:

"The entertainment—the various papers—deserve greater praise than we care to offer our own people. The truth would sound like exaggeration. But our Lewiston people were afforded a fine treat, and the question of audiences for our scientists is solved, so far as this city is concerned."

W. S. STRODE, Sec'y.

NOTED COLLECTIONS—NO. 1.

BY F. R. STEARNS.

This month I will begin a series of articles on some of the most noted collections in the United States. It will be well to begin with the mammoth collection owned by Mr. Wm. W. Adams, of Mapletown, New York, of whom you have all heard more or less. Although Mr. Adams has been a collector hardly five years, he has succeeded in gathering together a collection of relics which are coveted by all who see them.

The circumstances under which Mr. Adams became a collector are as follows: On the 28th day of February, 1881, he was arranging his books in a new case and found that a partition was unoccupied. So he told his wife that he would go to some woods near town, owned by a man named Hoskins, and see if he could find some Indian relics to fill the unoccupied shelf. He had heard when a boy that this was the site of an Indian burial ground, and after reaching the woods he proceeded to investigate the graves. The first grave he opened contained a fine Turkey head pipe. Then, he says, "I commenced talking Indian and inquiring about Indian relics. I soon found where there were more burying places and, whenever I found time, I would go and dig." The first year and a half he found about 7,500 specimens, which would be considered quite a collection by some, but which forms but a very small part of the present collection. Since then he has made some wonderful finds, of which we have only space to mention a few. Aug. 4th, 1886, he discovered a *cache* in which was found the following: One silver letter seal with crossed arrows and the letters "M. K." body of seal represents dolphin; 8 baldric beads; 5 bird shaped shell ornaments; 2 brass bells; massive shell bead; shell ornament, $2\frac{1}{2}$x$1\frac{1}{4}$x$\frac{1}{2}$. bird-shaped; 400 large colored beads; copper coin, 1650, and 19 Jesuit rings. The lot is valued at about thirty dollars. October 18, 1887, the following lot was found: 935 wampum and bugle beads on a string 294 inches long; three pint brass kettle in perfect condition; iron ax, and a perfect crania.

One of his luckiest finds was made August 15, 1887. This was a wampum belt about 3½ inches wide and 65 inches long, containing over 3,800 olivella shells, and valued at $40. It was found in a grave near Union Springs. N. Y., in company with three bone awls, doubtless the ones used to make it.

Last spring Mr. Adams spent several days searching for relics at East Cayuga, an old town about two miles north of his residence, where he found some wonderful things. One day's hunt brought him 6 kettles, about 2,500 beads and ornaments and a gun. The next day he found a chief's grave from which he obtained the following articles, May 2, 1888: a gun 4 feet, 8 inches long, two iron axes, 3 bars lead, melting ladle, 3 buckhorn implements, steel and flint, 3 arrows with brass points, 2 trigger guards warmer, piece of death paint, piece mica, numerous pieces of wood, iron and flint. 16 tusks, 4 rubbing stones, bone harpoon, 8 baldric beads, 2 gun flints, 6 bullets, 4 bullet moulds, 2 iron harpoons, six knives, 2,500 wampum beads, pipe, 47 pieces gun locks, 3 pair shears, and numerous other things. This was indeed a rare find and so Mr. Adams thought. He dug them all out in about two hours. Mr. Adams also visited the chief's burying place near Union Springs where the relics are all pre-European. On a spot not over forty feet square he found over 15,000 specimens.

For displaying his collection Mr. Adams has devoted a room 16 by 24 feet, which is completely filled. The specimens are each numbered and arranged in cases, each find being kept together as much as possible.

Although Mr. Adams devotes most of his time to the collecting of Indian relics, he also has a considerable number of war relics, old dishes, books, sea curiosities, etc. The collection at the present time numbers 50,000 pieces.

RIDGWAY'S
MANUAL OF N. AM. BIRDS.

By Prof. Robt. Ridgway, Curator of Birds, U. S. Nat. Mus., Washington, D. C.

Royal 8vo, Cloth, Gilt, 631 pages, 464 engravings, $7.50.
Sportsman's edition, bound in leather, $7.50

Contains consc's descriptions of every species of birds known to North America. Profusely illustrated with 464 outline cuts of the generic characters, and a portrait of the late Spencer F. Baird.

The classification, numeration and nomenclature conform strictly with the Check List of North American Birds recently published by the A. O. U. For the benefit of observers along our southern border, a synopsis of all Mexican, Cuban and Bahaman species of each North American genus is given.

THE ANALYTICAL KEYS

Are unlike those previously used for any ornithological work in America, and are models of concieseness and utility. Taken with the accurate outline cuts, giving the bills, claws, etc., no one can fail to use them with absolute certainty of satisfactory results.

Every genus has been worked up exactly as if it were the subject of a special monograph, based on all the material available, and not a single page, or part of a page, as printed, has been previously published in anything like the same form.

Not only are the essential characters of every species and sub-species given, with measurements, but the various plumage of each, depending on sex, age and season, are carefully distinguished. The nest and eggs are concisely described.

No active ornithologist, cologist or sportsman can afford to be without this book, as it will be the

STANDARD AUTHORITY

on North American Birds for many years to come.

E. B. WEBSTER, Cresco, Iowa.

OUR BIRDS IN THEIR HAUNTS.

BY REV. J. H. LANGILLE.

The most readable of all ornithological works, being written in a fresh and original manner and almost entirely from personal observations. It takes up the descriptions and habits of the birds as they appear in eastern North America, in order of the seasons, and being free from the classification of a text book or manual, begins by noting the arrival of the first feathered songsters of the winter, taking up each bird separately, and presenting all in FULL LIFE HISTORIES that are curious and fascinating in the lives of these wonderful creatures.

The Niagara River and St. Clair Flats receive the most attention, though a great deal of information is given on the interesting localities of Nova Scotia and Hudson's Bay.

Migration, instinct, the analogy of nidification, the specialized forms and adaptions of structure in birds is all made readable.

The illustrations, 25 in number, are by that prince of bird artists, EDWIN SHEPPARD of Philadelphia, whose connection with the Smithsonian Institute has given him a world-wide reputation, and assures accuracy.

There is no purer source of recreation than to go abroad and study the nature, habits and songs of the birds: and Mr. Langille has shown us what can be accomplished in that line by a quick eye and inquisitive mind, and that a persistent observer can cultivate an acquaintance with the birds which will prove alike pleasant, instructive and retaining.

IN CLOTH, and on FINE TINTED PAPER, $3.00.

E. B. WEBSTER, Cresco, Iowa.

FREE! FREE!! FREE!!!

My price list of Eggs, Minerals, Shells, Curiosities, etc., and sample copy of "The Old Curiosity Shop," an illustrated monthly journal devoted to the interests of collectors in all branches. E. M. HAIGHT,
311   Box 24, Riverside, Calif.

CLUBBING RATES.

—1889.—

Hawkeye O. and O. (50c) and any of the following publications at annexed price:

	Pub's. Price.	With H.O.
O. AND O., of Boston, Mass.,	$1.00	$1.25
West Am. Scientist, San Diego, Calif., $1.00 and Hoosier Naturalist, Valpariso, Indiana, 50c. together $1.50		.85
Above and Oologist with prem.		1.20
Oologist, Albion, N. Y.	.50	.75
Oologist's Exchange,	.10	.55
Agassiz Companion, Kansas,		
Old Curiosity Shop,	.35	.50
United States Philatelist,	.15	.60

EXCHANGES.

I will give any one of the following for every perfect Indian arrow head sent me labelled viz: Bird's Eggs, Cactus Wren, Western Lark Sparrow, Bullock's Oriole, Tricolored Blackbird, Red-shafted Flicker; Curiosities—Hawk Moth Coccoon, Skate's Egg, Silk Worm Cocoon, two Alligator's teeth, or 3 var. Calif. Bird wings.
          E. M. HAIGHT,
Box 24,   Riverside, Cal.

PROCURE THE PROPER
✢ CIRCUS MOVE ✢
IF YOU EXPECT TO
⇒ Secure Those Bargains ⇐
Advertised in last month's H. O.
Either singles, pairs or sets.
D. MEAD, Cresco, Ia.

~⊰ R. E. Rachford & Son, ⊱~
COLLECTING ✶ NATURALISTS
an wholesale dealers in
BIRD SKINS AND EGGS,
BEAUMONT, TEXAS.

BIRD SKINS AND EGGS
At Reasonable Prices. Send stamp for lists.
J. A. SINGLEY,
      Giddings, Texas.

THOUSAND DOLLAR
COLLECTION FOR $1.00.

A collection has been placed at our disposal and we intend to issue tickets and raffle it off. The collection contains 300 different varieties of American Bird's eggs, equal to one in all about 3000 specimens. A fair share of which are in sets, and series of sets. Lists furnished on application. Six hundred tickets will be issued and sold at $1.00 each. Duplicate of each of the eggs is sold will be placed in a box and when they are all disposed of a drawing will take place; let the last number drawn from the box will entitle the holder of the ticket corresponding with the number to this fine large collection of eggs. Some disinterested person live or two will be appointed to do the drawing which will be conducted fairly and squarely. The collection is worth twice what we will get for it, and advise you to send at once for one or more tickets as only the six hundred will be sold. There is hardly a naturalist in America that will not be willing to invest a dollar or more, thereby standing an equal chance of securing all this vast collection of specimens. Remember somebody will get them awful cheap. Will it be you? Send at once for tickets to

E. B. WEBSTER, Publisher H. O. O.,
          Cresco, Iowa.
Further particulars next month.

EXTRA COPIES.
I desire a few copies of October number of H. O. O. and will gladly pay 7c per copy.
W. RAINE, 6 Walton St.,
      Toronto, Canada.

Contents for February

Birds of Greenbrier Co., W. Va.,　-　-　-　-　-　T. Surber.
Notes on the Passeres of Fulton Co., Ky.,　-　-　-　L. O. Pindar.
Notes from Charleston,　-　-　-　-　-　J. Drayton Ford.
The California Road Runner,　-　-　-　-　-　Amalgam.
Noted Collections—No. 2,　-　-　-　-　-　F. R. Stearns.
Result of Walter Raine's Prize Drawing.
A Letter from W. C. Brownell.

THE HAWKEYE
Ornithologist and Oologist.

E. B. WEBSTER, Editor and Publisher.

The Leading Ornithological Journal of the Western States.

Successor to the "Geologist's Gazette," of Elkader, Iowa. Geological Department a leading feature.

Prominent writers, monthly; illustrated; second volume commenced January 1, 1889.

The HAWKEYE will appear on or about the first of each month.

All books and catalogues sent us will be carefully reviewed.

Papers desiring to suspend can have their lists filled by us at very low rates.

SUBSCRIPTION RATES:	ADVERTISING RATES:
U. S. and Canada, - 50c.	1 page, 1 insertion, - $5.00.
Foreign Countries, - - 65c.	1 col., " - 2.50.
Single copies, - - 5c.	2 in., " - 1.00.
Sample copy free.	1 in., " - .50.

ADDRESS:

E. B. WEBSTER, : : CRESCO, IOWA.

BIRDS OF GREENBRIER CO., WEST VIRGINIA.
(Continued from page 4.)

BY THADDEUS SURBER.

161. *Pyranga rubra.* Scarlet Tanager; "Soldier-bird." Summer resident; rare; breeds. Arrives in May; departs last of October. Food: seeds and insects.

E. S. *Passer domesticus.* English Sparrow. Resident; abundant. Food: grain and insects.

168. *Carpodacus purpureus.* Purple Finch. Occasional migrant.

172. *Loxia curvirostra americana.* American Crossbill. Occasional winter visitant.

181. *Astragalinus tristis.* American Goldfinch; "Flax-bird." Common resident; breeds. Food: insects, etc.

185. *Chrysomitris pinus.* Pine Goldfinch. Occasional winter visitant. Feeds largely among evergreens.

196. *Poæcetes gramineus.* Grass Finch. Common summer resident; breeds.

210. *Spizella montana.* Tree Sparrow. Common winter resident.

211. *Spizella domestica.* Chipping Sparrow, "Chippie." Abundant summer resident; breeds. Arrives first of April.

214. *Spizella pusilla.* Field Sparrow. Common summer resident; breeds. Arrives in April; departs in October.

217. *Junco hyemalis.* Black Snowbird, "Snowbird." Abundant resident, breeds.

231. *Melospiza fasciata.* Song Sparrow, "Vesper Bird." Common summer resident, breeds.

233. *Melospiza palustris.* Swamp Sparrow. Common summer resident, breeds. Arrives in April, departs in October.

235. *Passerella iliaca.* Fox-colored Sparrow. Occasional migrant.

238. *Pipilo erythrophthalmus.* Chewink. Towhee. Common summer resident, breeds. Arrives in April, departs in October. Food: seeds, worms, etc.

242. *Cardinalis virginianus.* Cardinal Grosbeak, "Redbird." Common resident, breeds.

244. *Zamelodia ludoviciana.* Rose-breasted Grosbeak. Occurs during migrations.

248. *Passerina cyanea.* Indigo Bunting, "Indigo-bird." Common summer resident, breeds. Arrives in May, departs in September. Food: insects, seeds, etc.

258. *Molothrus ater.* Cowbird. Summer resident, breeds. Arrives in April, departs in October.

261. *Ayelæus phœniceus.* Red-and-buff-shouldered Blackbird, "Swamp Blackbird." Common summer resident, breeds. Arrives in March, departs in November. Food: insects, worms, grain, etc.

263. *Sturnella magna.* Meadow Lark, "Field Lark." Common summer resident, breeds; occasionally a few winter here. Food: seeds:

270. *Icterus spurius.* Orchard Oriole. Summer resident, breeds.

271. *Icterus galbula.* Baltimore Oriole, "Hang-Nest," 'Gold-finch." Common summer resident, breeds. Arrives last of April, departs in September.

278. *Quiscalus purpureus.* Purple Grackle, Abundant summer resident, breeds. Food: young birds, grains, etc.

280. *Corvus corax carnivorous.* American Raven. Rare resident; breeds; formerly common.

282. *Corvus frugivorus.* Common Crow. Abundant resident; breeds.

289. *Cyanocitta cristata.* Blue Jay; "Jaybird." Common resident; breeds. Food: nuts, seeds, etc.

304. *Tyrannus carolinensis.* Kingbird, "Bee Martin." Common summer resident; breeds. Arrives last of April; departs in September. Insectivorous.

315. *Myiarchus crinitus.* Great Crested Flycatcher. Summer resident; breeds.

312. *Sayornis fuscus.* Phœbe Bird: Pewee. Common summer resident; breeds. Arrives in March; departs in Nov.

320. *Contopus vireus.* Wood Pewee. Occurs as a migrant.

322. *Empidonax flaviventris.* Yellow-bellied Flycatcher. Occurs during migration.

326. *Empidonax minimus.* Least Flycatcher. Common summer resident; breeds. Arrives in April, departs in Sept.

335. *Trochilus colubris.* Ruby-throated Hummingbird. Common summer resident; breeds. Arrives first of May, departs in September. Food: mainly insects.

351. *Chætura pelasgica.* Chimney Swift. Common summer resident; breeds. Arrives last of April, departs in September. Insectivorous.

354. *Caprimulgus vociferus.* Whip-poor-will. Summer resident; rare; breeds.

357. *Chordeiles popetue.* Night Hawk; "Bull-bat." Abundant summer resident; breeds.

[TO BE CONTINUED.]

NOTES ON THE PASSERES OF FULTON COUNTY, KENTUCKY.

(Continued from page 8.)

BY L. O. PINDAR.

The Maryland Yellow-throat, or Yellow-throated Ground Warbler, (*Geothlypis trichas*) is a common summer resident, arriving early in May.

A field covered with a thick growth of iron weeds is a favorite place for them and as you walk through the fields every now and then you see one thrust his head out of a thick clump and peer anxiously at you. But if you think you have found a nest you are mistaken. The nest is not so easily found. It is most carefully hidden, and he who finds it must be possessed of a good stock of patience, which, unfortunately perhaps, I haven't. The oologist will have many a long search, most likely, before he at last finds the nest, built of grasses and placed at the foot of a bush or tuft of grass, although Mr. W. Brewster found one nest two feet high in a juniper bush June 3d, 1875.

The eggs are white with spots of lilac, purple and light brownish shades, generally four in number and measure .70x.55. Pure white eggs are sometimes though rarely found.

The family *Troglodyticæ* includes the various Thrashers, Wrens, etc. First on the list is the far famed Mockingbird, "Prince of Song;" the rival, probably the superior from some accounts, of the wondrous musician, the Nightingale.

THE MOCKINGBIRD

is a resident, although much more common in summer than winter. He is very quiet in the winter months, but the warmth of spring soon thaws out the channels of song hidden in the plain drab throat.

I advise all admirers of the Mockingbird to read Maurice Thompson's charming little book "By Ways and Bird Notes." It contains a long chapter on the habits of this bird and much other interesting and instructive reading.

It is said that the Mockingbird can be taught to whistle a tune. And I suppose it could be easily done. Have any of the readers of the H. O. AND O. anything to offer on this subject?

I read Mr. Gibb's article on the "Foot Movements of Birds"

with great interest. Would like to state here that I have several times seen the Mockingbird walking on the ground, advancing first one foot and then the other, just like a Crow or other walking bird.

The Mockingbird builds a strong, substantial nest of small sticks, twigs etc., lined with dried grass and occasionally horsehair. The usual position is in an osage or other thorny tree, at a height varying from three to ten feet. It is occasionally placed on a stump covered with brush, but always in a place rather difficult of access from thorns, etc. The nest being bulky is easily found, and so many young ones are taken from the nest every year that I wonder any are left.

The eggs are four in number, greenish blue with large spots of dirty brown, chocolate and purple. They measure 1.00x.75.

NOTES FROM CHARLESTON.

BY J. DRAYTON FORD.

I have read with considerable interest the many interesting articles on birds in the H. O. AND O., and noticed that very few of them came from this State.

Among our Summer visitors is the Yellow-billed Cuckoo (*Coccyzus americanus*) the prettiest and the laziest of all the *Cuculidæ* family.

In the Spring of 1885 I found a nest of this bird at Summerville, S. C., containing two eggs. I took one and the next morning two more were there; again I took one and next day it still contained two. This was kept up until the bird had laid seven eggs, when she evidently became tired of her unprofitable laying and abandoned the nest, leaving me in full possession. It was then that I noticed that in the first egg laid, and which she had sat on during the seven days, incubation was considerably advanced. The variation in the size of these eggs was very considerable; the first being the smallest and the last the largest egg laid. Some of them were of a clear blue color, while others were covered with a white calcareous deposit. Average size about 1.28x.90.

The birds are very slovenly inclined, and have the peculiar habit of uttering their loud "Chow-Chow's" or "Coo-Coo's" while sitting on the nest, thus making it not a difficult task for the collector to find it. The nest, if so it can be called, is a very slight structure of dead sticks loosely laid to-gether with a little green moss in the center, and so frail that a brisk rain or sharp wind will overturn the whole affair.

They have three striking features, viz.: a snow-white breast, a long, graceful tail sloping downward, and a sharp, snake-like head, in all, giving it the appearance of a very handsome bird.

It is a very cowardly bird, and seems to be a particular enemy of the Blue-grey Nuthatch (*Polioptila cœrulea.*) I have often seen a pair of these tiny little birds chasing a pair of the Cuckoo's around the tree-tops and punishing them severely in spite of their diminutive size.

The Rain Crow, as it is commonly called, arrives here in May, and spends the Summer with us.

THE CALIFORNIA ROAD RUNNER.

BY AMALGAM.

This strange and rare bird, peculiar to California and some portions of Mexico, is sometimes called the Ground Cuckoo, to which family it belongs. At first sight it might be supposed to be a new kind of pheasant, so striking is the resemblance in color and pattern of the plumage to that genus; but upon closer examination it is soon discovered to be unlike it in every particular. Owing to its exceeding shyness and uncommon scarcity, there is probably less known about this singular bird than almost any other. The late Mr. Grayson, a loving student of ornithology, succeeded in catching, unobserved, the expression of eye and attitude of this bird just when preparing to spring, and the sketch shown me was the finest I have ever seen.

The following are from the late Mr. Grayson's notes:

"So far as I am acquainted, the Road Runner, or as it is called in Spanish, *Curier del Camini* or *Prsano*, has not been described by any ornithologist. It is a distinct and isolated species from all other birds, roaming over the barren plains and hills in search of lizards, snakes and other reptiles up on which it preys. It is almost always seen upon the ground, seldom in trees, unless pursued very closely, when it has been seen to spring from the ground to the branches, a height of from ten to fifteen feet, in a single bound; but it prefers running along a road or path, from which habit it derives its name.

When discovered it instantly runs off, with remarkable fleetness, to the nearest thicket or hill, where it generally escapes its pursuers, either by hiding or in sailing from one hill to another. It is very quick in its motions—active and vigilant; indeed its remarkable swiftness enables it to outstrip a horse.

The most remarkable feature about it is its feet, these being more like the feet of clinging birds, such as the Woodpecker or Parrot, having two toes before and two behind, armed with sharp claws. Its legs are strong and muscular, making it well adapted to running.

Its plumage is rather coarse and rough, of a dusky hue, marked with white and brownish specks on the neck and upper parts, while underneath it is of a dirty white. Its tail is long; the bill strong and slightly curved; eye of greyish brown, the pupil encircled by a light colored ring. A bare space extends from the eye to the back of the neck, of a pale bluish color, tinged with red. The body is about twenty-three inches in length from tip of bill to tip of tail, the tail being eleven and one-quarter, and the bill two and one-half inches long."

I have frequently met this bird in my travels over the country, and have never seen it in company with any bird, either of its own or any other kind. It is excessively shy and solitary, inhabiting the wildest and most unfrequented places.

It has no song to cheer its solitude. At times it utters a harsh note, not unlike the sudden twirl of a watchman's rattle.

It is exceedingly ravenous, and, like all birds of that class, has a disagreeable odor; and should be placed in the order of rapacious birds.

NOTED COLLECTIONS—NO. 2.

BY. F. R. STEARNS.

Another noted collection of Indian and Mound relics is that owned by Mr. G. U. Duer, of Millersburg, Ohio. His collection is finely displayed in a large, well-lighted room which is especially adapted to that purpose.

Mr. Duer pays special attention to displaying his collection to the best advantage, and he has met with great success in this line. His Indian implements, such as axes, celts, drills, spearheads, pestles, mortars, scrapers, pipes, ornaments and all rare pieces are displayed on a table with steps five inches high and twelve inches deep. By means of this arrangement the specimens are made to show off to the best advantage. Instead of having his arrowheads thrown together in a pile or in boxes, Mr. Duer has them neatly arranged in rows on long tables made especially for that purpose. In this way, what would otherwise form an unimportant part of his collection, is made to assume a front place and attract the eye of the visitor sooner than any other table in his cabinet.

In another part of Mr. Duer's cabinet is found a table containing his fine collection of minerals, and still another containing a fine assortment of miscellaneous curiosities. Space forbids a detailed enumeration of all the rare and curious objects to be found on this latter, but it contains nearly anything from a shark's or alligator's tooth to the old family Bible 200 years old (his great great grandmother's) or a six-shooter carried in the Mexican war.

I might continue to name a hundred or more of rare and valuable mementoes, such as autographs of great men, old coins and papers, war relics, etc., but as this would hardly be interesting to the readers of the H. O. AND O., I will desist.

RESULT OF WALTER RAINE'S (TORONTO, CANADA) PRIZE DRAWING OF JANUARY 11, 1889.

1st Prize, set of 2 Golden Eagles, No. 16, Mr. Gregory, New Haven.
2nd Prize, set of 2 Bald Eagles, No. 8, Mr. Sharp, Taunton.
3d Prize, set of 2 Iceland Gyrfalcon, No. 18, Wm. Woodruff, Montreal.
4th Prize, set of 2 Gray Sea Eagles, No. 14, Mr. S. Rand, Troy.
5th Prize, set of two Whistling Swan, No. 29, Mr. F. Lattin, Albion.
6th Prize, set of 2 Glancous Gull, No. 15, Mr. F. Harris, La Crescent.

PRIZES WON BY YOUNG OOLOGISTS.

1st Prize, an egg of Golden Eagle, No. M. 13, Mr. Rodey.
2d Prize, an egg of Bald Eagle, No. E 5, Mr. Rand.
3rd Prize, an egg of Gray Sea Eagle, No. N. 14, Mr. Shultes, of Berne, N. Y.
4th Prize, set of four Willow Ptarmigan, No. L. 12, Mr H. Long, Ohio.

PLYMOUTH, MICH., JAN. 1, '89.

PUBLISHER H. O. AND O.,

Dear Sir:—I noticed in the last issue of your paper some very depreciating letters against R. M. Gibbs, Kalamazoo, Mich.

Some time ago I sent said Gibbs some $16.00 worth of birds' eggs. He was to send me in return a pocket case of surgical instruments. He had previous to this sent me a scalpel supposed to belong to the case, showing style of handles of instruments, etc. It came about that he began to find fault with the eggs as soon as he got possession of them, and said he could not send the instruments for them. I then asked him to return the eggs and sent him back the scalpel.

I have written him several letters since sending scalpel, to which he pays no attention. I guess I am out about $16.00 in eggs. So you see he is an all-around cheat and scoundrel.

Yours truly,
W. C. BROWNELL.

MONTHLY BULLETIN
—OF—
BIRD SKINS
PLACED IN OUR HANDS
FOR SALE ON COMMISSION.

FEBRUARY.

All specimens of first quality (2d col. figures) guaranteed to be well prepared, of good plumage and labeled. Specimens will be carefully packed, but no risks are taken.

No.	Species		
69	Forster's Tern,	$ .25	.50
131	Hooded Merganser, m. ju.		.50
132	Mallard, m.,	.75	1.00
140	Blue-winged Teal,	.75	1.25
214	Sora Rail,	.30	.50
263	Spotted Sandpiper,	.20	.25
289b	**Texan Quail**,		.50
305	Prairie Hen,	1.00	
394	Downy Woodpecker,	.15	.20
433	Rufous Hummer, fm.	.25	
456	Phœbe,	.15	.20
461	Wood Pewee,	.15	.20
474	Horned Lark,	.15	
477	**Blue Jay**,	.10	**.20**
488	**Am. Crow**,	.25	**.50**
494	Bobolink, m.	.10	
498	Red-winged Blackbird,		.10
	English Sparrow,		.10
567	Slate-colored Junco,	.10	.15
595	Rose-breasted Grosbeak, m.,		.15
611	Purple Martin,		.15
652	Yellow Warbler,		.10
735	Chickadee,	.10	.15

Remittances must always be made by postal note or money order. Large specimens will be sent by express. Those under eight inches in length will be sent postpaid.

ADDRESS:
E. B. WEBSTER, : : CRESCO, IOWA.

WINKLEY.

I have gone over my large stock of Am. Birds' Eggs, and carefully selected several fine series of 100 SPECIES and specimens each. Figure it up, then look at our price, $12.50 NET, each.

They are not the most common varieties, of course not the rarest. Each egg is generally for 15 to 75 cents. They are all first class with full data for each.

We selected these because they are typical of many other species, uniformity of size, great diversity in color and markings and the kinds most in demand.

Besides data, each species will be described in an accompanying note book--description of bird, food, habitat, range, etc., author's description of egg, species, similar measurements, notes on balance of set, etc.

Satisfaction guaranteed; sent to known parties on approval. Will sell on installments: 50 species, $4; 25 for $1.50—same terms. 200, 300 and 600 species carefully selected, first-class, put up to order.

Advanced collectors should write to us for special offers. Are constantly receiving rare species, many not catalogued, which are first offered to preferred customers. Monthly lists to all who apply.

W. H. WINKLEY,
Clearfield, - - - Iowa.

R. E. Rochford & Son,
COLLECTING * NATURALISTS
and wholesale dealers in
BIRD SKINS AND EGGS,
BEAUMONT, TEXAS.

BIRD SKINS AND EGGS

At Reasonable Prices. Send stamp for lists.
J. A. SINGLEY,
Giddings, Texas.

THOUSAND DOLLAR COLLECTION FOR $1.00.

A collection has been placed at our disposal and we intend to issue tickets and raffle it off. The collection contains 300 different varieties of American Birds' Eggs, comprising in all about 3000 specimens, a fair share of which are in sets and series of sets. Lists furnished on application. Six hundred numbered tickets will be issued and sold at $1.00 each. Duplicate of each ticket as it is sold will be placed in a box and when they are all disposed of a drawing will take place and the last number drawn from the box will entitle the holder of the ticket corresponding with the number to this fine large collection of eggs. Some disinterested responsible person will be appointed to do the drawing which will be conducted fairly and squarely. The collection is worth twice what we will get for it, and advise you to send at once for one or more tickets as only the six hundred will be sold. There is hardly a naturalist in America that will not be willing to invest a dollar or more, thereby standing an equal chance of securing all this vast collection of specimens. Remember somebody will get them awful cheap. Will it be you? Send at once for tickets to

E. B. WEBSTER, Publisher H. O. O.,
Cresco, Iowa.

FREE! FREE!! FREE!!!

My price list of Eggs, Minerals, Shells, Curiosities, etc., and sample copy of "The Old Curiosity Shop," an illustrated monthly journal devoted to the interests of collectors in all branches.
E. M. HAIGHT,
Box 24, Riverside, Calif.

⇒PRIZE DRAWING.⇐

Everyone who subscribes for the COLLECTING SCIENTIST AND EXCHANGER will receive a ticket of chance for drawing one of the following: Egg of Richardson's Owl, Hollow Quartz, one year's subscription to this magazine, one year's sub. to my paper. Price of paper one year, 25 cents, with 50 cents worth of premiums. A. DINGS.
Hunters Land, N. Y.

IT PAYS

To advertise in the 'NATURALISTS' COMPANION," formerly the 'AGASSIZ COMPANION' established 1880.

For the coming year it will contain 20 neatly printed pages, finely illustrated, on first-class paper, etc.

It will positively be the best magazine of its class published.

If you want to see a copy of this excellent magazine send your name, together with the names of five of your brother collectors and you will receive a copy. Address:

PLANK & IRELAND, Pubs.,
Kansas City, Kansas.

N. B. Job Printing by mail a specialty. Send for prices.

I AM GOING INTO THE MOUNTAINS

Collecting Bird Skins and shall soon have some fine ones for sale. Send stamp for list.

CHAS. H. MARSH,
Dulzura, Cal.

CHEAPER YET,

Horned Lark, 10; Burrowing Owl 12; Road Runner, 20; Long-eared Owl, 25; Ruffed Grouse, 8; Am. Coot, 5; California Quail, 8; Am. Barn Owl, 30; Herring Gull, 5; Mallard, 2½; Blue-winged Teal, 30; Thick-billed Grebe, 5; White-rumped Shrike, 10, Rose-breasted Grosbeak, 5; Baltimore Oriole, 5; Western Meadow Lark, 5; Meadow Lark, 5 cents.

Eggs FIRST CLASS All with data. Orders under 25 cents declined.

F. D. MEAD, Cresco, Iowa

H. H. FIELD.   E. C. GREENWOOD.

FIELD & GREENWOOD,

BROWNSVILLE, CAMERON CO., TEXAS

Mr. Greenwood of this firm, who is well known as a naturalist and taxidermist, will give special attention to the collection for scientifical purposes, of all birds, beasts, reptiles and insects native to the interior and border of Mexico, and will furnish careful data in regard to same when desired.

Correspondence respectfully solicited.

FIELD & GREENWOOD.

THE SCIENTIST,

A Monthly Magazine for Naturalists.

50 cents a year, Sample free.

Advertising rates on application.

I. C. GREENE, Pub.,
Fitchburg, Mass.

---1889.---

CLUBBING RATES.

Hawkeye O. and O. (50c) and any of the following publications at annexed price:

	Pub's. Price.	With H. O.
O. and O., of Boston, Mass.,	$1.00	$1 25
West Am. Scientist,	1.00	.85
Oologist, Albion, N. Y.	.50	.75
Old Curiosity Shop,	.50	.80
Naturalist's Companion,	.50	.70

THE GARNER,

Of London, the official organ of the P. N. S., has a rapidly increasing circulation among science workers and lovers of Nature the world over. Annual subscription, post free, monthly, 2s. 6d. Vols. I, II and III, bound in cloth, 3s. 6d ea.

London, Eng., W. E. Bowers, 25 Wansey st., Walworth-road, S. E.

And thisite (cross-shaped crystal) for each Trilobite sent me, or for eight cents in stamps.   A. B. MORRILL,
Lancaster, Mass.

Entered at the Cresco Post Office as Second-class mail matter.

CONTENTS FOR MARCH.

Lay of the Whip-poor-will, - - - - - - Wm. L. Kells.
Notes on the Passeres of Fulton Co., Kentucky, - L. O. Pindar.
Nesting of the Maryland Yellow-throat in Southwestern Pennsylvania,
J. Warren Jacobs.
Birds of Greenbrier Co., West Virginia, - - - - T. Surber.
Noted Collections—No. 3, - - - - - F. R. Stearns.
The Hawkeye Ornithological Club.

THE HAWKEYE
Ornithologist and Oologist.
E. B. WEBSTER, Editor and Publisher.

The Leading Ornithological Journal of the Western States.

Successor to the "Geologist's Gazette," of Elkader, Iowa. Geological Department a leading feature.

Prominent writers, monthly; illustrated; second volume commenced January 1, 1889.

The HAWKEYE will appear on or about the first of each month.

All books and catalogues sent us will be carefully reviewed.

Papers desiring to suspend can have their lists filled by us at very low rates.

SUBSCRIPTION RATES:
U. S. and Canada, 50c.
Foreign Countries, - - 65c.
Single copies, - - 5c.
Sample copy free.

ADVERTISING RATES:
1 page, 1 insertion, - $3.00
1 col., " - - 2.50
2 in., " - - 1.00
1 in., " - - .50

LAY OF THE WHIP-POOR-WILL.

BY WM. L. KELLS.

In shady woods, by rippling brooks,
  I often love to wander;
And o'er the leaves of Nature's books,
  In solitude to ponder;
And often, too, at eve I sit
  When all around is still,
And hear its cheerless notes repeatt,
  The noisy Whip-poor-will.

By day this bird in silence sits,
  But when the light grows dim,
True to the call of Nature's voice,
  He sings his wild-wood hymn.
When most of all the feathered race
  In woods and fields are still,
Then, in the lonely sombre woods
  Is heard the Whip-poor-will.

Soon as the solar orb of day
  Is gone from human sight,
And coursing on her trackless way
  Appears the Queen of Night,
Beneath the maple's graceful shade,
  That grows on plain or hill,
Or where the cedar forms a glade,
  Starts up the Whip-poor-will.

And then, for many a lonely hour,
  While Night its mourning robe
Unfolds upon departed day,
  And follows 'round the Globe,
When men of toil in sleep do rest,
  And Summer sounds are still,
Near where his consort has her nest,
  Calls loud the Whip-poor-will.

The Indian, startled by the sound,
  Awhile in terror stands;
Perhaps it is his father's shade
  Come back from Spirit Land,
Lamenting for the hunting grounds
  Where once o'er plain and hill,
He used to take his daily rounds,
  Free as the Whip-poor-will.

But now, alas, another race
  Possess his ancient lands,
And he, downtrodden and oppressed,
  "No more his chief commands,"
What wonder, then, he should lament
  For all his race's ill,
And fear the spirit of the dead
  Was in the Whip-poor-will.

NOTES ON THE PASSERES OF FULTON COUNTY, KENTUCKY.

(Continued from page 17.)

BY L. O. PINDAR.

I have chosen the Tufted Titmouse as the representative bird of the family *Paridæ*, in this article. It is a common resident here, seen oftener in the winter, as it then gathers around the houses in search of food. In the Spring it takes to the deep woods to rear its young, and we see very few until in August, when they begin to come back to the orchards in search of the insects found there, which constitute the chief part of their bill of fare. Insects, however, do not form its entire diet, for I dissected one in June, 1886, whose stomach contained seeds, besides the remains of many unfortunate insects. And in January, the same year, I caught two in a trap baited with bread. I also caught a Chickadee. In fact, almost any thing one can say of the Tufted Titmouse is equally true of either the Black-capped or Carolina Chickadee (known as Crickadoo by some boys,) both of which are found here, the latter being most common. The nest is composed of grass, fine leaves, etc., and placed in a cavity in a tree, usually a natural cavity, sometimes excavated by the bird. The usual height of the nest is from ten to twenty feet. I know, however, of one in a deserted Downy Woodpecker's hole, at least fifty feet high, in a beech tree. The eggs are white, speckled with lilac and red, particularly at the larger end. Davie gives the measurement as .72x.54. The number of eggs is given by various writers as from five up to eight or even ten. A set may consist of less, however, for I found a nest May 12, 1888, containing four young about half fledged.

I will take the Wood Thrush and Bluebird from the last family on the list, the *Turdidæ*.

The Wood Thrush is a common summer visitant, arriving early in March. It is essentially a bird of the woods, frequenting especially a grove of trees through which a small stream runs, and is generally very common along the sloughs and bayous that intersect the bottoms. After listening to the delicious music to which this bird treats us in the cool of the morning, we would expect to find it building a very delicate and artistic nest. Such, however, is not the case. The nest is made of mud, covered with a few dry leaves and lined with fine twigs and perhaps a little dry grass. The average height is from ten to fifteen feet, but I have seen them at distances from the ground varying from eight to thirty feet. The same nest is often used twice. One nest was built and used in 1885, left empty in 1886, and May 11, 1887, I took a set of four fresh eggs from it. They probably raise two broods, as I found a nest containing one fresh egg, June 4, 1888, and the usual time for fresh sets is early in May. The eggs are four in number, deep blue, and measure 1.00x.75.

The Bluebird is a resident, and therefore cannot be called, in this climate, a "harbinger of Spring," as it was while I was living in Ohio, more than seven years ago. I never see a collection of eggs without thinking of this bird, for my first prize in the oological line was a set of five fresh eggs of this bird, taken one lovely afternoon early in May, 1886. This was rather late for fresh eggs, for I have seen young birds full grown as early at least as May 13, and took a set of five well inculated eggs April 28, 1887. These last were pure white, and the only set of white eggs I have seen. Also found a nest containing four young birds April 25, 1887. I do not suppose there is any one who does not know how and where the Bluebird builds. Surely the nest of grass, leaves, hay, etc., placed in a hole in a tree, stump or post, is familiar to all. The eggs are four or five in number, normally pale blue, sometimes white, as stated above, and measure .80x.60. These eggs in color form a notable exception to the general rule that the eggs of all "hole-breeders" are white. Perhaps, years hence, if the decrees of fashion and the omnipresent desire for slaughter have not swept the birds from the earth, and the student of ornithology does not have to study from skins collected to-day, the collector will, in writing up his notes, record as a rarity the set of blue eggs he has found. Who knows?

But, my readers, if you love the birds you study, as a naturalist should, if you really enjoy the bursts of melody that float through the forest aisles, if you wish the students of your favorite study in years to come, to love and enjoy them too, set your face against the reckless slughater going on from day to day. Be contented with fewer skins, with fewer eggs. I have no collection. I had a small one of eggs, but I gave it up, and I learn more now than then, for I can give to the birds themselves the time I spent in preparing specimens. Watch the birds build their nests, learn the materials they use in its construction, bend over the nest gently and note the number and color of the eggs, and then retire and let them rear their brood in peace; and when the Summer is over, and you see the young birds joyfully start with the old ones for the Sunny South, you will be thankful that on your account there is not one bird less.

NESTING OF THE MARYLAND YELLOW-THROAT IN SOUTHWESTERN PENNSYLVANIA.

BY J. WARREN JACOBS, WAYNESBURG, PA.

The Maryland Yellow-throat (*G. trichas*) is a common Summer resident here. Arriving early in May, he makes his presence known by his clear, musical notes, which ring from the brier, gulch and thicket. At this time of the season I am searching the wood and field in quest of the treasures of our feathered friends, and as I stroll along I am ever cheered by his lively song.

About the twentieth of the month quite a number of pairs are at nest building. The materials used seem to vary with the location. I have found the nests made of leaves with scarcely any lining, and some made of a mixture of leaves, hair, grass, moss, etc., and others made almost wholly of dry grass.

The number of eggs laid ranges from four to five. When the nest contains eggs of the Cowbird, the set of Yellow-throat's is usually incomplete, there being but two or three laid.

As the breeding habits are well known by most naturalists, and as the eggs vary but little in size, shape and coloration, I will describe but one set, which was taken by the writer the past season, 1888.

On May 22d I was out collecting, and as I was passing a clump of alders in a low, swampy place, I saw a Yellow-throat glide from the midst and disappear in the thicket. Knowing this to be a peculiar habit when an intruder is about, I made an examination of the bushes and found the nest, which contained but one egg. As it was but a few hundred yards from home I went my way, knowing there would be, in a few days, a nice set of eggs, if some small boy did not make a discovery. On the twenty-sixth I went back to collect the eggs, and as I approached, the female noiselessly disappeared as before. The nest contained four beautiful eggs of the Yellow-throat and one of the Cowbird, which had probably been laid after the foster bird had deposited her full complement.

The coloration is pure white, spotted as follows:

No. 1 has numerous spots and dots of black and umber brown seated on the larger end, and over the entire surface are distributed blotches of faint lilac. Measurement, .69x.53.

No. 2 resembles No. 1, but is not so boldly marked. Measurement, .66x.52.

The spots on No. 3 form a ring around the larger end. The black spots are entirely wanting. Measurement, .70x.53.

No. 4 is marked much like No. 2, and in addition has numerous black and umber blotches scattered over the entire shell. Measurement, .68x.51.

The nest was made of leaves, strips of weed stalks, bark, grass, etc., lined with fine grass and a small amount of hair, and was placed between two alders, four inches from the ground. Measures five by two and one-half inches outside.

BIRDS OF GREENBRIER CO., WEST VIRGINIA.
(Continued from page 15.)

BY T. SURBER.

360. *Picus villosus.* Hairy Woodpecker. Common resident; breeds.
361. *Picus pubescens.* Downy Woodpecker; "Sap Sucker." Common resident; breeds.
369. *Sphyrapicus varius.* Yellow-bellied Woodpecker. Occurs during fall and early spring as a migrant. Food: inner bark of trees.
371. *Hylotomus pileatus.* Pileated Woodpecker; "Log cock." Common resident; breeds.
375. *Melauerpes erythrocephalus.* Red-headed Woodpecker. Summer resident; breeds.
378. *Colaptes auratus.* Yellow-shafted Flicker; "Flicker;" "Yellow-hammer." Abundant summer resident; breeds. Arrives in April; departs in October.
382. *Ceryle alcyon.* Belted Kingfisher. Common in summer, occasionally a few in winter; breeds.
387. *Coccyzus americanus.* Yellow-billed Cuckoo; "Rain Crow." Summer resident; breeds. Arrives in May, departs in September.
388. *Coccyzus erythrophthalmus.* Black-billed Cuckoo. Same as *C. americanus.*
397. *Strix nebulosa.* Barred Owl. Rare resident; breeds. This species is very frequently called "Hoot Owl," a name more commonly applied to *B. virginianus.*
402. *Scops asio.* Little Screech Owl. Common resident; breeds. Food: small birds, mice, etc.
405. *Bubo virginianus.* Great Horned Owl. Resident; rare; breeds. Food: rabbits, etc.

417. *Aesalon columbarius.* Pigeon Hawk. Occurs occasionally; very rare.

420. *Tinnunculus spaverius.* Sparrow Hawk. Common resident; breeds.

425. *Pandion haliœtus carolinensis.* Am. Osprey; Fish Hawk. Occurs regularly.

430. *Circus hudsonius.* Marsh Hawk. Very rare; specimen secured 1880.

431. *Accipiter cooperi.* Cooper's Hawk; "Chicken Hawk." Common resident; breeds.

432. *Accipiter fuscus.* Sharp-shinned Hawk; "Pigeon Hawk." Common resident; breeds.

436. *Buteo borealis.* Red-tailed Hawk; "Chicken-Hawk;" "Squirrel Hawk." Abundant resident; breeds. Food: squirrels, poultry, etc.

439. *Buteo lineatus.* Red-shouldered Hawk. Occasional winter visitant.

448. *Archibuteo lagopus sancti-johannis.* Am. Rough-legged Hawk; "Black Hawk." Occurs occasiomally; very rare.

451. *Haliœetui leucocephalus.* Bald Eagle; Gray Eagle. Occurs during spring and autumn; rare.

454. *Cathartes aura.* Turkey Buzzard. Common summer resident; breeds. Arrives in March. Food: carrion.

459. *Ectopistes migratoria.* Passenger Pigeon; "Wild Pigeon." Rare; formerly occurred in immense numbers. Food: berrries, acorns, etc.

460. *Zenaidura carolinensis.* Mourning Dove; "Turtle Dove." Abundant summer resident; breeds. Arrives in February; departs in November. Food: grains, etc.

470a. *Meleagris gallopavo americana.* Wild Turkey. Common resident, breeds.

473. *Bonasa umbellus.* Ruffed Grouse; "Pheasant." Abundant resident; breeds.

487. *Ardea herodias.* Great Blue Heron; "Sandhill Crane." Occurs as a migrant.
489. *Herodias alba egretta.* American Egret; "White Crane." Two specimens secured Spring of 1878.
494. *Butorides virescens.* Green Heron; ,'Shikepoke;" "Fly-up-the-creek." Common summer resident; breeds. Arrives in April; departs in September. Food: fish, frogs, etc.
497. *Botaurus lentiginosus.* American Bittern. Specimen secured May 3d, 1888.
516. *Oxyechus voctferus.* Kildeer; "Kildee." Occurs regularly as a migrant.
525. *Philohela minor.* American Woodcock. Common; breeds.
526a. *Gallinago media wilsoni.* Wilson's Snipe; "Jack Snipe." Very rare. Breeds. (?)
557. *Tringoides macularius.* Spotted Sandpiper; "Tip-up," "Kildee." Common summer resident, breeds. Arrives in April, departs in October.
588. *Olor americana.* Whistling Swan. Two specimens cought by some lumbermen on Greenbrier River in October, 1876.
594. *Bernicla canadensis.* Canada Goose, "Wild Goose." Occurs during migration, common.
601. *Anas boscas.* Mallard. Winter resident, common.
602. *Anas obscura.* Black Mallard. Migrant, rare.
609. *Querquedula discors.* Blue-winged Teal. Common migrant.
612. *Nettion carolinensis.* Green-winged Teal. Common spring and autumn migrant.
613. *Aix sponsa.* Wood Duck: Summer Duck. Common Summer resident, breeds.
616. *Fulix collaris.* Ring-billed Blackhead. Very rare migrant.
621. *Clangula albeola.* Butterball: Buffle-head. Abundant migrant.

635. *Mergus merganser.* Am. Sheldrake; "Fish Duck." Common migrant.
673. *Larus atricilla.* Laughing Gull. Common migrant.
735. *Podylymbus podiceps.* Thick-billed Grebe; "Die-dapper." Formerly very common. Observed here Oct. 14, 1888, for the first time in about five years. Migrant.
736. *Colymbus torquatus.* Loon. Occurs occasionally as a migrant.

To the foregoing list may be added the following rare visitors:
60. *T. ludovicianus.* Carolina Wren. Specimens secured.
98. *D. cærulea.* Cerulean Warbler. Nest containing one young found in June, 1888.
550. *R. americanus.* Solitary Sandpiper. Specimen secured.
580. *F. americana.* Coot. Male shot Oct. 18, 1888.

NOTED COLLECTIONS—NO. 3.

BY F. R. STEARNS.

A fine collection of birds and their eggs is that owned by Charles F. Carr, of Madison, Wisconsin. Mr. Carr has made a particular study of the positions of birds in life, and, in consequence, his mounted birds are set up in life-like positions and present a much more pleasing appearance than the specimens handled by the majority of collectors. His collection of birds, both mounted specimens and skins, numbers over one thousand. Although not paying so much attention to oology, he has a collection of over two hundred fine sets of eggs. Among the birds which are rarely found in the North, the following will be found in his collection: Chestnut-bellied Scaled Partridge, Audubon's Oriole and the Texas Cardinal. He has also a fine lot of Southern Terns, Eagles of North America and specimens of Finches and Sparrows which are not often seen in collections. Mr. Carr has a way of labelling his skins which is peculiar to himself.

He keeps a journal in which is kept a duplicate of each label. The check list number is not used except for exchanging. Under the journal registry of the specimens he writes any miscellaneous remarks and notes concerning it—his field notes, etc. If it is exchanged, the name of the person to whom it is exchanged is added, or if received in exchange, the name of the person from whom it is received is added. Thus a full data of each skin is kept.

His sets of eggs are numbered in the same way and duplicates kept in the journal. The eggs are kept in trays in a cabinet of drawers. The number, date, locality and other data is written on a card three-fourths of an inch wide and the length of the tray. The card is placed in the back of the tray so the number, name, etc., face the front of the drawer. The numbers are all placed in rotation, and the card at the back of each tray, instead of being a hindrance, adds much to the beauty of the eggs. If complete particulars of any set are wanted, all he has to do is to open the journal at the set number. He also keeps the original data blanks of the sets, with the number written across the left-hand end in large figures. Mr. Carr informs me that he has tried several systems for arranging his eggs during the last eight years, but that this gives greater satisfaction than any he has yet tried.

Taking into consideration the difficulties he has labored under, Mr. Carr has built up a grand collection. Rising early in the morning before his day's work commenced, and going to the woods to collect birds, which were skinned in the evening, shows his love for the science. Many collectors would have soon tired of this kind of work.

While South in the employ of an expedition as taxidermist Mr. Carr learned considerable of bird life in the locality of Texas. Although his duties to his employers took most of his time, he managed to secure seventy-six skins with full data during the winter and spring he was there.

One of the rarest Wisconsin birds in Mr. Carr's collection is an American Velvet Scoter. It is the second that is on record of being captured in the State; the other was back in 1860. He also has many other species which are in no other collection in the State.

Mr. Carr is a member of the Wisconsin Academy of Sciences and intends to write up some of his observations for their meeting next Winter.

THE HAWKEYE ORNITHOLOGICAL CLUB.

A reorganization of the Howard County Ornithological Union, which flourished in '86 and '87, was completed on the 6th of March, 1889.

After the adoption of the constitution, submitted by a previously appointed committee, the following officers were elected: President, W. W. Searles, Lime Springs, Iowa; 1st Vice-President, John E. Light, Elma, Iowa; 2d Vice-President, Charles Burgess, Cresco; Recording Secretary and Treasurer, F. Dana Mead, Cresco; Corresponding Secretary, Wm. H. Tillson, Cresco; Curator, E. B. Webster, Cresco.

The objects of the organization are two-fold: the mutual advancement of its members in ornithological and oological matters, and the migration of birds.

The number of corresponding members is not limited, and all ornithologists or oologists who wish to become such are requested to communicate with our Corresponding Secretary.

Constitution and By-laws will be sent to all who may desire, as soon as they can be published. Bulletins will also be issued from time to time as the Club may direct.

Recognizing field work as an important factor in the science. a collecting trip will be had on March 30th, in which all the members are expected to take part.

Among our best exchanges we class the *Loon*, a bright and fresh monthly devoted to the interests of the students of birds, published by our old friend, Thad. Surber.

Taxidermists' Tools.

Anvil, 12 lbs.,	$3.00 Not malleable.
Bit-brace,	1.50 " "
Bits—12 sizes	1.25 Postage 25c.
Brain Spoons, fine finish 6in	.75 Post-paid.
cheapest	.25 "
Bone Cutters	2.50 "
Cutting Plyers:	
No. 1 for wire 1 to 8	3.00 Postage 50c.
No. 4 " " 9 to 16	1.75 Postage 25c.
Hall's double lever, 7 in	1.75 Post-paid.
" " 5 in	1.00 "
extra jaws .80 and	.60 "
German side cutters 6 in	.90
" " 5 in	.80
Files—8 in. 35', 4 in	.20
Hammers,	.35, .50, .75 Postg. extra.
Hooks and Chain brass	.25 Post-paid.
plated	.40
Mallets	.20 to .40
Needles, curved, each	.10
doz, astd	.75
straight each	.10
doz, astd	.75
long, 8 in	.15
12 in	.22
Oil Stones, fine	.15, .50 Postg. extra.
Probe, Surgeons,	.30 Post-paid.
Plyers, flat nose, 8 in	1.00
6 in	.50
5 in	.40
4 in	.35
long nose 5 in	.50
3 1-2 in	.30
round nose same sizes	
and price as flat nose.	
Rabbit's feet	.12
Scalpels ebony handle, l'ge	
medium & small	.75
asst steel, medium	.60
cartilage knife	.75
Screw Drivers	.25, .50
Stuffers,scissor h'd'ls,12in	1.75
9 1-2 in	1.50
spr'g lid'ls, 6 1-2 in	1.15
5 in	.75
Scissors, surgeon's dissecting, 7 in, $1.50; 5 in	1.00
curved, large	1.50
small	1.00
extra fine	.75
elbow, large	1.15
medium	1.00
Shears, extra fine make 7in	.75
Spring Forceps, 5 in.,	
serregated points	.75
fine "	.75
curved "	.75
common	.25
cheapest	.12
Steel rule, 4 inch and min.	1.00
Vise, b'nch	.85 $1.50, $2.60 Postg. extra.

E. B. WEBSTER, Cresco, Iowa.

R. E. Ruchford & Son,
COLLECTING * NATURALISTS
and wholesale dealers in
BIRD SKINS AND EGGS,
BEAUMONT, TEXAS.

—1889.—

CLUBBING RATES.

Hawkeye O. and O. (50c) and any of the following publications at annexed price:

	Pub's. Price.	With H. O.
O. AND O., of Boston, Mass.,	$1.00	$1.25
West Am. Scientist,	1.00	.85
Oologist, Albion, N. Y.	.50	.75
Old Curiosity Shop,	.50	.80
L'terary Visitor,	.50	.70

H. H. FIELD.   E. C. GREENWOOD.

FIELD & GREENWOOD,
BROWNSVILLE, TEX.

Mr. Greenwood of this firm, who is well known as a naturalist and taxidermist, will give special attention to the collection for scientific purposes, of all birds, beasts reptiles and insects native to the interior and border of Mexico, and will furnish careful data in regard to same when desired. Correspondence respectfully solicited.

FIELD & GREENWOOD.

Bird Skins and Eggs.
At Reasonable Prices. Send stamp for lists.
J. A. SINGLEY,
Giddings, Texas.

FREE!   FREE!!   FREE!!!

My price list of Eggs, Minerals, Shells, Curiosities, etc., and sample copy of "The Old Curiosity Shop," an illustrated monthly journal devoted to the interests of collectors in all branches
E. M. HAIGHT,
Box 24, Riverside, Calif.

THE LOON

A MONTHLY MAGAZINE
ooo   DEVOTED TO
ORNITHOLOGY AND OOLOGY

Best of reading matter relating to these branches.
50 cents a year. Sample copy free.

Address:
THAD. SURBER, White Sulphur Springs, W. Va.

RIDGWAY'S MANUAL OF N. AM. BIRDS.

By Prof. Robt. Ridgway, Curator of Birds, U. S. Nat. Mus., Washington D. C
—o—
Royal 8vo, Cloth. Gilt, 631 pages, 464 engravings. $7.50.
Sportsman's edition, bound in leather $7.50
—o—

Contains consise descriptions of every species of birds known to North America. Profusely illustrated with 464 outline cuts of the generic characters, and a portrait of the late Spencer F. Baird.

The classification, numeration and nomenclature conform strictly with the Check List of North American Birds recently published by the A. O. U. For the benefit of observers along our southern border, a synopsis of all Mexican, Cuban and Bahaman species of each North American genus is given.

THE ANALYTICAL KEYS

Are unlike those previously used for any ornithological work in America, and are models of conciseness and utility. Taken with the accurate outline cuts, giving the bills, claws, etc., no one can fail to use them with absolute certainty of satisfactory results.

Every genus has been worked up exactly as if it were the subject of a special monograph, based on all the material available, and not a single page, or part of a page, as printed, has been previously published in anything like the same form.

Not only are the essential characters of every species and sub-species given, with measurements, but the various plumage of each, depending on sex, age and season, are carefully distinguished. The nest and eggs are concisely described.

No active ornithologist, cologist or sportsman can afford to be without this book, as it will be the
STANDARD AUTHORITY
on North American Birds for many years to come.

E. B. WEBSTER, Cresco, Iowa.

A COLLECTION OF BIRDS' EGGS FOR SALE.

Owing to the extensive growth of my collection of European and American Birds' Eggs, I have concluded to dispose of half of my American Eggs, and now offer a very fine collection of 400 species, consisting of 3000 specimens, in first class sets with data, collected by well known and reliable oologists in the United States, Canada and Europe. This collection is especially rich in eggs of Birds of Prey and contains 50 species; very few private collections on this continent can show so many species.

During the past four years I have been at great expense and trouble in obtaining collectors in Greenland, Iceland, Lapland and other Arctic regions and have added to both private and public museums many very rare species, such as Knot, Sanderling, Black-bellied Plover, Eagles, rare Plovers, Ducks, Geese, and Sea Birds.

At regular cataloge rates of American dealers, this collection is worth $2500.00, but I am able to offer it at a great bargain. My price for this magnificent collection is only $1000.00, satisfaction guaranteed. This is a rare opportunity for some museum or wealthy naturalist to secure a good collection at half its value.

Apply to   W. RAINE, Toronto, Canada.

OUR BIRDS IN THEIR HAUNTS,
BY REV. J. H. LANGILLE.

The most readable of all ornithological works, being written in a fresh and original manner and almost entirely from personal observations. It takes up the descriptions and habits of the birds as they appear in eastern North America, in order of the seasons, and being free from the classification of a text book or manual, begins by noting the arrival of the first feathered songsters of the winter, taking up each bird separately, and presenting all in FULL LIFE HISTORIES that is curious and fascinating in the lives of these wonderful creatures.

The Niagara River and St. Clair Flats receive the most attention, though a great deal of information is given on the interesting localities of Nova Scotia and Hudson's Bay.

Migration, instinct, the analogy of nidification, the specialized forms and adaptions of structure in birds is all made readable.

The illustrations, 25 in number, are by that prince of bird artists, EDWIN SHEPPARD of Philadelphia, whose connection with the Smithsonian Institute has given him a world-wide reputation, and assures accuracy.

There is no purer source of recreation than to go abroad and study the nature, habits and songs of the birds; and Mr. Langille has shown us what can be accomplished in this line by a quick eye and inquisitive mind, and that a persistent observer can cultivate an acquaintance with the birds which will prove alike pleasant, instructive and reducing.

IN CLOTH, and on FINE TINTED PAPER. $3.00,

E. B. WEBSTER, Cresco, Iowa.

MONTHLY BULLETIN
OF
BIRD SKINS.

MARCH.

All specimens of first quality (2d col. figures) guaranteed to be well prepared, of good plumage and labeled. Specimens will be carefully packed, but no risks are taken.

No.	Species		
69	Forster's Tern,	$ .25	.50
131	Hooded Merganser, m. jv.		.50
122	Mallard, m.,	.75	1.00
140	Blue-winged Teal,	.75	1.25
214	Sora Rail,	.30	.50
263	Spotted Sandpiper,	.20	.25
289b	**Texan Quail,**		.50
305	Prairie Hen,	1.00	
394	Downy Woodpecker,	.15	.20
433	Rufous Hummer, fm.	.25	
456	Phœbe,	.15	.20
461	Wood Pewee,	.15	.20
474	Horned Lark,	.15	
477	**Blue Jay,**	.10	.20
488	**Am. Crow,**	.25	.50
494	Bobolink, m.,	.10	
498	Red-winged Blackbird,		.10
	English Sparrow,		.10
567	Slate-colored Junco,	.10	.15
595	Rose-breasted Grosbeak, m.,		.15
611	Purple Martin,		.15
652	Yellow Warbler,		.10
735	Chickadee,	.10	.15

Remittances must always be made by postal note or money order. Large specimens will be sent by express. Those under eight inches in length will be sent postpaid.

ADDRESS:
E. B. WEBSTER, : : CRESCO, IOWA.

IT'S NOW

The Literary Companion (formerly the Agassiz Companion.) An old paper under a new name.
Subscribe for it and keep posted. THE collector's paper, only 25c. per year. Exchange column free to subscribers. All the latest news will be found in it.
Advertise in it and get rich. Circulation 1000 or over copies every month. Sworn to. If you have anything to sell try our one cent a word column. Send for free sample copy.
THE LITERARY COMPANION.
Kansas City, Kansas.

EXCHANGE SETS.

Original, first-class and with complete data. For sale at greatly reduced rates, or for ex. at standard rates; many of the common species wanted.

FIELD PLOVER, SORA RAIL AM. COOT, PRAIRIE HEN, BLUE-WINGED TEAL, CANVASS-BACK, MALLARD.

One month only.

E. B. WEBSTER.
Cresco, Iowa.

We send you a personal letter, only it is in covers instead of an envelope:

No. 1.   *   *   *   We want to purchase rare and desirable objects of Natural History—all kinds. Please make an effort to obtain such specimens for us during the season.   *   *
   *   *   *   WINKLEY.

No. 2.   *   *   We will furnish to any Geologist or Paleontologist, on application, written lists. A great many of them rare and great bargains. We will keep an account with reliable naturalists and sell on the installment plan, or any other way. We make the same offer to Ornithologists, Oologists, Conchologists, and Entomologists.

We will execute all orders promptly, carefully, and to the best of our ability—and our reputation for supplying perfect authenticated specimens at bargains and in all cases exceptionally full data is good.

Our egg catalogues make capital exchange lists—they are the largest, cheapest, and are the standard. Send stamps for sample package.

We have another 100 species collections at $12.50, ready for shipment. Lists of contents on application.

W. H. WINKLEY,   -   -   Clearfield, Iowa.

The Hawkeye O. and O.

WILLIAM NIVEN,
739 AND 741 BROADWAY, NEW YORK.
WHOLESALE AND RETAIL DEALER IN
FOREIGN AND AMERICAN
MINERALS,
INDIAN RELICS, ETC.

ARIZONA PETRIFIED WOOD.

Polished Sections from 8 inches to 16 inches in diameter, at prices ranging from $8 to $50. Tiling from 1 to 8 inches, at $30 to $50 per square foot. Colors specially selected for mantels, wainscoting, etc. Cabinet specimens, showing bark, 25c and upwards. Rough specimens, all beautiful colors, 10c each. Objects cut from this wood: Paper weights, $1.25; Paper Cutters, $1.50; Charms, 50c; Sleeve Buttons, $1; Pen Holders, $1; Seals, $2; Scarf Pins, 50; Button Hooks, 50c; Ash Receivers, $2; Canes, $2.50; Blotters, $2.50; Jewel Boxes, $12; Tea Trays, $30 and upwards.

12 AMERICAN GEMS

For 50c., by mail, 60c. Cheapest and most attractive collection in the market. In partitioned box with cover, and catalogued.
ALASKA GARNETS.—Large consignment of the finest specimens ever received in the United States. Specimens from 2 to 12 inches, studded with garnets, from 25c. to $20.

FOSSIL FISH

From Wyoming, on white limestone. Scales, backbone, etc., as perfect as life, 25c. and upwards.
INSECTS IN TRANSPARENT AMBER.—Choice specimens from the Baltic Coast, 50c. to $3.

INDIAN ARROW HEADS

From Oregon, of jasper, obsidian, carnelian, etc., 25c, and upwards. From Georgia, North Carolina, etc., 5c. and upwards.

Estimates will be given at wholesale rates, for collections of Minerals, Indian Relics, etc. Special prices to the trade.

Entered at the Cresco Post Office as Second-class mail matter.

CONTENTS FOR MARCH.

To a Stormy Petrel, - - - - - - Wm. L. Kells.
Birds of Summerville, South Carolina, - - - J. D. Ford.
The Red-breasted Nuthatch, - - - - - Neil F. Posson.
Nesting of the Kentucky Warbler in South-western Pennsylvania,
   J. Warren Jacobs.
Noted Collections—No. 4, - - - - - - F. R. Stearns.
A Plea for Protection, - - - - - - J. D. Ford.
Editorial Notes.

THE HAWKEYE

E. B. WEBSTER, Editor and Publisher.

The Leading Ornithological Journal of the Western States.

Successor to the "Geologist's Gazette," of Elkader, Iowa. Geological Department a leading feature.

Prominent writers, monthly; illustrated; second volume commenced January 1, 1889.

The HAWKEYE will appear on or about the first of each month.

All books and catalogues sent us will be carefully reviewed.

Papers desiring to suspend can have their lists filled by us at very low rates.

SUBSCRIPTION RATES:
U. S. and Canada, - 50c.
Foreign Countries, - - 65c.
Single copies, - - 5c.
Sample copy free.

ADVERTISING RATES:
1 page, 1 insertion, - $5.00.
1 col., " - - 2.50.
2 in., " - - 1.00.
1 in., " - - .50.

The Hawkeye Ornithologist and Oologist.

TO A STORMY PETREL.

BY. WM. L. KELLS.

Loud is the tempest's dreadful roar;
  Men's hearts are filled with woe;
Their ship may sink to rise no more,
  Down in the depths below.

Fierce is the raging of the wind—
  The sea runs mountains high,
And seems, to the despairing mind.
  To reach the very sky.

Yet even here are to be found
  Who dread no tempest's roar;
The Petrels fly the ship around,
  As they did oft before.

The winds may blow, the storms may rave—
  No danger threatens thee,
Who walks upon the crested wave,
  And skims the raging sea.

Thy little brood is all thy care—
  Within the sea girt rock
Thy nest is found, and thou can't there
  The tempest's fury mock.

Oh, could I fly! I'd go with thee
  From all this world of care,
And make my home upon the sea,
  And find companions there.

BIRDS OF SUMMERVILLE, SOUTH CAROLINA.

BY J. D. FORD.

CHARLESTON, S. C., Nov. 10, 1888.

E. B. WEBSTER,

Dear Sir: I take pleasure in enumerating for you a few of the birds to be found near Summerville, S. C., and hope it will be of interest to your many readers.

Of the family *Turdidæ* we have: Wood Thrush, common resident; Hermit Thrush, very rare, only three specimens having ever been noted; Am. Robin, abundant winter visitor; Mockingbird, common resident, the sweetest songster we have in this locality; Catbird, common resident; Brown Thrasher, common resident.

Of the family *Saxicolidæ*, Bluebird, common resident.

Of the family *Syloviidæ*, Blue-gray Gnatcatcher, rare in winter and common in summer; Ruby-crowned Kinglet, occasional summer visitor.

Of the family *Paridæ*, Tufted Titmouse, resident, comparatively common; Black-capped Chickadee, comparatively common resident; Carolina Chickadee, comparatively common resident.

Of the family *Sittidæ*, White-bellied Nuthatch, rare resident; Brown-bellied Nuthatch, common resident.

Of the family *Troglodytidæ*, Carolina Wren, common resident; Bewick's Wren, rare resident, House Wren, common resident; Long-billed Marsh Wren, common resident throughout our marsh lands, Short-billed Marsh Wren, winter visitor.

Of the family *Mniotiltidæ*, Prothonotary Warbler, rare resident, Swainson's Warbler, rare resident, Worm-eating Warbler, casual winter visitor, Bachman's Warbler, coast-wise resident, Black-throated Blue Warbler, rare winter visitor, Yellow throated Warbler, common resident, Pine-creeping Warbler, rare resident; Yellow Red-poll Warbler, rare resident.

Of the family *Vireonidæ*, Red-eyed Vireo, common resident, White-eyed Vireo, common resident.

Of the family *Laniidæ*, Logger-head Shrike, common resident.

Of the family *Ampelidæ*, Cedar Waxwing, abundant winter visitant.

Of the family *Hirundinidæ*, Purple Martin, abundant resident; Bank Swallow, abundant resident.

Of the family *Tanagridæ*, Summer Redbird, abundant spring and summer resident.

Of the family *Fringillidæ*, Am. Goldfinch, rare resident; Grass Finch, rare resident; Tree Sparrow, rare winter visitor; Chipping Sparrow, rare resident; Field Sparrow, common resident; Song Sparrow, rare resident; Swamp Sparrow, rare resident; Cardinal Grosbeak, common resident; Painted Bunting, rare resident.

Of the family *Icteridæ*, Bobolink, or Ricebird, abundant summer and fall visitor; Red-and-buff-shouldered Blackbird, common resident; Meadow Lark, common resident; Baltimore Oriole, common resident; Orchard Oriole, rare resident; Purple Grackle, common resident.

[TO BE CONTINUED.]

THE RED-BREASTED NUTHATCH.

BY NEIL F. POSSON.

The Red-breasted Nuthatch (*Sitta canadensis*) occurs in this locality as a spring and fall migrant, although it may be rarely seen in midwinter in company with his white-breasted cousin. It is during the last of April or first of May that we are most apt to see his pleasing little form as he tarries a few days in his southward flight. He is by no means a plentiful species—quite the contrary—for five years of earnest ornithological research did not reveal a single species.

Never but once have I noticed them here in winter, and that was on February 22d last. With the thermometer at about 32°, and a brisk west wind filling the eyes with the snow that was rapidly falling. I leaped over a fence into a woods, having little hope of seeing anything interesting on such a day. As I did so I became aware of bird-life in a hemlock standing just before me. There were five or six Chickadees tilting this way and that, lisping and whistling to each other; then came the loud, sonorous "quank" of the White-breasted Nuthatch, and then another note similar to the last, but not so loud and in a higher tone. Then a Red-breasted Nuthatch came in view from among the thick foliage of the hemlock, followed soon by another. They seemed to be gleaning food from the recesses of the hemlock, now and then examining carefully a cone.

This smaller species of the Nuthatch is not much larger than the Chickadees, being about five inches in length. The upper colors on head and back resemble very closely the corresponding colors of *S. carolinensis*, but the under parts—how pretty! The throat is white. Thence, all the rest of the under parts are of a beautiful rust-red color, forming a pleasing contrast with the snow-covered ground as he approaches it, running nimbly along the lower rail of some forest-bounding fence. He is, indeed, a pleasing, pretty, and a striking form.

Sitta canadensis breeds well to the north of us, as the specific part of his scientific name would naturally suggest.

NESTING OF THE KENTUCKY WARBLER IN SOUTH-WESTERN PENNSYLVANIA.

BY J. WARREN JACOBS.

The Kentucky Warbler (*Oporornis formosas*) in this locality is not a rare bird, although they are not to be found nesting in every favorable spot in which they delight to haunt.

For a nesting site they select a swampy place, sometimes on low ground in mixed woods, at other times on high ground in open woods where tall, weeds abound, and usually near a small stream.

Twice have I had the pleasure of examining the nest of this golden-breasted Warbler.

On June 5th, '87, I was collecting in a large, gloomy woods, and after blowing and packing several sets, among which was a fine set of four eggs of the Louisiana Water Thrush, was returning home by a course which led through a piece of marshy ground near the border of the wood. This was overgrown with tall weeds, so that the ground and mud could not be seen only in spots where little dry knolls peeped up from among the weeds.

As I was skipping from one of these knolls to another, my foot struck a lonely clump of May apple and caused the large leaves to sway to one side, revealing for an instant a large and suspicious looking bunch of dry leaves. Upon examination I found a nest unlike anything I had ever saw before.

The base was composed of a mass of dry oak and maple leaves, six inches high. Upon this was placed a neat structure of leaves and fine black rootlets, with a heavy lining of long, brown hair. The whole structure was loosely bound to the stems of the plant.

As the eggs have since passed out of my possession, I cannot give a description.

The second nest was found on May 29th, '88. The foundation was just commenced, and for nearly an hour I stood watching the old birds bringing leaves and placing them in position.

The birds were very shy, and I had to keep several yards between us, and keep concealed too, in order to watch their movements, for when I would make any noise or motion, they would quietly disappear in the thicket.

As it was now growing late in the afternoon, I was compelled to move homeward; but all that evening, and in fact for more than a week, visions of nests containing from four to six eggs of *Oporornis formosus* would roll up before my eyes.

On the 31st, I called again, and found their nest nearly ready for the lining, and by the middle of the afternoon of June 1st, this was put in position.

The first egg was laid June 3d, and now as I had acted as overseer for several days, I decided on June 10th, as the day to finish up the job.

So early in the morning of the day set, I packed my traps and prepared for a long trip.

Before I arrived at the nest under discussion I had collected four or five sets of Acadian Flycatcher and a nice set of four eggs of the Scarlet Tanager and two nests containing young birds of a species of Warbler unknown to me.

And now arriving at the scene of action, I saw the female glide off the nest and disappear in the thicket. All along I had hoped for a large set—five or six eggs—but the nest contained only four. Notwithstanding four is the least number laid by this bird, I think I was well rewarded for my labors.

The nest was placed at the foot, or rather between, two small bushes, and was composed of a variety of materials. The base, or foundation was made of leaves and weed stalks, about three inches high. Upon this was placed, or rather sunken in the bed of leaves, the nest proper, made of leaves, rootlets, etc., lined with fine tendrils and horse-hair.

The eggs were perfectly fresh, and in ground color are white, with a very slight creamy tinge.

No. 1 has large spots of rich chestnut brown, thickest about the larger end, over which is distributed numerous pin points of lilac and reddish brown. Measures .77x.58 inches.

No. 2 is marked much the same way, the spots being smaller. Measurement: .77x.54 inches.

No. 3 is more heavily marked, and has numerous splashes of light chestnut, seemingly beneath the shell, in addition to the rich brown, lilac and reddish colors. Measures .77x.57 inches.

The markings on number four resemble those on numbers one and two, and have a tendency to collect on the end of the egg. This is the smallest egg in the set, measuring .74x.54 inches.

NOTED COLLECTIONS—NO. 4.

BY F. R. STEARNS.

One of the finest collections of shells in Kansas, and probably one of the finest in the United States, is that owned by Mr. Frank J. Ford, of Wichita, Kansas. He began collecting when only eleven years of age, and for eighteen years the most of his spare time has been devoted to collecting and exchanging. His especial hobby is conchology, but he is also interested in archæology and paleontology.

Mr. Ford's first collection consisted of a few land shells found in Maconpin Co., Ill., which he kept in a small box made of scraps of boards and with a cover hinged on with red leather. This little box, about six inches square and two inches deep, he still has in his collection; and it often serves to recall his early efforts at making a collection.

His collection has now far outgrown the little box, and consists of nearly fifteen thousand specimens, ten thousand of which are land, fresh-water, and sea shells. The remainder consists of Indian relics, of which he has about five hundred specimens, and numerous minerals, fossils, curios and relics.

Mr. Ford has his shells arranged in two cases which were made to order, one of them being seven feet high, four feet wide and two feet deep. This is divided into two parts, the upper being divided into four shelves having glass doors in front, and the lower into eighteen drawers, each twenty inches square. The other case is eight feet long, seven feet high and one foot deep, with four shelves having glass doors in front, and four drawers below. He also has a case of ten drawers each twenty inches square, with plate glass fronts, which contains his land shells, and is partitioned off to contain five hundred species.

Mr. Ford has made several quite lucky finds. In May, 1885, while proving up a claim in Kiowa County, he came across a bed of fossil oyster shells (*Gryphœa pitcheri*, Morton) in the bed of a small stream known as Soldier creek. From this bed he obtained several hundred fine specimens of this fossil which have been of great value in exchanging. He also at one time found fifty good specimens of the rare *Unio abiati* (Conrad) on the Fall river, near Neodesha, Kansas. He lately discovered an old Indian camp ground near the mouth of Chisholm creek, in Sedgewick County, where he found over one hundred stone relics consisting of arrow heads, scrapers, mauls, rubbing stones and flint hatchets. Last year Mr. Ford made a trip through Colorado, New Mexico, Arizona, Nevada and Utah, and many fine specimens were added to his collection.

Mr. Ford desires, through the H. O. AND O., to thank his friend and relative, Mr. John Ford of Philadelphia, Mr. J. R. Mead of Wichita, his father, E. P. Ford, and his brother, Fred L. Ford of Los Angeles, Cal., for their generous assistance, and for the many rare and valuable additions they have made to his collection.

A PLEA FOR PROTECTION.

BY J. D. FORD.

I have noticed that in some oological papers a great many of the young collectors boast of the number of eggs of each species they can collect in a day. For instance, one collector obtained nine sets of the Green Heron, eleven sets of the Long-billed Marsh Wren and a great many sets of Am. Robin and Red-and-buff shouldered Blackbird besides. Now this is only one instance, and a great many more such appear almost every month.

Now this is what I call wanton extravagance and cruelty. At that rate our birds would some become entirely depopulated, and it is a notable fact that some our best songsters are becoming very scarce.

I do not refer to the professional ornithologist and oologist, or or wholesale natural history and egg dealer, as they have to carry a large stock of eggs constantly on hand, and all such must see the advisability of protecting and promoting our bird life, but to young collectors and small boys who collect the eggs and destroy the nests and even the birds themselves as much as possible merely from idleness, having no love or interest in the sport but the cruelty that it affords them, exchanging and bartering the eggs like so many pretty beads, destroying them as soon as the novelty wears off or casting them aside for some other amusement.

Now what I would suggest is this: let every one begin by collecting single eggs, and if you do not get tired of them in one year then collect sets and exchange, sell or do as you wish with them, but use some moderation—collect sparingly.

It is a wonder to me that through the oologist for the eggs, the taxidermist for the skins, the milliner for the plumes and feathers, and the sportsman for the pot, we have any birds left at all.

EDITORIAL NOTES.

The *Scientist* is dead.

Commend us to A. E. Kibbe, of Mayville, N. Y., for fine taxidermal work.

Our thanks are due Wm. W. Adams, of Mapleton, N. Y., for a number of fine fossils.

The *Curlew*, published by O. P. Hanger & Co., of Orleans, Ind., as the organ of the Y. O. A., is a valued exchange.

We recently mounted a fine specimen of the Bald Eagle, which was killed in an adjoining county while attempting to carry off a large dog. The bird is quite a rarity here.

We can heartily recommend the *Loon* as an excellent advertising medium, having received most ample returns from our ad. Bro. Surber seems to be continually on the improve, and will, no doubt, make a great success. We extend our best wishes.

The Spring migration has fairly commenced in the Upper Mississippi Valley, and several species of birds have commenced to nest. Many fields now green with wheat were covered with snow at this time last year, and the roads now so dry and dusty were almost impassible.

We are sorry to say that one of our advertisers is unreliable, We have received information to that effect from reliable collectors and dealers, and would advise all of our readers to steer clear of him. We refer to R. M. Gibbs, M. D., of Kalamazoo, Mich. —*Old Curiosity Shop*.

We are indebted to W. H. Foote for a copy of his Ornithologists and Oologists' Semi-annual, Vol. I, No. 1., a 48-page journal of ornithology, presenting on the whole a very fine appearance. The article on collecting by Prof. Singley is alone worth the price of the number—35c. Sent postpaid on receipt of price by the H. O. AND O., Cresco, Iowa.

DAKOTA EGGS FOR EXCHANGE.

I have a few more sets of Plover, Rail, Teal, Mallard and Canvass-backs, as advertised in March issue of the H. O. AND O., for exchange. Both skins and eggs desired. E. B. WEBSTER.

THE LOON

A MONTHLY MAGAZINE
DEVOTED TO
✦∴ORNITHOLOGY∴AND∴OOLOGY∴✦

Best of reading matter relating to these branches.
50 cents a year. Sample copy free.

Address:
THAD. SURBER, WHITE SULPHUR SPRINGS, W. VA.

—1889.—

CLUBBING RATES.

Hawkeye O, and O, (50c) and any of the following publications at annexed price:

	Pub's. Price.	With H. O
O. AND O., of Boston, Mass.,	$1.00	$1.25
West Am. Scientist,	1.00	.85
Oologist, Albion, N. Y.	.50	.75
Old Curiosity Shop,	.50	.80
Literary Visitor,		.7

H H. FIELD.   E. C. GREENWOOD.

FIELD ✦ & ✦ GREENWOOD,
BROWNSVILLE, TEX.

Mr. Greenwood of this firm, who is well known as a naturalist and taxidermist, will give special attention to the collection for scientific purposes, of all birds, beasts, reptiles and insects native to the interior and border of Mexico, and will furnish careful data in regard to same when desired. Correspondence respectfully solicited.
FIELD & GREENWOOD.

✦ R. E. Rochford & Son, ✦
COLLECTING ✱ NATURALISTS
and wholesale dealers in
BIRD SKINS AND EGGS.
BEAUMONT, TEXAS.

✦ Bird Skins and Eggs. ✦
At Reasonable Prices. Send stamp for lists.
J. A. SINGLEY,
Giddings, Texas.

FREE!   FREE!!   FREE!!!
My price list of Eggs, Minerals, Shells, Curiosities, etc., and sample copy of "The Old Curiosity Shop," an illustrated monthly journal devoted to the interests of collectors in all branches.
E. M. HAIGHT,
3t] Box 24, Riverside, Calif.

For Sale or Exchange.
"The Lives of Harrison and Morton," by Gen. Lew Wallace. Write for particulars,
JOHN F. BOWERS, Wellsboro, Pa.

WANTED—Most any of the Warblers in sets with nests. Can offer some good sets for same.
H. W. DAVIS,
North Granville, N. Y.

NO. 674—FRANKLIN'S GULL.
Some fine sets of 3 eggs each of the above at $1.50 per set. Collected in Minnesota.
H. W. DAVIS,
North Granville, N. Y.

IT'S NOW The Literary Companion (formerly the Agassiz Companion. An old paper under a new name. Subscribe for it and keep posted THE collector's paper. Only 25 cents a year. Exchange column free to subscribers. All the LATEST NEWS will be found in it.

A COLLECTION OF BIRDS' EGGS FOR SALE.

Owing to the extensive growth of my collection of European and American Birds' Eggs, I have concluded to dispose of half of my American Eggs, and now offer a very fine collection of 400 species, consisting of 3000 specimens, in first class sets with data, collected by well known and reliable oologists in the United States, Canada and Europe. This collection is especially rich in eggs of Birds of Prey and contains 50 species; very few private collections on this continent can show so many species.

During the past four years I have been at great expense and trouble in obtaining collectors in Greenland, Iceland, Lapland and other Arctic regions and have added to both private and public museums many very rare species, such as Knot, Sanderling, Black-bellied Plover, Eagles, rare Plovers, Ducks, Geese, and Sea Birds.

At regular cataloge rates of American dealers, this collection is worth $2500.00, but I am able to offer it at a great bargain. My price for this magnificent collection is only $1000.00, satisfaction guaranteed. This is a rare opportunity for some museum or wealthy naturalist to secure a good collection at half its value.

Apply to W. RAINE, Toronto, Canada.

OUR BIRDS IN THEIR HAUNTS.
BY REV. J. H. LANGILLE.

The most readable of all ornithological works, being written in a fresh and original manner and almost entirely from personal observations. It takes up the descriptions and habits of the birds as they appear in eastern North America, in order of the seasons and being free from the classification of a text book or manual, begins by noting the arrival of the first feathered songsters of the winter, taking up each bird separately, and presenting all in FULL LIFE HISTORIES that is curious and fascinating to the lover of these wonderful creatures.

The Niagara River and St. Clair Flats receive the most attention, though a great deal of information is given on the interesting localities of Nova Scotia and Hudson's Bay.

Migration, instinct, the analogy of nidification, the specialized forms and adaptions of structure in birds is all made readable.

The Illustrations, 25 in number, are by that prince of bird artists, EDWIN SHEPPARD of Philadelphia, whose connection with the Smithsonian Institute has given him a world-wide reputation, and assures accuracy.

There is no purer source of recreation than to go abroad and study the nature, habits and songs of the birds; and Mr. Langille has shown us what can be accomplished in this line by a quick eye and inquisitive mind, and that a persistent observer can cultivate an acquaintance with the birds which will prove alike pleasant, instructive and refining.

IN CLOTH, and on FINE TINTED PAPER, $3.00.

E. B. WEBSTER, Cresco, Iowa.

Contents for May.

To A Snowbird,	Wm. L. Kells.
Robins Ahead Again,	S. A. Ball.
My First Owl's Nest,	W. C. Brownell.
Birds of Summerville, South Carolina,	J. D. Ford.
The Red-tailed Hawk As A Pet,	Fred Jones.

THE HAWKEYE ORNITHOLOGIST AND OOLOGIST.

E. B. WEBSTER, Editor and Publisher.

The Leading Ornithological Journal of the Western States.

Successor to the "Geologist's Gazette," of Elkader, Iowa. Geological Department a leading feature.

Prominent writers, monthly; illustrated; second volume commenced January 1, 1889.

The HAWKEYE will appear on or about the first of each month.

All books and catalogues sent us will be carefully reviewed.

Papers desiring to suspend can have their lists filled by us at very low rates.

SUBSCRIPTION RATES:		ADVERTISING RATES:	
U. S. and Canada,	50c.	1 page, 1 insertion,	$5.00.
Foreign Countries,	65c.	1 col., "	2.50.
Single copies,	5c.	2 in., "	1.00.
Sample copy free.		1 in., "	.50.

TO A SNOWBIRD.

BY WM. L. KELLS.

Harbinger of coming winter,
   Herald of approaching storm,
How know you the appointed time
   Your annual journey to perform.

When fallen are the summer leaves,
   And the freezing, wintry blast
Nature of its charms bereaves
   And earth seems a dreary waste.

When the snow is falling fast,
   And the azure vault of Heaven
I' dark clouds is overcast,
   Oft before the tempest driven.

When the pure-white garb of winter,
   Hills and valleys cover o'er,
Silent are our summer songsters,
   And we hear their lays no more.

Then we see your frost-proof plumage
   Mingling with the fallen snow,
Or we hear your cheery wild notes
   As before the wind you go.

But when spring the snow is melting,
   And our spring birds come again,
You return towards the Northland,
   Where the winters ever reign.

ROBINS AHEAD AGAIN.

BY S. A. BALL.

To be as big a bird as it is, I don't think the Robin can be excelled for shyness and expedition in nest building.

You may make up your mind each succeeding spring to see the first straw carried and watch the plastering process go on, but they get ahead of you every time—or, at least, of me. Generally the first thing I know, a flutter of wings in the apple or cedar tree attracts my attention, and stepping under it, there, in a crotch, is a nest big enough to accommodate a crow, and nothing has been said about it. That tree, too, may stand within ten feet of your door.

This is the 26th of March, with not even a wild cherry in leaf, and yet I have just returned from the discovery of a Robin's nest all completed, and Mrs. Redbreast snuggled down on it laying, looking as pleased as Punch. It beats the Jews.

How it may be in other places, I can't say; but here on the prairie in south-west Missouri, the 26th of March is the earliest date I have any record of Robins nesting. This pair have selected, as far as my knowledge goes, a most unusual place for building, namely: an old storm-wrecked Martin box. I never before knew a Robin to build anywhere but in a tree or a grape arbor. This old box has blown down and fallen from the top of a tree, in the lower branches of which it has lodged, bottom upward. A part of the bottom was knocked off in falling, and this has made an opening sufficiently large to admit the Robins. When I stepped up to make an examination with a view to making repairs for the Martins, Mrs. Robin cocked her head over the edge of one of the windows, and eyed me with a coolness that reminded me of how many points in law possession constitutes. I instantly withdrew my claim and walked away thinking of what L. O. Pindar says in the H. O. AND O. for this month, where he strikes a note but seldom heard, when he enters a protest against collecting.

To read our current ornithological literature, it certainly does look as if most of us are Nature's betrayers instead of her disciples—have rather the instincts of the cat and the weasel than the fine sympathies that mark the true bird lover and student.

L. O. Pindar in speaking of the Bluebird notes May as being late for finding its eggs fresh, but the fact is, these little fellows hatch three broods a year when things are favorable; and I have known them to often bring out nestlings in the latter part of June. February 12th is the earliest date I have recorded of their nesting here, but that was most uncommonly early I think. This spring they did not begin to build until the 7th of March, though I suppose this winter will be cited for its phenomenal mildness for a hundred years to come.

MY FIRST OWL'S NEST.

BY W. C. BROWNELL, W. OF. M., ANN ARBOR, MICH.

[Extract from "The Oologist's Camp Around the Great Lakes and Inland."]

We entered the swamp by a path known only to myself, and after much laborious tramping through the tangled underbrush at last emerged into a particularly clear space, the center of which was occupied by an immense dead pine stub which loomed up far above the surrounding trees.

Seating ourselves on an old moss covered log not many yards distant from the dead pine, and while the smoke from our pipes curled lazily upward, mingling with the balsam scented air, gave out its fragrant aroma, I related to my friend the circumstances connected with the collection of my "first owl's nest."

During the preceding fall and winter, on most dark, cloudy days and nights I had heard what I took to be the call of some species of Owl, issuing from various portions of this self-same timber tract.

Often on some clear, cold night, when the full moon shone on the snow clad hills, would I start from my chair, scattering books and papers in my eager haste to catch the full import of that startling cry—but would invariably be too late. Fain would I wait to hear it repeated; just on the verge of despair I would turn to re-enter the house, but again coming from the deepness of the swamp would that wierd, long drawn, muttering cry awake the stillness of the night. I would listen spellbound till the last echoing note died away, then turn back feeling well repaid for my vigil, that I had heard the cry in its fullness.

Back in my cosy, fire-lit room, I resolved that when the proper time came I would visit that particular swamp and find, if possible, the eggs of that pair of birds, that I knew would be deposited somewhere within its limits. Time flew by almost unawares, so occupied was I with my books, till I awoke to the realization that it was time to be up and doing, or my hopes would not materialize.

One morning past the middle of February, with a light tracking covering the ground and signs of a thaw overhead, found me equipped for the search. Encumbered with collecting box, climbers and gun, I started for the swamp, determined to do my utmost to discover "the chosen spot." I entered the swamp at its outer third, purposing to make a complete circuit and again circling the swamp nearer its middle, thereby covering as much ground as was possible in so short a time as one day.

I had at last after much tramping made my way through the swamp, coming out near the part where four hours earlier I had started on my search so full of hope and expectancy. I stopped to rest awhile before resuming the search, as I was much exhausted from the rough walking the ground afforded

Again resuming the hunt I started down through the swamp nearer the middle—this time with many misgivings—not doubting the presence of a nest in the swamp, but rather my inability to find it.

The sun, which had been tardy in appearing during the earlier part of the day, now shone full down through the trees, just melting the snow underneath, destroying my foot prints except on occasions where, at the foot of some slight eminence, the snow was deeper.

I shuddered at the possibility of becoming bewildered and lost in all that wild, dreary waste; and, losing my way, be compelled to spend the night in the swamp, seeking shelter as best I could among the thick brush, with only my light gun for protection against the possible attacks of numerous gray timber wolves known to infest the swamp.

The day was waning and as yet I had discovered nothing that looked like an Owl's nest. Many times I was on the point of giving up, take the shortest cut out of the swamp and make my way home; but was prevented from so doing by my dogged determination to do my duty with the hope of its reward.

I was following a small stream that ran in a winding course through the swamp, and had entered a small opening occupied only by several trees larger than the rest, when my attention was attracted by the passage overhead of some object that flitted past and struck on the large limb of a tree some way off to my right. Cautiously I made my way within full sight of the object, and my heart was gladdened and my hopes arose, for there sat a fine specimen of the Barred or Round-head Owl, his big black eyes blinking bewilderingly at having been disturbed. I immediately began to search among the neighboring trees in hopes of locating the nest, but could discover nothing. I traveled some distance away, until I lost my bearings and could not have found my way back to where I had first seen the owl, but for my tracks left in occasional patches of snow. Further I traveled, my hopes gradually sinking the further I went, till at last I made a headlong plunge through an unusually tangled thicket, and with a rush came standing at the foot of this very same old pine stub. Looking up the tree I saw the opening just over that broken limb, as you see, and thought it the most likely place for an Owl's nest I had seen that day. Raising my climbers high over my head, I gave the tree a resounding whack, and was just drawing back for a more vigorous assault, when, with a flapping of wings, an Owl made out of the hole and flew quickly out of sight among the neighboring trees. I gave utterance to my delight, never stopping to think that after all the nest might prove barren, for I knew instinctively that the cavity out of which the bird had flown contained the treasures I sought. I had a hard, perilous climb before me, but was finally rewarded by reaching the ground safely with a set of three round, pearly white and very fine eggs of *Strix Nebulosa*.

BIRDS OF SUMMERVILLE, SOUTH CAROLINA.
(Continued from page 37.)

BY J. D. FORD.

Of the family *Corvidæ* we have: Common Crow, comparatively common, more abundant in summer; Blue Jay, an abundant resident.

Alaudidæ: Shore Lark, occasionally seen in winter.

Tyrannidæ: Kingbird or Bee Martin, arrive in March and are common throughout the spring and summer, departing in September; Great-crested Flycatcher, arrives late in April and are quite numerous during the spring and summer months, departing about August or September; Wood Pewee, a common resident; Acadian Flycatcher, in the last two years I secured three sets of three eggs, $\frac{2}{3}$-$\frac{1}{2}$, hitherto I had never noted any in this locality.

Trochilidæ: This family is represented by the Ruby-throated and the Anna's Hummingbird, common throughout the spring and summer, but nests hard to obtain on account of the high and precarious places in which they build; feed mostly on the honey from the flowers, but sometimes catch insects.

Cypselidæ: Chimney Swift, common resident.

Caprimulgidæ: Chuck-will's-widow, common in spring and summer, eggs deposited in a slight depression in the ground, but are hard to find, being so nearly the color of the leaves that surround them; Night Hawk, or Bull Bat, as it is called here, is very common during the spring and summer months, departing about the first of October. They lay two eggs on the bare ground in a corn or cotton field or sometimes in the pine land, the same color but smaller than those of the preceding species. The two birds have often been confounded, although there is not the slightest resemblance when seen together. The Chuck-will's-widow has been mistaken by some of our local oologists for the Whip-poor-will, but the latter bird is seldom, if ever, seen below the North Carolina boundary.

THE RED-TAILED HAWK AS A PET.

BY FRED JONES.

A few years ago a friend of mine had a novel pet in the shape of a Red-tailed Hawk. Joe had been out of the nest only a few days when he was captured by a farmer and sold to my friend.

Joe never became quite reconciled to a life of captivity, but he knew his friends and could be handled and carried about by them. It was dangerous for a stranger to go near him especially when he was hungry or feeding, and woe betide the cat or dog that came within his reach.

Joe's greatest accomplishment was catching rats. We used to catch the rats in a box trap and then take them out on the common and let the hawk catch them. Joe always seemed to know what was expected of him when he saw the trap. He would hop round and round it, all the while uttering piercing screams. As soon as the rat was loosened from the trap and tried to escape, he would pursue it, not on the wing, but taking great leaps by aid of his wings. He always seized his prey by striking the talon of his great toe into the neck of the rat, and by this means held it securely and prevented it from injuring him. When he had seized his prey, he drew his wing around in front of him, concealing it from view and then make a meal of it.

Joe was very fond of frogs. It was a funny thing to see him try to catch five or six at once. He would get one with each foot, and the others would escape.

My friend often let Joe loose to fly around for exercise, but he always gave him this liberty just before feeding him. He would sail around high in the air, but would always come down like an arrow when called, for he knew food awaited him.

One day my friend went on a visit and forgot to feed him. Joe escaped from his coop and went on a foraging expedition and made great havoc among the chickens. When my friend returned he discovered Joe making a meal from one of his favorite hens.

This angered him so that he disposed of him to a German boy who lived in the upper end of the town. He soon tired of his pet and neglected to feed him. In the next yard was a pen in which there were some pigs about a week old. Joe, on one of his expeditions for food discovered them and carried one off. He repeated the visit two or three times. One day the owner of the pigs saw Joe on the roof of the neighboring shop making a meal off one of his young porkers. He at once sent for a policeman, and Joe came to an untimely end by means of a bullet from the officer's revolver.

THE LOON

A MONTHLY MAGAZINE
DEVOTED TO
ORNITHOLOGY AND OOLOGY

Best of reading matter relating to these branches.
50 cents a year. Sample copy free.

Address:
THAD. SURBER, White Sulphur Springs, W. Va.

H. H. FIELD.   E. C. GREENWOOD.

FIELD & GREENWOOD,
BROWNSVILLE, TEX.

Mr. Greenwood of this firm, who is well known as a naturalist and taxidermist, will give special attention to the collection for scientifical purposes, of all birds, beasts, reptiles and insects native to the interior and border of Mexico, and will furnish careful data in regard to same when desired. Correspondence respectfully solicited.

FIELD & GREENWOOD.

R. E. Rachford & Son,
COLLECTING NATURALISTS
and wholesale dealers in
BIRD SKINS AND EGGS,
BEAUMONT TEXAS.

CLUBBING RATES.

Hawkeye O. and O. (50c) and any of the following publications at annexed price:

	Pub's Price.	With H. O.
O. AND O., of Boston, Mass.,	$1.00	$1.25
West Am. Scientist,	1.00	.85
Oologist, Albion, N. Y.	.50	.75
Old Curiosity Shop,	.50	.80
Literary Visitor.	.50	.75

THE CURLEW.

Published for the Wilson Ornithological Chapter Agassiz Association, also the official organ of the Y. O. A.

Filled with interesting matter.

Only 25c. per year. Sample copy free. Address,

O. P. HANGER & CO.,
Orleans, Ind.

WHY NOT

Give me a trial order for
SOUTHERN CALIFORNIA BIRD SKINS AND EGGS

collected this season and first class in every respect. Price list for

CHARLES H. MARSH,
Dulzura, San Diego Co., Cal.

Bird Skins and Eggs.

At Reasonable Prices. Send stamp for lists.

J. A. SINGLEY,
Giddings, Texas.

WANTED: Specimens of all classes of objects of Natural History. Our trade is founded on our reputation for fair dealing and honest representation. We guarantee every specimen we sell and make our guarantee good, too. 'Tis this that makes our trade so good. Others come and go; we come stay and grow. So we want to get more material and spread out faster. Our trade is so good just now that we can use many of the more common species—we always want rare ones. If you have a collection you would like to dispose of, or wish to sell your duplicates or exchange them we would like to hear from you.

W. H. WINKLEY, Clearfield, Iowa.

MUST BE SOLD
WITHIN
THIRTY DAYS!

Having received a fresh invoice of several hundred fine Dakota eggs in complete sets with full data, which must be sold within thirty days, we are closing them out at the following rates:

500 Am. Coot's in sets of 9, 10, 11 and 12, at 2c each.
100 Field Plover in sets of 4, at 7c. each.
Blue-w. Teal in sets of 9 and 11, at 8c. each.
Mallard, 1 set of 11 at 10c. each.
Short-eared Owl, sets of 4 and 6, at 25c. each.

Sent securely packed in wooden boxes on receipt of amount in postal note. As they are sold on commission, stamps will be strictly refused. Ten cents extra must always be inclosed for postage, balance not used will be returned with data.

A SET OF SIX FINE CANVASS-BACKS at $1.25 each in exchange for first-class skins at usual rates. Flycatchers or Plovers and Sandpipers preferred.

E. B. WEBSTER,   CRESCO, IOWA.

A NEW DIRECTORY

We are engaged in complying a NEW Oologists' and Ornithologists' Directory, to be issued August 5, 1889. We desire the addresses of all Collectors. Do not neglect this opportunity to increase your collections by exchanges from all parts of the world. Exchange notices a special feature, 10n for 25 words or less. Extra words at same rate. This will be the largest and best Directory ever published. Order now. A limited number of reliable advertisements inserted at reasonable rates. Write for terms. Address all communications to

MENEFEE & CORLESS,
San Jose, Calif.

OUR $1 A WEEK Club System while as convenient to the buyer as any instalment system, is *a wholesale spot cash system* to us. The co-operation of the club members sells us 28 watches in each $28 Watch Club, and we get cash from the Club for each watch before it goes out, though each member only pays $1 a week. This is why we give you more for your money than any one else and why we are doing the largest watch business in the world. We sell only first quality goods, but our prices are about what others get for second quality. Our $10 Silver Watch is a substantial Silver (*not imitation of any kind*) Stem-Wind American Lever Watch—either hunting case or open. Our $25.00 Watch is a Stem-wind, Open Face, first quality, stiffened Gold American Lever Watch, *guaranteed to wear 20 years*. It is fully equal to any watch sold for $33 by others. We find a first-class Stiffened Gold Case much more satisfactory and serviceable than any Solid Gold Case that can be sold at less than double the money, as cheap solid cases are invariably thin, weak, of low quality, and worthless after short use. Our $28 Watch contains numerous important patented improvements, of vital importance to accurate timing—*Patent Dustproof, Patent Stem Wind, &c.*, which we control exclusively. It is fully equal for accuracy, appearance, durability and service, to any $75 Watch, either Open Face or Hunting. Our $43.00 Railroad Watch is especially constructed for the most exacting use, and is the best Railroad Watch made, Open Face or Hunting. All these prices are either all cash or in clubs, $1.00 a week. *An Ajax Watch Insulator given free with each Watch.*

The Keystone Watch Club Co.
Main Office in Co's Own Building
904 WALNUT ST. PHILADA. PA.
Agents Wanted.

Ajax Watch Insulator, $1.00
A perfect protection against magnetism. Fit any Watch. Sent by mail on receipt of price. We refer to any Commercial Agency.

PRESERVATIVE TAXIDERMY by E. B. Webster. A New Treatise on the Embalming Method. Gives Complete and Concise Explanation. A Child can Understand. Also contains Recipes for Compound, and Chapters on Making Skins and Skeletons. The Only Work on the Method Yet Published. Price only fifty cents. Send for sample pages.   E. B. W., Cresco, Iowa.

THE RETURN OF THE KINGLET.

BY WM. L. KELLS.

Back again to our wild-wood lands
Comes the Golden-crested Kinglet;
Still the days are warm and sunny
And the air is soft and balmy.
Misty smoke hangs o'er the hollows,
Cattle roam the fields and fallows,
'Tis the time of Indian Summer,
Nature greets its gay newcomer.

Still the woods are in their glory,
And the leaves yet keep their greenness,
For the chilly winds of Autumn
Scarce are felt among the woodland,
And the hoar-like frost of midnight
Vanishes before the sunlight,
Like the dripping dews of morning
In the sun-shine of the June day.

Still some wild flower shows its beauty
In the deep and sheltered forest,
Where the bee is yet heard drumming
As it gleams among the blossoms.
But the Thrush has ceased its solos,

And the Whip-poor-will is silent,
And no more in woody glens
Do we hear the Winter Wrens.

Now most other birds are silent,
Or have vanished toward the tropics,
And no more we hear their warbles
Till the voice of spring recalls them.
Now among the cedar branches,
Or amid the wavy limblets,
In the balsam and the hemlock.
In the pine, the birch and maple
We may hear the cheery wild-notes
Of the Golden-crested Kinglet.

In the golden sun-lit Springtime
When the wild-flowers of the woodland
Just were peeping through the mosses
And the fallen leaves of Autumn;
When the crow was loudly cawing
O're the tree tops and the fallows;
When the Winter Wren was singing,
And the Saw whet's notes were ringing,
In the deep, dark, sheltered wildwood
Did we miss the Golden Kinglet.

Then off to the northern woodland,
Where the dwarfish birds and fir tree
Clothe the borders of the lakelet,
And the margins of the streamlet,

Where no voice of man disturbs it,
Even that of Indian hunter,
There amid the tangling branches
Of some evergreen or birchwood,
To raise its future nestlings
Goes the Golden-crested Kinglet.

There her nest so firm and downy
Waves she in the tangled brushwood,
There her eggs are incubated,
And her young are fed and guarded
Till they follow through the tree-tops,
And they need her care no longer,
Then the impulse which there brought her,
Dies within the happy mother,
Then she thinks of the wood-land
Where she passed the previous winter.

Then the heralds of the winter,
Breezes from the snow-capped highlands,
From the West-land and the Arctic,
From the frozen shores of Greenland,
With black frost and cloudy mornings
Makes her hasten from the North-land.

Down along the south bound streamlet,
Over hill-tops, lakes and valleys,
So with young and faithful consort,
Back returns the Golden Kinglet.

THE BIRDS OF MINER CO., DAKOTA.

BY FRANK A. PATTON.

Bird life is very abundant here in the spring, summer and fall months, especially about the small lakes that dot the surface of the prairie. The most noticeable of these to a collector may be

THE AMERICAN COOT.

This bird, more commonly known as the "Mud Hen," arrives with us in April; through April and the first of May it is very abundant, the surface of most of the small lakes and marshes being literally covered with them. As June approaches they disappear to a common observer, the rushes having grown up enough to give them concealment. Then, in the open spaces, heaps of dead rushes will be seen, which increase in size until they very often reach the size of a bushel basket. These heaps of dead rushes are the nests of the American Coots, the eggs being placed in a slight hollow in the top. The nests are sometimes well concealed, but more often placed in open places or where the rushes are thin, which makes them easy to find. Some are placed in shallow water and rest firm on the bottom, while others are placed in deeper water, float clear and are rocked by the waves. I notice a great difference in the number of eggs found in the different nests, ranging from six to fourteen. Last season, I collected about six hundred eggs of this bird, the sets ranging thus, two sets of fourteen, four of thirteen, eleven of twelve, and so on down, the most common being ten. It is very seldom the birds are seen on or near their nests after the first egg is deposited, and I have good reason to think they often commence laying before their nests are completed. The young of this bird cannot fly till they are full grown, but are remarkable divers and swimmers, and are also very good runners. As these birds nest in small ponds that dry up during the summer months, the young birds start out on foot in search of water and roam about over the prairie and through the towns like so many chickens.

BIRDS OF SUMMERVILLE, S. CAROLINA.
(Continued from page 51.)

BY J. D. FORD.

Of the family *Picidæ* we have: Ivory-billed Woodpecker, resident though rarely seen, inhabitating thick and heavily wooded swamps; Downy Woodpecker, a common resident; Red-cocaded W., resident and common, but nests and eggs very rare; Piliated W., resident, rare, frequenting thick swamps and secluded places; Red-h. W., resident, common; Yellow-s. F., resident, common.

Family *Alcedinidæ*: Belted Kingfisher, seen in winter only.

Family *Strigidæ*: Am. Barn Owl, a rare bird in this locality; Barred O., a very common resident; Little Screech O., very common resident. There is a superstition that if the notes of this owl are heard near a bed-room window after the hours of retiring, there will be a death in the house shortly; on that account the colored people have a mortal hatred for the bird.

Family *Cuculidæ*: Yellow-b. Cuckoo, or Rain Crow, arrives here in April, spends the spring and summer and departs about September.

(TO BE CONTINUED.)

CORRESPONDENCE.

BY W. H. WINKLEY.

I was much pleased with the tone of Mr. Ford's article in the April No. of the H. O. AND O., and with the permission of the editor I would like to express my opinions on the same subject.

The true naturalist is enthusiastic in the pursuit of authenticate information and the acquisition of facts having a direct baring on the objects of his special study—the collection of specimens is always secondary. In the field he collects and preserves specimens, seting them aside that he may examine them more carefully at his leisnre, and to compare them with others collected in other localities or at different times. The specimens themselves probably posess no intrinsisk value to him. I would advise all persons who are making a collection "just for the fun of it," or because it suits their *soi distant* character of being "a naturalist, sir," to quit at once or to study up their specimens untill they become an authority on those subjects.

I care not what strange relics are exhumed from the ice of Rusia or the cave dens of paleothic man in Franc; what undiscribed forms of animal and vegitable life are found in the depths of the swamps of the Amazon or on the heights of the Sierras; wherever and by whomsoever these objects of interest may be collected, they will finely pass into the pose-sion of those who can comprehend their marvles and appreciate their value. The wholly ignorant are no more responsible for the distruction and mutalation of valuable specimens, and what is worse the loss of much valnable data, than are the hobbiest.

There is another class of persons who are a constant manace o the advancement of the cause, and they are those who have no interest in the cause but only care for financial profit. This may sound strange coming from a dealer, but it is true. Here is the point: from the circumstances it is evident that there can be only a very few persons who can gain a living by buying and selling nat. hist. specimens and of the many who fail there will be some who will resort to illegitimate tricks to gain their ends; and there is no buisness that I know of that offers such oppertunities for trickery as this does. Indevidnals of many allied species closely resemble each other and as in nine cases out of ten the receiver of these specimens has not the specimens at hand to make any comparison. He is easily cheated.

In a recent letter from a certain dealer of this class, he stated that he had sold 7,000 bird's eggs last year. Allowing this to be true, what an imense damage he has done to the cause of the sciense!

The position of a dealer is a perticularly advantagous one for a person who wish to study a large series of specimens of one kind and I belive the majority of the better class of dealers are taking advantage of the oppertunities presented to them.

Some time ago I noticed a discription of the collection of Mr. Carr of Madison, Wis. I study very carefully the thousands of specimens of all kinds that are constantly passing through my hands and make a record of my observations in much the same way as he does. My plan is this: I have one book in which I paste in or write an exact discription of a type specimen of any varicty that I have in my collection. I number this and below keep a record of the name, auther, Vol.. No and page of all books magazines etc that in my reading I find contains articles on this perticular subject. In a second journal I keep a copy of all datas received and as each specimen passes through my hands,

I write in this book a discription of its variations from the type specimen. I also have a portefolio whare I keep my pen and colored drawings, carfully drawn engravings, etc. After I have thus used a specimen, I do not care for it any more, but wish to get others instead. It is not much trouble to keep up this system of records, and if carried on for several years their value would indeed be great. I would like to see others adopt it. Being acquainted with the type form I can not see what benifit or use a specimen is to a person after he has examined it and made a note of its pecularities or variations, and in the case of animal skins, skeletons, etc., this can quite often be done without the distruction of life; at any rate it would reduce collecting to a proper minum.

I have noticed lately the tendency among students twords specialism. That is right. The whole field has been examined too thouroughly for the probability of a general student picking up any new facts; but patient and persistant investigation in and especial branch will be *shure* to bring to light many new facts, some of which may revolutionize the science.

BY WALTER RAINE.

To the Editor of the H. O. AND O.

Dear Sir:—Mr. Winkley has advertisements in March and May issues of the H. O. AND O., in which he wishes to purchase natural history specimens from collectors, and I think it my duty to let naturalists know how he has used me, so that they may avoid a wolf in sheep's clothing. Early last November, Winkley ordered birds' eggs at one third his catalogue rates as pre arranged. I filled his order, sending him first-class European and

Icelandic eggs to the value of $38. I wrote a month afterward to know if he had received the eggs, as I had not heard from him, and got the reply that the eggs had arrived some time ago, but that they were not first-class, and that I had charged him for 24 European Buzzard's but only sent him three eggs, and he could only pay me $32 for the eggs. I replied to the effect that I had sent him strictly first-class eggs and was sure I had sent him 24 Buzzards, but as he promised to be a good customer I would accept $32 instead of $38. I waited several weeks and got no money and wrote to Winkley several times, when one day a card board box arrived with lid smashed in, containing one third of the eggs which Winkley alleged were not first class. Now the idea of a Professor returning a lot of valuable eggs in a card board box, any school boy would have known better, but Winkley intended the eggs to get broken on the way and the result was most of them were broken.

I then looked for the alleged imperfect eggs and was astonished to find a lot with chipped blow holes, which a lense at once showed had been recently done. I then wrote accusing Winkley of tampering with the blow holes to try and convince me I had sent them in that condition and was astounded when he admitted it, making the excuse that he had been trying to remove the inner lining of the eggs. I will leave my readers to draw their own conclusions. The box also contained 11 European Buzzard's eggs, Winkley having forgotten he had said I had only sent him three eggs; he evidently wanted to cheat me out of 21 Buzzards.

I asked Winkley to pay for the eggs he admitted he had damaged and he then threatened to return all the eggs, saying he never ordered them, that they were a poor lot and not true to name and he was in financial difficulties and could not sell the eggs as he had no trade or use for them. By his heavily bluffed advertisements one would think he was doing all the trade in America, but by his conduct he apparently does not possess sufficient funds or brains to run a peanut stall.

However for several weeks I tried coaxing and threatning but could get no money out of him and as I was helpless in his clutches I offered to take back the eggs he still had; after having them in his possession three months he returned them, but on examination I found that he had detained over $10 worth of eggs and upon enquiring he said they had got broken by a box falling upon them. I have written Winkley several times for compensation for the eggs he admits he damaged about the blowholes and those he detained, but only got abuse and insults. I will leave my readers to form their own opinions on Winkley's way of dealing with collectors, and if Winkley thinks I have here stated anything that I cannot prove by his own letters he must seek satisfaction through the law courts. Yours truly,

W. RAINE.

BY W. WINKLEY.

* * I am glad you spoke about Mr. Raine. I had never given any order for any specimens in the lot Mr. R. sent. I refused to accept them and returned them to him He said that I injured some of the specimens and that others was missing. I agreed to pay for the latter if he would make out a list and bill of them Also for the first class if he would show that I had damaged any. This he has refused to do and has made an insulting demand for $12 alleged damages and now threatens to blackmail. If he is half the gentlemen he pretends to be, he would act more honorable I am willing to leave the matter for settlement in your or any other honest man's hands. Is that fair? * *

Resp. yours, W. H. WINKLEY.

Remarks on the above are unnecessary, further than that we have always found W. Raine to be a thorough gentleman and more than square in his business relations with us. We have published both sides, having followed copy closely, but we have not the correspondence and cannot, as yet, act as judge.

NOTES.

Owing to a change in business life we will not be able to continue the H. O. AND O. with more than ten pages for the present. Hence we reduce the subscription price one-half, making it 25c per year. Present subscribers will have their account carried forward a year. By the coming winter we expect to be so situated that we can readily make the increase to sixteen pages, with ample illustration. We trust our friends will avail themselves of this opportunity.

'Tis said that at last we are to have a long-felt want supplied a directory, to be published by Messrs. Menefee & Corless of San Jose, Calif. Davis & Bakers edition of 1885 and Henry Coale's are the only good directories extant, and these are considerably out of date. The gentlemen write that their directory will be the largest and finest of the kind ever published, containing addresses of all the leading ornithologists of the world, besides exchange notices and a directory of the periodicals devoted to the subject. We wish them every success in their undertaking.

Arthur E. Pettit, of New York, has assumed control of the Oologist's Exchange. Vol. II, No. 1, is presented in a very creditable manner and we wish it all success. The present address is Box 2060.

RECREATION, for June, opens with a brilliant article on "Salmon Angling in the Abstract," by Charles Hallock, senior editor of the magazine. The essay is written in the author's happiest vein, and describes noteworthy personages and places dear to salmon fishers and interesting to the entire angling brotherhood. The Maiden Hunt, The Cruise of the Thetis, Florida Field Sports Association, and other interesting articles make up the balance of the number. Single copies 20c, 2 00 per year. Charles Hallock, 2218 Penn. Ave., Washington, D. C.

The Curlew of Orleans, Ind., has made such rapid growth of late as to require a new coat and in a number of other respects present a much more creditable appearance. Published for the Wilson Ornithological Chapter of the A. A.

DAKOTA EGGS

A FEW REMAINING SETS

Will be sold at a very low rate until disposed of. Specimens guaranteed first class with full data. Ten cents extra must be enclosed for postage.

Am. Coot, sets of 9, 11, 12, at 2c each.
Prairie Hen, sets 12, at 75c per set.
Mallard, set 11, $1.10.
Canvass-back, set 6, $2.00.
Am. Bittern, set 7, $2.00.
Golden Plover, set 2, $1.00.

———ALSO THE FOLLOWING SETS———

Golden Eagle, 1-1, $4.   Roseate Spoonbill, 1-1, 75c.   Am. Long-e. Owl, 1-4, $1.00.   European Buzzard, 1-2, 50c.   Red-b. Rail, 1-7, 75c.   Red-t. Diver, 1-2, 1.50.   Herring Gull, 1-3, 50c.   Double-c. Cormorant, 1-3, 75c.   King-fisher, 1-5, 50c.   Woodcock, 2d, 1-4. 1.00.   Rough l. Hawk, 1-2, 1.50.   SINGLES —Caracara Eagle, 1.00; Flamingo, 50c; Wild Turkey, 75c; Turkey Buzzard, 50c; Egyptian Vulture, 1.25.

E. B. WEBSTER,   CRESCO, IOWA.

THE LOON

A MONTHLY MAGAZINE DEVOTED TO ORNITHOLOGY AND OOLOGY

Best of Reading Matter Relating to These Branches.
50 cents a year. Sample copy free.

Address:
THAD. SURBER, White Sulphur Springs, W. Va.

VALUABLE RECIPES.

Price, one cent each. If less than ten are ordered at a time two cents extra must be included for postage.

New Method of Preserving Birds. How to Clean and Polish Shells. How to Clean Silver and Copper Coins. How to Press Autumn Leaves, a florist's secret. How to Tan Skins with the Fur on. How to Preserve Small Birds Entire. To Preserve Starfish. To Polish Stones and Agates. To Skeletonize and Bleach Leaves. To Make a Copying Pad and Ink. To Make a Fluid Ink Eraser. To Polish Sea Beans. The Great Secrets of Trapping Foxes and Other Game. Trappers and Anglers Secret for Game and Fish.

E. M. HAIGHT, Box 24, Riverside, Calif.

$2.00 SAVED

by buying your Shoes of the Manufacturer.

SATISFACTION GUARANTEED!

ONLY $2.50

for Shoes that usually retail at $4.00 and $5.00.

BUTTON.　　LACE.　　CONGRESS.

On receipt of $2.50 and twenty-five cents to pay expressage we will send one pair of our **Fine Calf Shoes**. Seamless Vamps, either Button, Lace or Congress. We Use only selected stock and the best workmanship. Every pair Warranted. Try our Shoes once and you will buy no others.

☞Mention Size and Width wanted. Send postal note or N. Y. draft. Write your address plainly,—Town, County and State.

CUSTOM BOOT & SHOE CO.,
EAST WEYMOUTH, MASS.

THE OOLOGISTS' EXCHANGE

A monthly paper for Oologists and Ornithologists. Send for a sample copy and see what it is.
OOLOGISTS' EXCHANGE,
P. O. Box 2060,
New York.

C. E. CURTIS,
Stamp and Curiosity Dealer,
Sawens, N. Y.

Stamps on approval at 35 per cent com. Catalogue of Relics, Curiosities, etc., FREE.

☞The Standard, a 12 page magazine for collectors, one year on trial only 5c. Adv. rates 3c per line. Address, The Standard. Sawens, N. Y.

Circulars mailed for dealers at 10c per 100. Star Mailing Agency, Sawens, N. Y.

Budget of over 450 different things and one pound of story papers and magazines for 10c. Star Supply House, Sawens, N. Y.

FOR EXCANGE.—Two 50c mineral collections, made up by Wm. Niven. H O., Cresco.

R. E. Rachford & Son,
COLLECTING * NATURALISTS
and wholesale dealers in
BIRD SKINS AND EGGS,
BEAUMONT, TEXAS.

H. H. FIELD.   E. C. GREENWOOD.
FIELD & GREENWOOD,
BROWNSVILLE, TEX.

Mr. Greenwood of this firm, who is well nown as a naturalist and taxidermist, will give special attention to the collection for scientifical purposes, of all birds, beasts, reptiles and insects native to the interior and border of Mexico, and will furnish careful data in regard to same when desired. Correspondence respectfully solicited.
FIELD & GREENWOOD.

☞Bird Skins and Eggs.☜
At Reasonable Prices. Send stamp for lists.
J. A. SINGLEY,
Giddings, Texas.

WHY NOT

Give me a trial order for
SOUTHERN CALIFORNIA BIRD SKINS AND EGGS
collected this season and first class in every respect. Price list for
CHARLES H. MARSH,
Dulzura, San Diego Co., Cal.

SPECIAL PREMIUM

For One Mouth Only we will offer Preservative Taxidermy and the H. O. for price of the former, 50 cents.

PRESERVATIVE TAXIDERMY.

◀ BY ・ E. ・ B. ・ WEBSTER. ▶

A manual setting forth in a clear, concise manner the process of "Embalming," so called. Gives recipes for compound and contains chapters on making skins and skeletons. Price 50 cts.

FROM J. A. SINGLEY.

I have looked over your "Preservative Taxidermy" carefully and can only say that if those who prefer preserving their birds by this method instead of skinning and mounting will carefully read and follow your method they cannot fail to do creditable work. The main objection to the preservative method is the liability of the birds to shrink while drying but I believe the method you give will obviate this defect.

FROM OLIVER DAVIE.

In regard to this method I cannot speak to any degree from practical experience. Have never done a great deal with it myself but I know of some who make a grand success in preserving birds and the smaller quadrupeds. I have some specimens of birds which I prepared ten years ago with the Embalming Process and they appear to be in as good shape as the day they were preserved.

I have carefully read over your treatise on the Embalming Method and find it indeed very clearly and concisely stated. I do not see how any person, even the greenest hand, can fail to do satisfactory work with the clear manner in which you have laid it down in your treatise. I congratulate you on the same.

E. C. GREENWOOD.

Have read your manual over carefully and although you express many good ideas regarding taxidermy there is a part of your method with which I have never had any experience as I always remove entire body and insert a substitute of hard wound grass. I would suggest that clay is far better than putty for modeling; also paint legs and bills first with arsenical soap, then a second coat of crude carbolic acid preserves the natural color of beak and legs. This I have tried of late with fine result on some Roseate Spoonbills. Stains are preferable to pains. From your humble servant,

E. C. G.

R. E. RACHFORD & SON.

We have carefully examined Manual of Taxidermy and heartily endorse it and will cheerfully recommend it to our brethren in the ornithological field.

A. E. KIBBE.

Am pleased to say that it makes the process very plain and distinct. It will speak for itself.

The Hawkeye Ornithologist and Oologist.

THE SONG SPARROW.

L. OTLEY PINDAR.

In the early part of winter
When the woods are bare and leafless,
And the gaily feathered songsters
All have left the woods and meadows
Where they sang throughout the summer,
When the Cardinal is silent
And the Mockingbird is moping
Waiting the return of summer;
Comes a singer from the Northland,
Rather small and plainly colored,
But he perches on the branches
Of some tree along the wayside,
And he sings throughout the winter,
Never caring for the bitter
Winds that whistle all around him.

But when spring returns, and with her
Comes the host of forest singers,
Who had left us in the autumn,
When the Cardinal's rich whistle
And the Mockingbird's sweet music
Loudly sing from all directions;

Then the Sparrow quietly leaves us,
For his notes will not be listened
To, while louder strains are sounding
From each wood and field and orchard;
And his song is soon forgotten,
E'en his name is unremembered
Till the sunny days are over;
Then he comes again to cheer us,
Knowing he will then be welcomed.
   April 24, 1889.

A FAIR SIZED SET OF FLICKER'S EGGS.

NEIL F. POSSON.

I have read at different times in different periodicals of collectors securing large sets of eggs of the Flicker, but never dreamed that any such good fortune should be mine.

However, my luck began on the evening of May 22, this year, when I found a Flicker's nest containing four eggs. Fearing lest the nest should be visited by some of the "small boy" collectors, with which this locality is burdened, I returned early next morning with my "egg-scoop" and found that there were now five eggs, which I secured, leaving in their place two Pigeon's eggs and a Kingfisher's. Two days later I visited the nest and found one more Flicker's egg. Just one week later, June 1st, I again visited the nest and found that two of the "sham eggs" I had put in the nest had been removed, and that there were three more eggs of the Flicker, which I took. These made nine in all, and, as the last two were runts, I concluded that this ended the set, and so I made out my data and marked my eggs as a set of nine.

However, on June 6 (just five days later) happening to be in the vicinity of the nest, I thought I would simply climb up and look in, when, imagine my surprise, to find five more eggs.

June 13 netted me one more egg and June 18 five more, making twenty in all. After this the birds evidently concluded that laying eggs in that nest wasn't a paying business as they left the spot for good, and now the pearly white set of 412 1-20 graces my cabinet.

The nest was but twelve feet from the ground in a natural cavity in an apple tree in one corner of an old orchard. The cavity was about four feet deep.

MY FIRST WHITE-WINGED CROSSBILL.

W. S. JOHNSON.

The sixteenth day of last February, ('89) I was taking a snow-shoe tramp through a small stretch of woods when suddenly I heard some birds overhead. On looking up I saw a flock of about 30 or 40 birds alight in a tall evergreen tree near which I standing. Upon seeing them I immediately raised my gun and fired at one, a red bird, the only one of that color that I saw. At the report of the gun they all flew up except the one at which I had fired, which laid on a thick bough near the top of the tree. At the time that I shot it began to rain hard and it was so cold that the rain would freeze as fast as it fell on my gun and my clothing, but in spite of the rain I determined to secure the bird that I had killed to identify it. After throwing many sticks at it with no effect, I took off my snow-shoes and started to climb the tree. It was a hard task, as the tree was swaying from side to side in the strong wind which was now blowing. I at last reached the top, however, and was rewarded by finding that I had procured a fine male White-winged Crossbill, a bird which is quite rare here, and only visits us in the severest winter weather.

The male Cross-bill is a beautiful bird, being carmine red, tinged across the back with black, and black wings and tail, with two bands of white across the wings. But the the most peculiar thing about the bird is that its mandibles, which are curved, cross each other, the upper one being the longest.

BIRDS OF SUMMERVILLE, S. C.
(Continued from page 57.)

J. D. FORD.

Of the family *Cathartidæ*: Turkey Buzzard, a very common resident; Carrion Crow, a rare resident.

Columbidæ: Mourning Dove, common resident and highly gregarious except in the breeding season, when they go in pairs; Ground Dove, a rare resident.

Meleagridæ: Wild Turkey, a very common resident.

Percididae: Bob-White, Am. Quail, a very common game bird and highly gregarious.

Ardeidae: Louisiana Heron, rare in this locality; Little Blue Heron, comparitively common; Green Heron, a winter resident; Am. Bittern, rarely seen here.

Ibididae: White Ibis, a rare resident.

Charadriidae: Killdeer, a good observer can perceive a great decrease in these birds, five years ago they were very common in this county and highly gregarious, now it is rare to see five in a flock. I notice to that they are shifting their quarters, formerly they were to be found mostly in corn fields or around some inland pond, now they are more numerous around the salt marshes in the lower part of the state. Piping Plover, a rare resident. American Woodcock, common resident.

Scolopacidae: Wilson's Snipe, a winter resident; Red-breasted Snipe, a rare winter resident; Sanderling, a rare winter resident; Greater Yellow-legs, a very rare winter visitor, occasionally a small flock is seen.

Rallidae: Clapper Rail, common resident; Sora Rail, seldom so far south.

Anatidae: Black Mallard, Blue-w. Teal, Am. White-fronted Goose, rare winter visitors.

Pelecanidae: White and Brown Pelicans, rare residents.

Laridae: Common Tern, a comparitively common resident.

Additions and corrections to the above list will be thankfully received.

J. D. FORD, 10 Mill St., Charleston, S. C.

RAINE-WINKLEY CONTROVERSY.

Last month, it will be remembered, we published letters from Walter Raine and W. H. Winkley regarding a transaction between those parties. We had held Raine's letter for some time as we did not wish to meddle with their private affairs, but when we received the "correspondence" from Winkley containing one or two slaps as some one (whom we judge to be Raine) we asked Winkley for the other side of the case and presented it as fairly as possible. We also had another reason for so doing. Our readers will remember that we accused R. M. Gibbs of being a swindler and then published a part, though amply sufficient, of our proof. We did this to prevent Gibbs from swindling our readers further, as he had been an extensive advertiser with us. We now have the same case again; both gentlemen having frequently used the H. O. as an advertising medium, and not wishing to run the ads of those not strictly honest, we took it upon ourselves to clear up the difficulty.

The case, as well as one can judge from the correspondence sent us by both parties, stands about as follows: A proposition was made by one or the other of the parties that Raine sell Winkley a quantity of eggs at one-third the latter's catalogue rates for cash. Winkley now claims that he never *ordered* the eggs, and—Raine fails to send the order sheet. If we let the matter rest here Raine cannot complain so very much at his subsequent treatment. But in a letter written December 10th, after he received the eggs, Winkley complains that some were not sent, some were 2d class and three broken, hence he can only pay Raine $32 instead of $38, the amount of the bill. Now, suppose there was no positive order, does it seem reasonable that an order was deemed necessary by the parties, when the consignment is accepted with the exception of the claimed irregularities.

Farther than this nothing remains to be said except that Winkley's letters fully bear out Raine's statements in his letler regarding the pasteboard box, broken holes, Buzzard's eggs, etc.

PECULIAR NESTS.

The HAWKEYE has lately added to its collection two oddities in the way of nests. Several weeks ago a pair of wrens commenced investigating the premises of the writer and finally settled for a nesting site on the pocket of a pair of overalls which had been left hanging under one of the porches. They labored a long time with the first twigs, but in spite of frequent interruptions, they finally managed to prop the pocket open wide enough to build the nest, and soon laid a set of five handsome eggs. Not long afterward the family were very much astonished, and displeased as well, upon hearing that the eggs were all gone—but they were not told that five tiny birds had taken their places. In an amazingly short time they had doubled again and again in weight and are now enjoying themselves amongst the shrubbery.

The other nest was built by a Baltimore Oriole and was supported, in addition to a number of twigs, by a piece of twine, about 55 inches long, which was passed over a limb above, the ends being firmly woven in opposite sides of the nest. Though nests have occasionally been supported in this manner before, (see Vol. II, No. 1, H. O.) still it may well be considered quite a rarity.

NOTES.

The July and August issues of the H. O. are necessarily combined, owing to the continued illness of the editor, but in the future we hope to issue about the first of each month, and also to present a better appearance as we have recently purchased a new dress and have also added a Challenge press. When our immediate rush is over we will be able to print catalogues, circulars, and all classes of fine job work and can give our ornithological friends a letter or note head in the latest grotesque styles or a strictly plain, neat job, as they may wish.

We would call attention to the opinions of some of the leading field collectors on our pamphlet entitled "Preservative Taxidermy." A few taxidermists have endeavored to teach the method by mail, charging for the written process and also for the recipe, but we are not aware that the method has ever before been embalmed in type.

Our list of Dakota eggs is nearly exhausted though we still have a set of six fine eggs of 617 for sale or exchange on very liberal terms, also have left two sets of 1-12 Prairie Hen at 6c each, postage 10c extra.

We are sorry to notice that the Oologists' Exchange has discontinued its supplements. They promised to prove of great value to the ornithological library.

We we were greatly grieved to learn of the death of Mr. E. C. Greenwood, which occurred July 21st, 1889. Mr. Greenwood was the junior member of the firm of Field & Greenwood, collecting naturalists, of Brownsville, Texas. We learn from Mr. Field that he will continue the business of the firm.

J. A. Singley writes that he has returned from his collecting trip, having had great success. He has collected some very rare eggs, besides one species never taken heretofore. He secured a duck new to science which will be described in the Auk. With shells and fossils he was none the less successful, having discovered new species of each.

We must congratulate Bro. Surber on the improved appearance of the Loon. He now uses an appropriate engraving for a heading and the typographical appearance is much better. The contents, as usual, are very interesting.

Vol. I of the H. O. cannot be furnished by us at any price; of the January, May and October numbers we would like to buy several copies.

The Literary Companion has again prssed into W. H. Plank's hands and will he issued as formerly. Vol. I, No. 2 is before us.

Our thanks are due the Oologists' Exchange for the first prize on ornithological articles entered in their recent contest.

May we ask what the publisher of The Oologist is ashamed of? Or perhaps we may guess?

Where is the Curlew?

DAVIE'S "KEY."

Our thanks are due Oliver Davie for a copy of the third edition of his very valuable work on "Nests and Eggs of North Am. Birds." He has greatly enlarged the work (it now consists of 475 pages) having entirely re-written it and added a number of fine full page illustrations by Theodore Jasper and W. Otto Emerson. It now includes all the species that occur north of the southern U. S. boundary including Lower California and Greenland, giving the breeding range, time of nesting, number of eggs laid, color and size, together with the chief characteristics of the birds. This latter point makes the work very interesting to read as well as being a manual for referrence. The new nomenclature of the A. O. U. code is used, but Ridgway's numbers are given. There are a vast number of common names given and these are also arranged in an index of twelve pages. The work concludes with brief directions for collecting nests and eggs. It is certainly invaluable as an aid for the identification of specimens to all those collecting in the field. In fact, it may be safely said that the oological world owes more than it can ever realize to Mr. Davie for his labors in this direction.

CHAS. K. WORTHEN,
NATURALIST .'. AND .'. TAXIDERMIST,
···DEALER IN···
BIRD • AND • MAMMAL • SKINS,
WARSAW, ILL.

CARRIES a large stock of rare native and foreign Bird Skins. Rare Alaska species, brilliant plumaged Tropical Birds, handsome Decoration Pieces, Game Birds on Panels, Bird Medallions on silk plush and velvet panels, Owls, large or small, on gold crescents and books, feather fire screens, lamp screens, etc., made to order. Animal Rugs, with heads mounted, mounted Buck Heads, Flying Terns, White Doves, White Owls, Arctic Horned Owls, Dusky Horned Owls, Emperor Geese, Spectaled Eiders, Parrot Auks, Horned Puffins, Flamingoes, and thousands of others. A large invoice of the beautiful Long tailed Resplendent Paradise Trogans just received and for sale cheap. Can also fill orders for Geodes. Refer by permission to Prof. Ridgway of Smithsonian Institute, Prof. J. A. Allen, Mus. Nat. Hist., N. Y., and many others. Enclose stamp with inquiries.

THE • • • •
OOLOGISTS EXCHANGE

A monthly paper for Oologists and Ornithologists. Send for a sample copy and see what it is.

OOLOGISTS' EXCHANGE,
P. O. Box 2060.   New York.

JUST PUBLISHED.

THIRD EDITION.

OLIVER DAVIE'S
 NESTS * AND * EGGS
—OF—
NORTH .·. AMERICAN .·. BIRDS.

RE-WRITTEN AND GREATLY ENLARGED.

To those who have used the former editions it needs no recommendation. Suffice it to say that it is now *complete* and forms an invaluable book as an aid for the identification of specimens to all those collecting in the field. 475 pages and 13 full page illustrations. Paper edition 1.25, cloth 1.50.

For sale by E. B. WEBSTER, Cresco, Iowa.

BIRDS' SKINS. & EGGS
at Reasonable Prices. Send for lists, enclosing stamp.
J. A. SINGLEY,
Giddings, Texas.

R. E. RACHFORD & SON,
COLLECTING-:-NATURALISTS
AND WHOLESALE DEALERS IN
· BIRDS · SKINS · AND · EGGS, ·
BEAUMONT, TEXAS.

BIRDS' EGGS CHEAP!

Eggs are all first class, with full data in sets or singly, one hole side blown. The figures in parenthesis indicate the number of eggs in a set. Orders in amount less than 25 cents must contain 4 cents additional for packing and postage.

A.O.U.	Per egg
365 Barn Owl (4-5 6)	.12
378 Burrowing Owl (5-6)	.15
385 Road Runner (4-5-6)	.12
448 Cassin's Kingbird (4-5)	.20
458 Black Phœbe (4)	.10
505a Ariz. Hooded Oriole (3-4)	.75
508 Bullock's Oriole (4-5)	.07
510 Brewer's Blackbird (4-5)	.04
519 House Finch (4-5)	.05
531 Lawrence's Goldfinch (5)	.12
552a Western Lark Sparrow (4)	.07
574 Bell's Sparrow (3)	.75
* California Shrike (4-5-6) new var.	.10
710 California Thrasher (2)	.12
713 Cactus Wren (4 5)	.07

E. M. HAIGHT, RIVERSIDE,
BOX 24. CALIF.

WHY NOT

Give me a trial order for SOUTHERN · CALIFORNIA · BIRD SKINS · & · EGGS collected this season and first class in every respect. Price list for stamp

CHAS. H. MARSH,
DULZURA, CALIF.

W. E. LAIDLAW,
CRESCO, IOWA.

WHY NOT

Give me a trial order for
SOUTHERN · CALIFORNIA · BIRD
SKINS · & · EGGS
collected this season and first
class in every respect. Price
list for stamp.

CHAS. H. MARSH, Dulzura, Calif.

R. E. RACHFORD & SON,

COLLECTING-:-NATURALISTS

AND WHOLESALE DEALERS IN

· BIRDS · SKINS · AND · EGGS, ·

BEAUMONT, TEXAS

BIRDS' SKINS & EGGS

At Reasonable Prices. Send for
lists, enclosing stamp.

J. A. SINGLEY,
    Giddings, Texas.

Birds Eggs Cheap!
· · · ·

Eggs are all first class, with full data in sets or singly, one hole, side blown. The figures in parenthesis indicate the number of eggs in a set. Orders in amount less than 25 cents must contain 4 cents additional for packing and postage.

A.O.U.	Per egg
378 Burrowing Owl (6 9 10)	.10
385 Road Runner (4 5-6)	.09
448 Cassin's Kingbird (4-5)	.14
505a Ariz. Hooded Oriole (3-4)	.35
531 Lawrence's Goldfinch (5)	.09

Send stamp for further list.
E. M. HAIGHT,   RIVERSIDE,
BOX 24,   CALIF.

THE LIGHT RUNNING
NEW HOME
SEWING MACHINE

HAS NO EQUAL.

THE LADIES' FAVORITE.

THE ONLY SEWING MACHINE
THAT GIVES
PERFECT SATISFACTION

NEW HOME SEWING MACHINE CO. ORANGE, MASS.
CHICAGO — 28 UNION SQUARE, N.Y. DALLAS,
ILL.   ATLANTA, GA.   TEX.
ST. LOUIS, MO.   SANFRANCISCO. CAL.

W. E. LAIDLAW,
CRESCO, IOWA.

Send Lists
of skins of sandpipers and flycatchers with lowest rates to the H. O.

Hawkeye Ornithologist and Oologist.

TO A BOBOLINK.

WM. L. KELLS, LISTOWEL, ONT.

When the grass is green and wavy,
   And the yellow dandelion
Dots the meadow and the wayside,
   And the wind is gently sighing

Through the orchard white with blossoms,
   And the woods their leaves assuming
Where the wild flowers, pink and purple,
   Through the fallen leaves are blooming.

Then is heard the Bobolink's music,
   Rattling, jingling as he goes,
Over meadow, field and fallow,
   Lately clothed with winter's snows.

O'er the pasture, by the woodland,
   Wafts the gay and gladsome bird;
From the dawning to the evening
   Is his jingling music heard.

There is not a trace of sadness
   In his clear, metallic ring;
Summer would lose half it's gladness
   If we did not hear him sing.

While the female in the clover
   Well conceals her grassy nest,
He the field is wandering over,
   Scarcely taking time to rest.

Now he ruffles out his plumage,
  Then outspreads his wings and tail,
While his mates unceasing rattle
  Like an ancient coat of mail.

Thus are passed the days of summer,
  Till the haying time is o'er,
Then he's silent, and his music
  For the year is heard no more.

But the female with her offspring
  Lingers late among the grain,
Till the voice of nature calls her,
  To the sunny south again.

A PAIR OF RED-EYES.

BY WILL. H. PLANK, "FURGUSON."

A pair of red eyes, coat of olive-green, with vest and pants to match, attracted my attention, one afternoon in early May, some years ago, as I was slowly meandering through a forest seeking the curious and wonderful stores that nature has *cached* everywhere, was the first time I ever saw the Red-eyed Vireo, or Greenlet, as it is sometimes called. Since then in nearly all of my rambles from early spring to autumn, I hear its sweet song full of melody and spirit. We are no longer strangers, but friends. This little feathered friend of mine has taught me many a lesson of patience in looking for her nest, and when found I was fully rewarded for the hours spent in its search. It happened this way. Coming through a grove my eyes fell upon a little bunch of grass, fibers, etc., supported from a forest tree just overhead. This nest whose form and make-up I had never before seen caused me to pause and examine it. It looked like a completed structure or nearly so. So I waited for these handless carpenters to resume labor on the dwelling, but in vain. It was either dinner-time, or they preferred to work in secret, for I was unable to make the much desired (on my part) acquaintance, after marking the tree, I resumed my walk. About a week later I called again, when, presto! my nest was gone or else some magic wand had changed it into one of the most beautiful forms of bird-architecture we have, Where I had expected to find a *rara avis* was my oldfriend Red-eye, who scrutinized me with a what-is-your-business look that showed I was not wanted; after eyeing one another for a short time and after an apology from me, and my stating I was not an "egg hog," and had neither egg-box or drill, she permitted me to look and behold the five little pearls encased in a shell of her own making. This was my first acquaintance with the Red-eyed Vireo and since then I have seen many little pendant nests hanging from a low bush or high forest trees.

The Curio Informant, a new journal devoted to archæology, and also containing articles of interest to collectors in oology and many other branches, is presented by James McBride. It will certainly be a valuable addition to the archæological students library and merits a hearty welcome.

Vol. 1, No. 2 of the O. and O. Semi-annual is before us. W. H. Foote, publisher, 50 pages and cover; best edition 35c, cheaper 25c.

A SNIPE HUNT.

J. CLAIRE WOOD, DETROIT, MICH.

I had always longed for a day in the field with a well trained dog but it was not until October 1888, that my wish was realized. One day about the middle of that month, father came to me and said "Claire, Patterson and I were going snipe hunting to-morrow but I find it impossible to get away so have arranged with him to take you, meet him at the Grisworld House before day-break to-morrow morning." "But school?" I asked—"Oh! never mind, I will see the teacher myself," he replied. So the gun was brought out, cleaned, oiled, and with fifty shells in each pocket of my coat I hung it on the foot of my bed and tumbled in. Several times during the night I crawled out, struck a match to look at the clock and peered out of the window to see the state of the weather, which by the way was anything but promising as the rain was pouring down with a violence almost tropical. I was out of the house next morning long before the rest of the family were astir. The horizon was lightened with the dim, gray tint of early dawn when I reached the place appointed. P. soon made his appearance and we lost no time in starting on our way. As I said before it had rained heavily all night, but the morning was clear and cool indeed almost chilly despite the sparkling rays of the silvery sun that shone so brightly from the heavens above. I found Mr. P. to be a very agreeable and entertaining gentleman. The time passed pleasantly and I was so busily engaged asking questions and hearing accounts of camp life and adventure that it surprised me greatly when he pulled up before a half grocery and half hotel, facing the lake, with the tallest tamarack pole in front I ever saw, on the top of which a Cleveland and Thurman flag floated to the wind and announced our destination reached. When the horse was taken care of and the carriage drawn under the shelter of a friendly shed I went into the house and inquired what the prospects for snipe shooting were. I was told that only a few birds had been seen during the whole season as the marshes were so uncommonly dry, in fact so dry as to in no part afford a boring place for these birds. When I communicated this information to P. he expressed his surprise and could not account for such dryness after the numerous heavy rains we had had of late. Never-the-less we determined to go over the ground and as we started out, Don, P's setter, flushed a meadow lark from the grass in the field back of the barn. It flew to a fence near by and perched upon the top rail, cast glances of inquiry over first one shoulder and then the other until I was within 15 feet of him, when with a fare-well jerk of his tail he started away. I threw the gun to my shoulder, glanced along the barrel, and pressed the trigger, but the only visible effect it had on master lark was to quicken his speed although like bo-peep's sheep he left his tail behind him. The landlord's statement was correct. We tramped over two miles of marsh land and found not a drop of water. A sand hill crane came flying slowly towards us from the north. When first seen he was a long way off and the stilt-like legs stretched out behind made me mistake him for a Gt. Blue Heron, but as he neared us he gradually sank lower, evidently with the intention of lighting in the reeds when a fellow shot at him with a rifle, causing him to rise and pass over us at a great height. Convinced that no game was to be had here we retraced our steps to the hotel, hitched up and took the first road going north to try our luck with the partrige and woodcock.

[TO BE CONTINUED.]

THE NORTHERN SHRIKE.

NEIL F. POSSOM, MEDINA, N. Y.

Every winter, as sure as the last days of January or the first days of February come around, bringing with them their pleasant, sunshiny hours; almost so sure am I of a visit from the Northern Shrike.

In a certain suburb of our village, on the main street leading into the country toward the west, I am always sure of finding a shrike, generally before January closes. This suburb seems to be a favorite of *L. Borealis*.

In 1887, a pair of shrikes remained in this locality all through January and long into February when I lost track of them. In the preceding year and every year since, I have noted them regularly. I have also noted them Nov. 11 and Dec. 16, showing that they are here in the early part of the winter, as well.

The Northern Shrike is a very shy bird, not allowing one to approach at all near, although by stealth, he may get comparatively close.

Perched on the very topmost twig (as he always does) of some tall tree by the roadside, giving vent to his peculiarly entertaining warble, on some bright, crisp morning; he is, indeed a pleasant feature of our winter landscape. Most ornithological writers say but little about the notes of the shrike; passing over them as unattractive and unimportant; but to me, as I hear them from some tall tree-top of a winter's morning they constitute a warble, which is, indeed sweet, pleasing, and somewhat continued.

But the most interesting of his performances, is to watch him, as he pursues some pugnacious sparrow, diving madly at him and generally catching him and pecking out his brains, apparently from pure spite.

Be that as it may, I know of no bird-brains that we can better spare than those of *Passer domesticus*, and so I say, long live *Lanius Borealis*. The Northern Shrike summers far to the north of us and, in very severe winters, I think he goes farther south than this.

E. A. Browne, of Florence, Wyoming, found a brood of ten Monkey-faced Owls a short time ago. The largest has become tame and is both intelligent and amusing. Their faces are simply ludicrous and would make a dyspeptic laugh.

PRIZE COMPETITION.

Desiring to issue 1000 extra copies of the October issue for circulation in Cresco and vicinity and wishing to secure a considerable quantity of manuscript of interest to the general reader we make the following prize offer:

Best article on collecting experiences—Languill's "Our Birds in Their Haunts."

2d best—Davie's "Nests and Eggs."

Best article on bird protection as viewed by the orinthologist—250 handsomely printed letter heads and envelopes.

Best article on taxidermy—Maynard's Manual,

Best article on geology—The "Great Divide," one year.

All articles to be in on or before the 28th of October, to contain about 700 words, rather less than more, and to become the property of the magazine.

In the awarding of the prizes the best will be those of most interest to the general public, though other articles will be entered and considered fairly as well; uninterested judges will be secured to decide upon the relative merits.

SPECIALIZING.

The question of specializing often occurs to the mind of the student of nature, and unless he has a very strong will power, the chances are that he will fiind himself unable to fix his energies on any one branch. It may be more pleasing to change from one object to another, but in the end little is gained. Again, the specialist need not confine his attentions to the one thing he is studying, to the neglect of all others, but to make that his specialty, as it were, the study of which he looks forward as a duty which claims a greater part of his investigations. Some may come forward with the argument that some of the world's greatest naturalists were not specialists, devoting their time to all or several branches of science. But the rapid advancement which science has made since their time has made it impossible to attain a knowledge of the whole; and that there are few minds at this day which are competent to grasp and digest as much as either of these great scidntists, and probably it would be difficult to find half a dozen scientists to-day, who have studied and attained a clear comprehension of the elements of all the natural sciences. The specialist has one great advantage, that of being well versed on at least one subject, while the non-specialist has a very feeble idea of, perhaps, all, but at the same time being unable to discourse fluently about any one thing. In the near future we may look for a more general turning toward specialization in the various branches of science, and for a larger amount of work than could be accomplished by the same individuals under other circumstances.—Ex.

Star fish should be first immersed in fresh water for four or five hours, to kill them, and then extended on a board. The rays may be held in place by pins placed each side of them.

www.ingramcontent.com/pod-product-compliance
Lightning Source LLC
Chambersburg PA
CBHW020812230426
43666CB00007B/981